WORKING SITES

* These volumes have been produced for the European Association for American Studies (E.A.A.S.).
** This title is not a volume in the series, but closely connected with it.

WORKING SITES
Texts, Territories and Cultural Capital in American Cultures

edited by

John Leo and William Boelhower

VU UNIVERSITY PRESS
AMSTERDAM 2004

EUROPEAN CONTRIBUTIONS TO AMERICAN STUDIES

This series is published for the Netherlands American Studies Association
(N.A.S.A.) and the European Association for American Studies (E.A.A.S.)

General editor:
Rob Kroes
Amerika Instituut
Spuistraat 134
1012 VB Amsterdam

VU University Press is an imprint of
VU Boekhandel/Uitgeverij bv
De Boelelaan 1105
1081 HV Amsterdam
The Netherlands
E-mail: info@vu-uitgeverij.nl

ISBN 90 5383 917 8 (ECAS no 56)
NUR 686

Design cover: De Ontwerperij (Marcel Bakker), Amsterdam
Printer: Wilco, Amersfoort

CONTENTS

ACKNOWLEDGMENTS

The Editors intellectually owe much to the intelligence and scholarship of the contributors to this volume—to merely mention their patience in putting up with what often appeared to be stylistic challenges or incomprehensible delays with multiple "beta" versions coursing through the ether and from two continents. If this adventure in what's been described as "critical internationalism in American Studies" offers merit and promise, its "birth site" is in the European Association for American Studies, where these essays were first heard and critiqued in Graz (2000). That Association is justifiably known for truly international activities, networking, and collaborative work, all gifts that keep giving. Certainly a major "presence" in all senses here, and without whom this volume would have been inconceivable, is Rob Kroes, who has more than any editor and international champion of American Studies worked to expand and build the field's outreach by publishing a remarkable range of voices within.

No task as arduous as fine-tuning a pile of manuscripts with inconsistent formats, fonts, critical apparatuses, and the like, should ever proceed without a skilled super editor. We have been most fortunate in having Dr. Kerstin Gallant be equal to the task. A freelance translator (she's Norwegian and competent in a number of languages as well as editorial languages), her own training in literary studies made for astute suggestions and, heaven knows, "intuitive" divining of infirm or murky intent (something we all were guilty of!). The staff at the Informational and Instructional Technology Services office at the University of Rhode Island—Providence, gave us access to equipment and expertise. In particular we wish to thank its manager Vincent Petronio, and André Charpentier, Peter Decesaro, and Lynn Petronio. Numerous student helpers were always cheerful when called on.

John Leo, Providence
William Boelhower, Venezia

INTRODUCTION

The defining issues of our day—such as the emerging network of world cities, an increasingly globalized economy, new conceptualizations and also practices of empire, and the diasporas of migrant and deterritorialized peoples—have indirectly shaped the set of questions raised by the contributors to this collection of essays. The contributors gathered here address the above scenarios with varying degrees of directness but consistently with heightened senses of place, with renewed curiosity toward those intersections where historical, national, and global concerns merge with local standpoints. The outcome is a geocritical "extended site" that we have titled *Working Sites*. As for their immediate crossdisciplinary ambience, these essays form part of an ongoing discussion already staked out by some of the cartographic and microphysical genealogies of Michel Foucault, the postmodern geographies of Edward Soja, the urban and largely sociological savvy of Michel de Certeau and Mike Davis, the marxist critiques of Fredric Jameson, David Harvey, and Henri Lefebvre, and the travel theory and anthropological reflections of James Clifford, Clifford Geertz, and Mary Louise Pratt, to mention only a few of the luminaries whose work has revived and extended the range of implications connected with geocultural critique.

More to the point, each of our contributors has chosen a site that especially interested them and then proceeded to work it within the referential boundaries suggested and yet problematized by the volume's subtitle: text, territory, and cultural capital. While each of these admittedly porous categories already assumes a set of established as well as contested functions, our specific aim was to assemble and juxtapose them in new relations the better to reconceptualize them. Above all, it was the idea of carrying out a "dig"—admittedly as literary anthropologists and geocritics of our own making—that was to bring these three terms into productive relations. Hence our fundamental commitment to the notion of site in its many different facets. Spatially, the sites dealt with here range from North America's west coast (present day Los Angeles) to its east (present day Boston and Gloucester; and the northeastern or New England landscape). Sites in between embrace an iconically resonant set of western mountain ranges (the photographs of the US Geological and Geographic Survey of the Territories, 1869-1878; lithographs and paintings such as Thomas Moran's "Mountain of the Holy Cross"; and the revisitations of the Rephotographic Survey Project of the late 1970's). Other North American sites include both "capitals" of the Midwest: Chicago the capitalist metropolis, and intriguingly "Middletown" (locally known as Muncie, Indiana), the heart of the "average."

In addition, there are also important discussions of a well-defined archive of early images of South America that index as well colonial fantasies of the others' bodies, a reminder of how sites function as both locales and as cultural repositories. Similarly, another working site examines a different sort of early encounter, namely that of the Amazon River as celebrated above all in Sir Walter Raleigh's travel report blending classical mythology with a New World environment. But besides considering a number of exemplary colonial encounters between English explorers, Spanish settlers, and indigenous peoples, several of our contributors also peel back the temporal layers of more recent sites only to discover the embedded and apparently indelible traces of earlier cultures and multiple acts of colonial dispossesion. Thus the reader is inevitably sent back and forth between the early 1500's and the present day—between the European discovery of "America" and exemplary moments of nation-building and, say, the freeway system and cinematic dreams of a uniquely postmodern city like Los Angeles. Indeed, the discoveries discussed reveal, again and again, how much a "place" captures its beholder, and how this reciprocity that is also a disruption in turn informs the joint acts of re-searching and reading. Sites beget "sites," and frequently in different orders and registers.

But this is another way of saying that the contributors here raise questions regarding descriptions of the hermeneutic circle between subject and object. As essay after essay in this collection demonstrates, sites (phenomena, texts, archives) by nature are collective phenomena and often untamable at that; by putting these first, the subject's traditional privileges become less useful and more self-conscious. Given a site's inherently critical nature—its always constructed and arbitrary perimeters and often seemingly illegible stratifications—the researcher must learn how not only to fathom but also make positive use of its depths and opacities. As Tadeus Sławek points out in his essay on Charles Olson's poetic meditations on Gloucester via the paintings of Fitz Hugh Lane, Dogtown (an earlier archaeological strata of Gloucester) can also evoke an oriental or "Phoenician eye-view." In Sławek geography gives way to grammography as he studies the importance of place in the very placelessness of the everyday. Again, in William Handley's essay the Los Angeles freeway system, apparently an ideal biotope of the city's quest for cultural amnesia, is a material palimpsest of the old Spanish Camino Real and its rail and auto successor paths as well as the inspirational source for much of the city's fiction and cinema.

In Susanne Rieser's discussion of Los Angeles as the epicenter of the cinematic spectacle, the city's screen self-portrait is shaken by earthquakes, volcanoes, wildfires, racial violence, and all kinds of lesser (if proleptic) apocalypses. As if caught in a nightmare it can never shake off, Hollywood has consistantly portrayed the city as a cinematic disasterville, the capital of catastrophes. Rieser goes on to explore why this is so and in the process reveals how disaster films and action movies help the city to forget the very real problems that are staring it in the face. Or perhaps more accurately, by representing and formalizing the city's general thwart, film "manages" metropolitan edginess by reproducing it as an entertainment commodity. In her finely layered essay on Muncie, Martha Banta correlates what was famously meant to be a workable definition of a typical American town with three different moments of its history. In the end, however, we are left with not one but three truly engrossing narratives which she identifies as so many different realities: Buckongahelastown, Munseytown, and Middletown. Refusing to stop here, Banta continues to dig into Muncie's past, until we are ultimately left hovering over an ancient Indian mound and litte more than a handful of eloquent archaeological traces.

When properly investigated, though, even such scattered clues are capable of yielding not only an hypothesis but also a conviction of America as God's book. John Leo, for example, discusses how popular media work to produce and publicize sites as iconic spectacles for dispersed beholders. In his view sites can be at once places that are made legible in ideological, religious, and national ways by the operations of discourses made to seem as if they are immanental to places themselves. Thus "God" is co-present if not co-terminal with the "American" landscape: a deconstruction of perception by privileging the transcendental. This is the logic of "Manifest Destiny," which Leo argues can also be understood as the signifying work of perspectival systems in American early mass culture. As all of these essays demonstrate, there is a special challenge in working sites: they invariably require multidisciplinary forms of critical response as well as methods adequate for the discursive representation of the scene. If complex perception initiates the encounter with sites, the critical reflection on that perception resituates the archive and its appropriations.

* * *

But what, after all, is a site? What, for that matter, do we mean by text and territory? And finally, how do these produce cultural capital? In this collection of essays, rarely are these fundamental concepts obvious or dealt with in the same way. Let us begin with the first. For archaeologists, a site traditionally has stood for a basic empirico-analytical unit; it was an activity area which the researcher defined unproblematically through surface reconnaissance. In effect, the concept of site was once considered a rather self-evident and relatively well-defined space that seemingly produced its own definition as the fieldworker uncovered it. Today, however, this is not the case. With the contribution of disciplines such as semiotics it has been overhauled and greatly enriched. Viewed as a semiotic entity, a site comes into being as much through the intentions and procedures of the archaeologist as through the simple process of "finding" it.

Taken to its extreme, this approach leads us to equate the activity of working a site with the site itself. In a sense, then, there are as many versions of a site as there are overdetermining explanations of it. And how could it be otherwise? In his essay Anthony Marasco mentions that photographs of a number of western sites taken during several United States Geological Survey exeditions during the last quarter of the 19th century were eventually canonized under the rubric of art photography in the 1930's. Then in the late 1970's these same sites were resurveyed and rephotographed, with highly ambiguous results. Some considered the new set of photographs a revisionist attempt to finally define the west as a distinct region and not just a stage for confirming the archetypal processes of nation-building. But Marasco argues that it is not that simple. Not only did the Rephotographic Survey Project reproduce those early monumentalizing images; they now suggest an arbitrary process of ruin and decline. In these latest photographs, in other words, nature in the United States is now a momento of its past.

In effect, studied in place, sites form a memory theater of the nation or the territory in which they are located. As John Leo, Anthony Marasco, and Martha Banta suggest, the most famous of them provide us with our culture's common places and function rhetorically both as productive images and as the *mise-en-scène* of our most cherished cultural subjects. In his essay on Chicago and its premier architect, Louis Sullivan, William Boelhower discusses how Sullivan embraced the surrounding agricultural wealth of the Midwest and summed it up in his theory of ornament in an attempt to commemorate the very territory that made Chicago nature's metropolis. In the hands of a Sullivan, the tall office building and the modern department store came to represent the city's eagerness to invest in cultural capital commensurate with its new national and world stature. Spilled across the territory in formations perhaps only a map would help us to chart, such sites provide us with a sort of thematic reserve of our culture's most compelling narratives and topics. In order to read them, though, we must respect their complexity not only as anthropological and historical concretions but also as recycled and already circulating cultural representations.

In his essay on the highly stylized images of early America as the site of a feminized utopian idyll, Mario Klarer also sheds light on the equally familiar images (colonial fantasies or projections) of the cruel cannibalistic practices of the natives. He seeks to trace the origins of both sets of images, which he draws mostly from 16th century travel narratives, back to similar sets of images in ancient and medieval texts. This inevitably leads him to trace an earlier European genealogy for such practices as "sealing anuses and devouring men." In other words, the practice of literary anthropology or geocultural critique means reading territories as palimpsests of all sorts of historical residues, including the fantastical. If each site has its own story (or stories) to tell, a sequence of them may lead to a larger and ultimately quite different narrative, as several of the essays in this collection demonstrate. Any given site may also be part of a larger network involving county, state, region and more. Writ large, these sites give witness, indeed are the testimonies of a history of modernity as institutionalization and instrumentality of everyday practices.

For poststructuralist literary critics and cultural studies scholars, this polarization between site as a paradigm for empirical data and site as a theoretical and also practical construct of the fieldworkers and their choice of tools will sound familiar. In fact, over the same period of time the notion of text has undergone the same transformation as that of site. Up until around the late 1960's in the field of literary studies, the dominant concept of the text derived from largely formalist and humanist assumptions—as a kind of well-wrought urn, the text was an immanental aesthetic object sufficient unto itself, a bearer of universal, transcedental meanings. "Intertextuality" at most consisted of echoes, allusions among coteries, outright thefts. Today, even the older generation of humanists and New Critics accept some such version of literary texts as tethered to the ground and conditions of their making. For cultural studies scholars these conditions entail the vectors certainly of class, ethnicity, and gender and also those of the production, circulation, distribution, and consumption of cultural artifacts—in other words, "texts" in the broadest sense. In his book *Culture and Imperialism*, for example, Edward Said writes: "Texts are protean things; they are tied to circumstances and to politics large and small, and these require attention and criticism." In a bid to suggest the current challenges which the heavily loaded concept of text now embodies, he then goes on to say: "No one can take stock of everything, of course, just as no one theory can explain or account for the connections among texts and societies." Once again, perhaps it is indirectly due to the long-term, crossdisciplinary influence of cultural studies that all of our contributors have apparently evoked and then critiqued an originary notion of text as a basic cultural activity (however "mythic" or fictive such an "imaginary" may be): thus, not text understood as a noun (Lat. *textus*) but primarily as a connecting activity (*texere* to weave). And so we have identified a fundamental operative link between the notions of site, text, and culture.

As we have already implied in our discussion of these two terms above, neither can be fully appreciated without taking into account the notion of territory. In effect, if we do not want sites to appear as isolated atoms or scholarly monads—as if they too could be read as well-wrought urns—then we must place them in context. In this volume of essays, context stands for territory, whether that be a mountain peak, a freeway system, a midwestern metropolis, a small average town in central Indiana, but also for that web of archives and discourses marking and mapping the landscape. It is this enhancement of territory that allows us to speak of both sites and texts as already positioned and caught up in a series of already determining frames. Moreover, it is perhaps this broad notion of territory that best evokes the kind of intractability which the hermeneutic circle must now tolerate as it seeks to withstand the physiosemiotic pressures involved in working sites. In addition, how can we fail to recognize issues of a geopolitical nature impinging upon and crisscrossing any given site, however intimate and unexplored? In his detailed essay on how the Amazon River got its name, Robert Lawson-Peebles takes us through a fascinating history of how geographical and textual representation often function as both a chivalric quest and a practical colonizing guide. In the hands of Sir Walter Raleigh, the old-world myth of the Amazons is used to project a new-world utopia in which the power of a virgin queen (Elizabeth) has legitimacy and dominion over a lesser known virgin land (the "Large and Bewtiful Empyre of Guiana").

In its most rudimental form the notion of territory implies an extension of terrain, a surface, a form, and a zone of competence, whether these be understood as phenomena or the cultural discourses invested in those phenomena. In the political and administrative context of modernity, territory thus may become "charged" by the any number of discursive effects and emotions, including competing versions of sovereignty, citizenship, shifting notions of human rights and privileges, or varieties of patriotism. Territory is invariably the subject and the object of these conflicts; the land literally their ground and horizon.

Having made specific claims for the terms site, text, and territory, let us briefly comment on this final category shaping the workgathered here. This would be the suggestive concept of capital, especially as it is developed and deployed in the work of Pierre Bordieu. While it may seem self-apparent that all forms of capital work on the basis of "exchange," that is that values, things, places and conditions not only change but may be substituted for each other (and not always as equivalences), as practicing scholars we are aware of how knowledge "works" as social and cultural capital (to just mention economic). As Bourdieu might remind us, there is nothing innocent about working sites (we may substitute here the phrase "critical objects") like Middletown, the Amazon River, or the Mountain of the Holy Cross. These choices involve exclusions, risks, professional investments, and sometimes struggles, although scholars also may choose territories and topics because they find them personally attractive or appealing. Most probably find their interests piqued and shaped by global concerns and passions, for example, the roles played in public life by contradictory and even delusory conceptions of "nationalism" and "territory." Some forms of symbolic or cultural capital formation, then, are counter-hegemonic: they seek to restore or to maintain cultural memories by showing how a self-effacing and seemingly self-generating (or self-legitimating) present got where it is. On this view it's a truism to say that all sites by definition are contested, that is, they are complex *places* in which and over which conflicts of signification and representation occur. Inasmuch as they belong to an *image-repertoire* of by now *trans*national scenes, topics and mass produced visualizations, sites *work* to invite and produce the expressive reactions of their global beholders. In these extended senses of the always changing locations of capital and of site, let us say that the international roster of contributors here demonstrates a commitment to "critical internationalism" as one of the "futures of American studies." We find that the diversity of viewpoints offered here, the number of surprises attending a deliberately international collaboration, strengthens American studies as an enterprise in self-critique: it gets past its past and learns from it.

William Boelhower, Venezia
John Leo, Providence

Foucault's Mirror, the Amazon Basin, and the Topography of Virginity

Robert Lawson-Peebles
University of Exeter

1

Naming is one of the earliest stages in the process of taking possession. The Vinland Sagas tell us that when Leif Eriksson sailed west, he first reached a barren country that he named Helluland ("Flat Stone Land"; probably Baffin Island). Then he reached a land which "was flat and wooded, with white sandy beaches," and which he called Markland ("Forest Land"; probably Labrador). Finally he arrived at the land that he called Vinland (the land of vines), which almost certainly was the northern tip of the land which was later, in ignorance of Viking presettlement, called Newfoundland.[1] In this essay I want to discuss one instance of naming, that of the Amazon River. It is a process much more labyrinthine than the descriptive topographies of Viking colonialism, is deeply rooted in textual transmission and comprises, in addition to taking possession, a dynamic involving national and religious rivalries and the redirection of the pre-existing tropes of European eastward expansion.

Foucault's mirror gives us an initial access to the complexities involved in the toponymy of the Amazon. At an age considerably greater than Lagan's median of 12 months, Michel Foucault imagined himself in front of a mirror. During a lecture given in 1967 he playfully reconfigured the most significant moment in Lacanian psychoanalysis by suggesting that the consequence of seeing oneself in the mirror was not the decentering of the self, but rather an awareness of the complex relation of the self and space. Foucault suggested that the sight in the mirror produced "a sort of mixed, joint experience" that typified the relation between the two forms of space, which he characterized as a utopia and a heterotopia:

> The mirror is, after all, a utopia, since it is a placeless place. In the mirror, I see myself there where I am not, in an unreal, virtual space that opens up behind the surface; I am over there, there where I am not, a sort of shadow that gives my own visibility to myself, that enables me to see myself there where I am absent: such is the utopia of the mirror. But it is also a heterotopia in so far as the mirror does exist in reality, where it exerts a sort of counteraction on the position that I occupy. . . . [I]t makes this place that I occupy at the moment when I look at myself at once absolutely real, connected with all the space that surrounds it, and absolutely unreal, since in order to be perceived it has to pass through this virtual point which is over there.[2] (Foucault 22)

At first glance, this seems to give us a complete, as well as a complex, account of the interplay of self and space. The "virtual space" in the mirror's silvered surface, its area of virtuality, describes an angle of almost 180 degrees and extends theoretically to infinity. Its opposite, the area of actuality, occupies the remaining space and includes the mirror itself. To develop this duality as a metaphor of the process of exploration, it would seem that as the experience of new environments develops with the written record of them, the area of actuality would increase in inverse ratio to the area of virtuality.

This is, however, far too schematic. The literature of exploration shows that the areas of virtuality and actuality overlap, are more flexible, less geometrically precise in their relation to each other. In recent years, cultural critics have suggested two reasons. The first has usefully been called the "textual system." It is the network of pre-existing texts which may condition the viewpoint of the explorer, and with which the explorer's own text is in tension—sometimes contention.[3] The second reason, which has received greater critical attention, are the values of the explorers themselves, possibly including sensitivities to and prejudices about religion, nationality, gender, and social status; those elements which constitute their self-image and their sense of their differences from others. In The Wretched of the Earth, Franz Fanon drew attention to this Manichean mode of thinking apparently inherent in colonialist thought. The colonist, he suggested, conceived himself as the *maker*, creating temporal and spatial structures, which were then applied to indigenous peoples, and the lands they inhabited:

> The settler makes history; his life is an epoch, an Odyssey. He is the absolute beginning: "This land was created by us"; he is the unceasing cause . . . The natives were *made*. They were imagined by the colonist to exist outside those structures, "interminably in an unchanging dream."[4] (39-40)

Yet again, the schema suggested by Fanon and some other analysts of colonialism may still be too rigid. Firstly, I will suggest later in this essay that colonialist and native tropes may well have overlapped. Secondly, the colonialist "dream" was itself subject to change over time. When Foucault analyzed the mirror he used only the pre-Columbian definition of "utopia": no place, derived from the Greek *ou-topos*. That definition is, in other words, confined within the ambit of the so-called "Old World." The arrival of the "New World" on European consciousness led directly to a new, and now the more common, meaning of "utopia." That meaning began its life in 1516 in More's Utopia, as a pun exploiting the homonymic qualities of *ou-topos* and *eu-topos*, a "good place." The pun is a structuring device of Utopia, a complex and guileful text whose only certainty lies in its opening gambit. Peter Giles tells of one Raphael Hythloday, a learned traveler who "accompanied Vespucci on the last three of his four voyages, accounts of which are now common reading everywhere." This last statement is correct. The First Four Voyages of Amerigo Vespucci was initially published in Lisbon in 1504, quickly appeared in several editions, and was widely read. Giles is also correct about the limit of Vespucci's fourth voyage, a fort at Cabo Frio, on the coast of Brazil east of Rio de Janeiro. Such references to text and place are mere vehicles for a grand geographical flourish. After leaving Cabo Frio Hythloday "traveled through many countries" until "by strange good fortune, he got, via Ceylon, to Calicut, where by good luck he found some Portuguese ships; and so, beyond anyone's expectation, he returned to his own country." In other words, Hythloday completed an eastwards circumnavigation of the globe some fifteen years before the Magellan expedition, and within one sentence. That sentence is symptomatic of two aspects of European writing about the New World. Firstly, imagination precedes fact. One could say that, after that sentence, Utopia is unusually faint-hearted: after the opening geographical detail it makes little claim to be grounded in reality.[5] Second, that sentence joins the West with the East. I will argue that the written record of the New World took on some of the imaginative structures that had previously been applied to the East, added some of its own, and maybe even some of the denizens of the land it recorded. The naming of the Amazon River is symptomatic of a network of cross-cultural relations of even greater complexity than had existed before.

2

The river system to which we now give the collective title of the Amazon is the largest in the world by volume. Over 4,000 miles long, it is second in length only to the Nile's 4,187 miles—although Mark Twain, with typical panache, treated the Missouri and Mississippi as one, and claimed that the result, at 4,300 miles, was the longest in the world. Bigger ships can navigate the Amazon from the Brazilian Atlantic coast for 2,306 miles to the Peruvian port of Iquitos. The river has more than one thousand tributaries. Its precise sources are unclear, but they certainly begin in the Peruvian Andes less than one hundred miles from the Pacific Ocean. It is likely that the Amazon drained into the Pacific until the upraise of the Andean range, between 15 and 4 million years ago, caused those sources to reverse direction, feeding a river that crossed a much greater landmass and became much more powerful. The Amazon's discharge into the Atlantic is so great that it turns the salt water brackish for more than one hundred miles offshore.[6] Superficially, it seems fitting that a *lusus naturae* should be named after the warrior-woman, long regarded in Western culture as a *lusus humanae*.

This discussion of Foucault, More and Fanon indicates, however, that the river did not simply gain its title because, like the warrior-woman, it was regarded as a freak. An account of the textual transmission of the myth of the Amazons, from the earliest Greek writers to the authors of chivalric romances of the sixteenth century, will suggest that the River was named for more complex reasons. The Homeric poem the Iliad notes that the Amazons are "men's equals," and that they "fight men in battle." Later writers and artists perpetuated a myth of the women-warriors that had four or five components. The first, apparent in the Iliad and also Plutarch's Life of Theseus, is that they were formidable fighters. The second is that they maintained an independent, all-female state. This component is to be found, for instance, in the writing of the Roman Marcus Junianus Justinus, as is the third, which is that to maintain the state beyond one generation the Amazons imported males for a brief mating season, killing or expelling any male children resulting from this brief union.

The fourth component of the myth of the Amazons was the subject of much debate. It derived from the Greek root of their name: *mazos*—the breast. The Greek geographer Strabo, for example, suggested that each Amazon woman underwent a mastectomy so that she could shoot arrows or throw javelins more easily. In The Campaigns of Alexander, the Greek historian Arrian was more reserved, noting that "according to some writers, their right breasts were smaller than their left, and were bared in battle." (356-357) Greek painters, perhaps on aesthetic grounds, tended not to show any amputation. A frieze from the Temple of Apollo at Bassae reveals an Amazon with both breasts bared, while a vase, by the Niobid Painter, shows a fully clothed Amazon, wearing Greek corselets and oriental tights. The Niobid Painter hints at the fifth and final component of the myth. The Amazons represented an alternative, antithetical way of life, and were therefore placed at the edge of the Greek world. It was part of the cult of Alexander the Great that the Amazon Queen Thalestris was among his many conquests as he marched eastwards beyond Asia Minor. Usually, stories of the Amazons placed them at a safe distance from the patriarchal order of the Greek world. Another Greek historian, Diodorus Siculus, put them on the Isle of Hespera "in the western parts of Libya, on the bounds of the inhabited world," an appropriate place for women "who followed a manner of life unlike that which prevails among us." Dionysius Scytobrachian, a grammarian who lived in Alexandria during the second century BC, located Hespera at the far western edge of the world.[7] (1-4)

Jacob Burckhardt, in the lectures on Greek culture first given at Basle in 1872, remarked that "it was to this magnificent or awe-inspiring fringe of their world that the Greeks clung longest."[8] (22). It follows that their belief in the occupants of that fringe influenced their successors. A survey of some later texts reveals that the myth of the Amazons is flexible, thus allowing adjustment to disparate societies both in time and place. Two romances concern Alexander. The Alexander Romance, which may date back to the third century BC, was first translated into Latin around 338 AD. It subsequently appeared in eighty versions in twenty-four languages, including Hebrew, Serbian, Czech, Italian, Spanish, French, German, Russian, Irish and English. The text asserts that "the Amazons, larger than other races of women, and remarkable for their beauty and strength . . . live in the hinterland across the river Amazon . . . beyond the edges of the world." (143-146). The river completely encircles their land, "and it takes a year to travel around it." In short, a *lusus humanae* is protected by a *lusus naturae*. Despite this defense, and despite being armed in overwhelming numbers, the Amazons agree to obey Alexander and pay him tribute. The Alexandreis works harder to integrate Alexander into the Amazon myth. It was written in Latin between 1178 and 1182 by Gautier de Châtillon, and translated into Czech, Dutch, Spanish and—as Alexanders Saga—into Old Icelandic.

The Alexandreis retells the story of the visit by Thalestris "with virgin retinue," their left breasts bared, their right seared "to ease their wielding of the pliant bow, and leave them unencumbered for the javelin." Alexander agrees to "sire a kingdom's heirs." If Thalestris produces a daughter, she will "attain her mother's realms." If it is male, "he'd be returned/for nourishment under his father's tutelage."[9] (131-133). There is no Alexander to reassert a patriarchal order in the Amazon city-state of Ariosto's Orlando Furioso (1532). The 1591 translation by Sir John

Harington acts as a bawdy satire of the government of his godmother, Queen Elizabeth:

> Here women guide, and rule, and govern all,
> The men from government they do expell,
> Some they do kill, the rest keep bond and thrall,
> He sole shall scape that runs at tilt so well,
> As first to make ten men of theirs to fall,
> And next in Venery and flesh delight,
> Can satisfie ten women in one night.[10] (216)

The tale of Freydis likewise inverts the patriarchal order, and is responsible for the first landing of an Amazon in the New World. The tale is contained in a Viking Saga—not Alexanders Saga, of course, but rather Erík's Saga (The Saga of Eric the Red) which, with the Grænlendinga Saga (The Greenlanders' Saga), treats the Norse arrival in America. Freydis, the sister of Leif Eriksson, is amongst those who settle Vinland. She is "an arrogant, overbearing woman," married to a "feeble" man called Thorvard. She taunts the other male settlers, claiming that she can fight better than they. She soon gets her chance. During a battle with the Native Americans, whom they call Skrælings (savages), Freydis is cut off from her party because she is hindered by her pregnant condition:

> The Skrælings closed in on her. In front of her lay a dead man, Thorbrand Snorrason, with a flint stone buried in his head, and his sword beside him. She snatched up the sword and prepared to defend herself. When the Skrælings came rushing towards her she pulled one of her breasts out of her bodice and slapped it with the sword. The Skrælings were terrified at the sight of this and fled back to their boats and hastened away. (108-111)

Understandably, the Skrælings do not wish to enter combat with an Amazon. The tale of Freydis extends the myth of the warrior-women. Viking society was as patriarchal as the Greek, despite evidence of well-to-do Viking women. In contrast, America from the earliest settlement provided opportunities for the modes of behavior symbolized by the Amazons. Freydis therefore became the virago within. The episode with the Skrælings is just the first overt expression of a temperament which, given that margin of freedom in the New World, continued to trouble Viking males, but did not lead to her expulsion. Erík's Saga tells how Freydis breaks trading agreements and, coveting a larger ship, kills the owners, their crew and wives. She returns to Greenland rich and unrepentant.[11]

The Travels of Sir John Mandeville taught Columbus to expect to find Amazons when he sailed westward. It was first written in French about 1357, and by the end of that century had been translated into every major European language. Scholars revealed Mandeville as a fraud in 1888. In contrast, Columbus treated it as a traveler's handbook, as did others such as Raleigh's contemporary Sir Martin Frobisher, who carried Mandeville on his first attempt in 1576 to find the Northwest

Passage. The text retells the story of the origin of the Amazon state, and locates the women on an island in the Caspian Sea. It adds detail about Amazonian democracy, and suggests that social status determines the precise nature of the mastectomy:

> Next to Chaldea is the land of Amazoun, which we call the Maiden Land or the Land of Women; no man lives there, only women. . . . If they have a girl child, they will cut off one of her breasts and cauterize it; in the case of a woman of great estate, the left one, so that she can carry her shield better, and, in one of low degree, they cut off the right, so that it will not hinder them shooting—for they know very well the skill of archery. There is always a queen to rule that land, and they all obey her. The queen is always chosen by election, for they choose the woman who is the best fighter. These women are noble and wise warriors . . .[12] (116-117)

Felipe Fernandez-Armesto noted that Columbus was "evidently obsessed by the legend of the Amazons," and guessed that they might perform a decorative function on his maps, or might be used to flatter Isabella of Castile, who saw herself as a strong woman.[13] Mandeville's description of the warrior-women, both less frightening and more law-abiding than the Viking account of Freydis, could be used by Columbus to honor to his patroness.

3
The textual evidence for Columbus's voyages was, for a very long time, slight indeed. His journals were kept secret by the Spanish royal court, and were then lost. The abstract made by the Dominican historian Bartolomé de Las Casas remained unknown until 1791. Martin Fernández de Navarrete first published it in a Spanish collection of documents in 1825. It was not until 1828, with Washington Irving's The Life and Voyages of Christopher Columbus, drawing on Navarrete's collection, that the personal fame of Columbus was finally established. For almost three centuries, then, the only primary source detailing Columbus's landfall was "an account of the facts, thus abridged" to slightly less than 3,000 words, dated 15 February 1493 and written shortly before he arrived back in Spain. The popularity of the "First Letter," as it is now known, was in inverse proportion to its length. The response to it was almost telegraphic. It was promptly translated into Latin, French, German, Italian and Catalan, and by 1500 had spread, in at least seventeen editions, throughout Europe. The Letter was successful because it conveyed reports about the West in terms of the East, including the story of the warrior-women:

> I have found no monsters, nor had a report of any, except in an island "Carib," which is the second at the coming into the Indies, and which is inhabited by a people who are regarded in all the islands as very fierce and who eat human flesh. They have many canoes with which they range through all the islands of India and pillage and take whatever they can. . . . They are ferocious among these other people who are cowardly to an excessive degree . . . These are they who have intercourse with the women of "Matinino," which is the first island met on the way from Spain to the

Indies, in which there is not a man. These women engage in no feminine occupation, but use bows and arrows of cane . . . and they arm and protect themselves with plates of copper, of which they have much.[14] (125-127)

This is the first appearance of New World cannibalism in European consciousness, and it is partly derived from Columbus's second travel handbook, the Pipino Latin edition of Marco Polo's Travels that he annotated. The report of the copper armor may also have been influenced by Polo, and probably by Columbus's awareness of the West African copper trade, dominated from about 1480 by the Portuguese.[15] "These women" interest Columbus, then, for martial and mercantile reasons as well as sexual. His report is notable for its plausibility. Columbus does not say if they have undergone mastectomies nor—perhaps for that reason—does he call them Amazons. Yet, alone amongst the denizens of what are now known as the Antilles, the warrior-women seem able to control the Caribs; they might also give Isabella the means to loosen the Portuguese grasp on a valuable metal.

There are good reasons, then, why Columbus should include information about warrior-women in his report. But critics have tended to assume that he reported only what he wanted to hear, or what he misheard, from frightened or complaisant native captives. There is, however, another possibility, suggested by the anthropologist Neil Whitehead, that the natives may have had their own pre-Columbian myths of a matriarchal society, which in due course had an impact on the naming of the Amazon. Those myths may have been the reason why Columbus left the name "Matinino" undisturbed, although its first syllable could be taken from the Latin term for "mother." Otherwise, as did the Vikings five centuries earlier, Columbus began the process of assimilation by renaming. Some of the names reflect the devotional structure of the Catholic Church. One of the islands had the aboriginal name of Guanahani; Columbus called it "'San Salvador,' in remembrance of the Divine Majesty, Who has marvelously bestowed all this." Another island he called "Santa Maria de Concepcion." Yet other islands, like Fernandina, Isabella and, most obviously of all, Hispaniola, imprinted Spain upon the New World.[16]

In contrast, the European naming of the river now known as the Amazon is more complex, and has been the subject of some enquiry. Its first name reflected both Catholicism and topography. The initial European sighting of the river was credited to Vicente Yanez Pinzón, who had captained the Nina on Columbus's first voyage and led another expedition westwards in 1499. According to the 1504 Libretto of the Italian historian Petrus Martyr Anglerius—known to the English as Peter Martyr—in February 1501 Pinzón had noticed a stream of fresh water flowing into the Atlantic. Pinzon named the river "Santa Maria de la Mar Dulce," while a map of the world apparently printed that year stripped the river of its Catholic connotations by naming it simply "Mar Dulce." From 1513 "Mar Dulce" was gradually replaced by the name "Marañon."[17] It is not entirely clear how the river came to be given that title. Robert Southey, the British Poet Laureate and friend of Coleridge, wondered about some of the more vivid reasons. They included a version of the native name; the "villainies" of Lope de Aguirre; even a negation of the river Marah in the Book of Exodus, so called because the Israelites found the waters bitter. Southey concluded that the river had probably been named "after some person in that [Pinzón] expedition, . . the man who first tasted its waters, . . or who first ascertained they were in a river." At the end of the nineteenth century, the Spanish historian José Toribio Medina made a much more painstaking examination of original documents and decided that, while the river could have been named for a Spanish captain, it was finally impossible to explain the origin of the name "in a satisfactory way."[18] Present-day maps seem to achieve a compromise by calling the river the Marañon from the Peruvian Cordillera Central until where it joins the Ucuyali, shortly before Iquitos; and the Amazon or Amazonas thereafter.

The Amazons, although no European had yet seen them, still waited in the wings. A further chivalric romance, published in 1510, placed them on the Pacific coast. Garci Rodriguez de Montalvo wrote _Las Sergas de Esplandian_ (The Labors of the Very Brave Knight Esplandian) as the sequel to _Amadis de Gaula_. In part the text deals with the Amazon queen Calafia, who occupies a stronghold that bears her name:

> . . . on the right-hand side of the Indies there was an island called California, which was . . . inhabited by black women, and there were no males among them at all, for their life style was similar to that of the Amazons. The island was made up of the wildest cliffs and the sharpest precipices found anywhere in the world. These women had energetic bodies and courageous, ardent hearts, and they were very strong. Their armor was made entirely of gold—which was the only metal found on the island—as were the trappings of the fierce beasts that they rode once they were tamed. They lived in very well designed caves. (456-458)

Esplandian united Columbus's First Letter with some of the tales in Mandeville, and used the myth of Eldorado, begun with the First Letter, to increase the value of the warrior-women's armour.[19] The text also made the first overt comparison between the New World warrior-women and the Amazons. The convergence of image and evidence seemed so compelling that it could not be long before the real Amazons were found.

4

In December 1541 Francisco Pizarro, the Spanish conqueror of Peru, sent his lieutenant Francisco de Orellana down a river now called the Napo (a tributary of the Amazon) in search of food. According to the scribe of the party, the Dominican friar Gaspar de Carvajal, the strong current of the river prevented them from returning upstream. Unaware of its length, they decided "to go forward and follow the river . . . trusting in Our Lord that He would see fit to preserve our lives until we should see our way out." One month into their journey they are told "of the existence of Amazons and of wealth further down the river." On Thursday 24 June 1542, seeking a place to celebrate the feast of Saint John the Baptist—Carvajal is both precise in his dates and punctilious in observing the Catholic calendar—the party "came suddenly upon the excellent land and dominion of the Amazons." The local natives threaten "to seize us all and take us to the Amazons," and a fight breaks out. The natives give such a vigorous account of themselves that Carvajal feels it necessary to explain:

> I want it to be known what the reason was why these Indians defended themselves in this manner. . . . they are the subjects of, and tributaries to, the Amazons, and, our coming having been made known to them, they went to them to ask help, and there came as many as ten or twelve of them, for we ourselves saw these women, who were there fighting in front of all the Indian men as women captains, and these latter fought so courageously that the Indian men did not dare to turn their backs, and anyone who did turn his back they killed with clubs right there before us, and this is the reason why the Indians kept up their defense for so long. These women were very white and tall, and have hair very long and braided and wound about the head, and they are very robust and go about naked, [but] with their privy parts covered, with their bows and arrows in their hands, doing as much fighting as ten Indian men . . .
>
> Our Lord was pleased to give strength and courage to our companions, who killed seven or eight (for these we actually saw) of the Amazons, whereupon the Indians lost heart, and they were defeated . . . (213-214)

This passage twice enjoins belief. Because Orellana's party "actually saw" these women, Carvajal is able to correct both the account of the pigmentation of the warrior-women in Esplandian, and the social analysis of the mastectomy in Mandeville. (Carvajal comments on the nakedness of the women, and therefore would not have omitted the detail of any mutilation.) The result is an increase in the sense of wonder. Leaders of male warriors, the women are more stalwart than those in Columbus's First Letter and even those in Esplandian. Later, Carvajal reports an interrogation conducted by Orellana. The native's answers coincide with four of the five components of the European classical myth. The missing component, the mastectomy, is replaced by a story, also to be found in Esplandian, of "very great wealth of gold and silver." In Carvajal's account there seems to be a complex set of overlapping components: between the European classical account of the Amazons; topography and Amazonian beauty in the Alexander Romance; the myth of Eldorado; a native matriarchal trope; and personal experience. The title that they are now given, "Amazon," is as a result more an accolade than an etymology.

Orellana's party escaped to complete their journey to the Atlantic along "this river, which we hold to be the Marañon."[20] (234). They returned to Seville, where their account of their experience was met with skepticism. Gonzalo Fernandez de Oviedo y Valdes, who knew Columbus and who had lived much of his life in the West Indies, reserved judgment. Carvajal's claims were included in Oviedo's La historia general de las indias, but in a section which remained unpublished until the mid-nineteenth century. Oviedo wrote that the women "may well be called Amazons (if I have been told the truth); but they do not cut off their right breasts, as did those whom the ancients called Amazons." Antonio Herrera y Tordesillas, in the Historia General de las Indias published in Madrid between 1601 and 1615, repeats

Carvajal's account, but leaves "the credibility of it to the judgment of others." The judgment of Francisco Lopez de Gómara was clear. Hernán Cortés employed him as secretary-chaplain on the conquistador's return from Mexico. Lopez de Gómara published his *Historia de las Indias* in 1552, largely in praise of Cortes. Despite—or perhaps because—he had never visited the New World, Lopez de Gómara was categorical in his statements. He defined the Amazons in terms of the story most recently refined in Mandeville. To be sure, there were warrior-women in the New World, but they were not Amazons:

> I do not believe either that any woman burns and cuts off her right breast in order to be able to shoot with the bow, because with it they shoot very well; or that they kill or exile their own sons; or that they live without husbands, being as they are very voluptuous. Others besides Orellana have proclaimed this same yarn about the Amazons ever since the Indies have been discovered, and never has such a thing been seen, and never will it be seen, along this river. Because of this imposture, already many write and say the "River of the Amazons" . . . [21] (34)

Lopez de Gómara's attempt to achieve diagnostic clarity was doomed to failure. As we shall see, the river was for a while renamed the Orellana, following the convention mentioned by Southey, in honor of the first European leader to travel its length. But the one that Lopez de Gómara detested so much eventually superseded that name.

The Amazons occasionally continued to appear in Old World environments. A Report of the Kingdome of Congo, published by the Portuguese Odoardo Lopez in 1588 and translated into English in 1597, asserted that the King of "Monomotapa" (situated approximately where Zimbabwe is today) maintained:

> Legions of women, whom he esteemeth very highly, and accounteth them as the very sinewes and strength of his military forces. The women do burn their leaft [sic—left] papes with fire, because they should bee no hinderaunce unto them in their shooting, after the use and manner of the auncient Amazones . . . (195)

Samuel Purchas reprinted the account in the compilation, Purchas his Pilgrimage (1626). Unlike Lopez, Purchas had read Mandeville, for he added a dryly-noncommittal marginal note: "Left-Handed Amazons." [22] (508). Purchas was less cynical elsewhere in his compilation, because the English translations he provided, of accounts of Spanish and Portuguese exploration in the New World, were part of a colonial agenda.

5

Joyce Lorimer has shown that, at least from 1553, the English had been interested in sending an expedition to the Amazon. But at that time any thoughts of English colonization of America were, in the words of the early twentieth-century literary scholar Sir Walter Raleigh, "not likely to bear fruit while Mary reigned and

Philip governed."[23] (1-9). The translators therefore preceded the colonizers. When in 1553 Richard Eden published A Treatyse of the New India, his first translation of Peter Martyr's *De Orbe Novo*, he blended Columbus's First Letter with the comparison in Esplandian: "he [Columbus] passed by many Ilandes: among the whiche was one called Matinina, in whyche dwell only women, after the maner of them, called AMAZONES." In the longer translation he made two years later, he warmed to his theme, uniting the First Letter with the stories told in Mandeville and Esplandian. While sailing from Guadalupe to Hispaniola, Columbus saw:

> A great Ilande . . . called MADANINO, or MATININO . . . inhabited only with women. To whome the CANIBALES have accesse at certain tymes of the yeare, as in owlde tyme the THRACIANS had to the AMAZONES in the Ilande of LESBOS. The men children, they sende to theyre fathers. But the women theye kepe with them selves. They have greate and strange caves or dennes in the ground, to which they flye for safegarde if any men resorte unto them at any other tyme then is appoynted. And there defende them selves with bowes and arrowes, against the violence of such an attempte to envade them.[24]

When the tale was repeated in Eden's 1577 edition, completed by Richard Willes, Elizabeth had been Queen for nineteen years. She reversed Mary's prohibition of English involvement in the New World, and began the period when the English colonizers flourished together with the translators.

One translation included by Purchas in his collection was an account by the Bavarian Ulrich Schmidt of his travels in Brazil and Peru in the twenty years from 1534 to 1554. Schmidt's account had first been published in German in 1567, maybe because his frequent comments on the voluptuary women appealed to vernacular tastes. Purchas made an abridgment from the Latin translation of 1599, quaintly rendering the author's name as "Hulderike Schnirdel." There was nothing droll about Purchases translation of the tale of the Amazons by the king of the "Scherves," doubtless because the king had chosen the correct breast:

> he made mention of the Amazones and of their riches, [which] was very pleasing to us to heare. . . . These women the Amazones, have only one of their pappes, their Husbands come unto them three or foure times in the yeere. And if the woman beeing with child by her Husband, bring forth a Male child, she sendeth him home again to his Father, but if it be a Female, she keepeth it with her: and seareth the right pap of it, that it may grow no more, which she doth for this purpose, that they may be more fit to handle their Weapons and Bowes. For they are warlike women, making continuall war with their Enemies.[25]

Schmidt's account was also interesting to Purchas because of the connection, to be found in both Esplandian and Carvajal, between Amazons and untold wealth.

The foremost English authority on the Amazons, as well as the most enthusiastic seeker for gold, was Sir Walter Raleigh. During his long second sojourn in prison, from 1603 to 1616, he wrote The History of the World, taking some one million words to reach 130BC, and publishing the book in 1614. After an account of Alexander's campaigns in the East, Raleigh devoted a lengthy "digression" to a discussion of the sources for "this Amazonian business." He named several of "the many authors making mention of Amazons that were in the old times," including Plutarch, Justinus and Diodorus Siculus. From sixteenth-century writers he chose Odoardo Lopez, Ulrich Schmidt and Lopez de Gómara, ignoring the vehement denials of the secretary-chaplain to Cortés. Raleigh concluded:

> I have produced these authorities, in part, to justify mine own relation of these Amazons, because that which was delivered me for truth by an ancient cacique of Guiana, how upon the river of Papamena (since the Spanish discoveries called Amazons) that these women still live and govern, was held for a vain and unprobable report.[26]

Raleigh's reasserted belief in the existence of the New World Amazons is a good example of the double life of Foucault's mirror. Raleigh looked back into the heterotopic past of the Old World to create a utopia in the New. In the process he flouted the fine distinctions insisted upon both by Lopez de Gomara and his own earlier work, doing so with such force that his beliefs became inscribed upon representations of the environment. It was an irony, which may have added to his forcefulness, that he was defending his view in a Jacobean age of which he was not emotionally, and shortly would not be physically, a part.

Celeste Turner Wright and Winfried Schleiner have demonstrated the frequent use of Amazonian imagery in England during the reign of Elizabeth.[27] Although there are suggestions that the Queen was not entirely pleased with Harrington's bawdy satire, she did allow Harington to dedicate it to her. She herself occasionally used Amazon imagery to advantage, most notably during her appearance at Tilbury in 1588 to inspect defences against the Armada. In a poem published that year, James Aske recorded the sight of her at Tilbury, like "the *Amazonian Queene . . .* beating downe the bloodie Greekes."[28] Raleigh, more than others within the charmed inner circle of Elizabeth's subjects, paid court to her in a manner which combined myth with realism, distinguished Protestant worship from Catholic idolatry, and moderated ardour with an imagery of chastity. The Discoverie of the Large, Rich and Bewtiful Empyre of Guiana is a fine example of Raleigh's style, and it was rewarded appropriately. Four different editions of the text appeared in 1596. De Bry included it in the eighth part of his America, as did Richard Hakluyt in the 1600 edition of his Principall Navigations. By that time it had been translated into Latin, German and Dutch. Raleigh's text aims to be both a hymn to Elizabeth and an advertisement for colonization, a chivalric quest and a practical guide.

This delicate process is achieved by means of an allegory of virginity.[29] Raleigh therefore reported that he presented Elizabeth to Trinidadian chiefs as "the great *Casique* [chief] of the north, and a virgin, and had more Casiqui under her than there were trees in their Iland." He linked virginity with freedom in order to distinguish

English and Spanish modes of colonization. The Spanish, he wrote, took the wives and daughters from the natives "and used them for the satisfying of their own lusts," while because it is the Queen's command, the English, even under provocation, never "knew any of their women . . . woonderfully to honour our nation." The image of chastity is then extended to the land itself, presenting it as undefiled in order to make it the rightful inheritance of the Elizabethans. The sentence has become notorious: "*Guiana* is a Countrey that hath yet her Maydenhead, never sackt, turned, nor wrought, the face of the earth hath not been torne . . ." The virginity of Guiana is contrasted with the description of the Amazons, related with a scholarly, judicious blend of classical myth and contemporary detail, and apparently a close attention to the natives. In another "digression," Raleigh tells that he met "a Casique or Lord" who had been to the river *"Topago"* (now known as the Rio Tapajos, a tributary of the Amazon) where the warrior-women dwelt:

> The memories of the like women are very ancient as well in *Africa* as in *Asia* . . . in many histories they are verified to have been, and in divers ages and provinces: But they which are not far from *Guiana* do accompanie with men but once in a yeere, and for the time of one moneth, which I gather by their relation to be in Aprill. At that time all the Kings of the borders assemble, and the Queenes of the *Amazones*, and after the Queens have chosen, the rest cast lots for their Valentines. . . . If they conceive, and be delivered of a sonne, they returne him to the father, if a daughter they nourish it, and reteine it . . . all being desirous to increase their owne sex and kinde, but that the cut of the right dug of the brest I do not finde to be true. It was farther told me, that if in wars they tooke any prisoners . . . in the end for certaine they put them to death: for they are said to be very cruell and bloodthirsty, especially to such as offer to invade their territories. These *Amazones* have likewise great store of these plates of gold . . .

Raleigh is likewise judicious about the environment of the Amazons. They live at the southern edge of Guiana and to the north of the river, which Raleigh identifies as "the *Amazones* or *Oreliano*." The *"Maragnon,"* he asserts, "is but a braunch" of the larger river. Raleigh's careful description succeeds in being of service to topographical exactitude, to his promotional needs, and to his Queen. The distinction between the South American Amazons and the English Amazon allows him to close his text with a flourish that is both a promise and a threat:

> Her Majesty heereby shall confirme and strengthen the opinions of al nations, as touching her great and princely actions. And where the south border of *Guiana* reacheth to the Dominion and Empire of the *Amazones*, those women shall heereby heare the name of a virgin, which is not onely able to defend her owne territories and her neighbors, but also invade and conquere so great Empyres and so farre removed.[30]

Raleigh, more than his predecessors, succeeded in transferring a name from classical mythology onto a New World environment. Later writers would not heed the complaint of Lopez de Gómara. When Purchas included in his compilation the 1597 account of the journey of one "Master Anthony Knivet" into "the Countrie of the Amazons," he added the marginal note: "Amazons, not a one-breasted Nation, but warlike women." In 1639, twenty-one years after Raleigh was beheaded, the Jesuit Father Cristoval de Acuña explored the river from Quito, in Peru, to the Atlantic. Two years later he published his findings in Madrid as the _Nuevo Descubrimiento del gran Rio de las Amazonas_. He repeated Raleigh, and noted: "Time will discover the truth, and if these are the Amazons made famous by historians, there are treasures shut up in their territory, which would enrich the whole world."[31] The South American Amazons never were found but, as Acuña's title shows, those who sought them left their mark permanently on the river.

NOTES

[1] The Vinland Sagas: The Norse Discovery of America, trans. and ed. Magnus Magnusson and Hermann Pálsson (Harmondsworth, Middx.: Penguin, 1965), pp. 55, 95.

[2] Michel Foucault, "Of Other Spaces," trans. Jay Miskowiec, Diacritics 16 No 1 (Spring 1986), 22.

[3] Christopher Mulvey, "Ecriture and Landscape: British writing on post-revolutionary America," Views of American Landscapes, ed. Mick Gidley and Robert Lawson-Peebles (Cambridge: Cambridge University Press, 1989), p.100.

[4] Franz Fanon, The Wretched of the Earth, trans. Constance Farrington (1965; rpt. Harmondsworth: Penguin, 1967), pp. 39–40. See, for instance, Tzvetan Todorov, The Conquest of America: The Question of the Other, trans. Richard Howard (New York: Harper & Row, 1984); Stephen Greenblatt, Marvelous Possessions: The Wonder of the New World (Chicago: University of Chicago Press, 1991); and Anthony Pagden, European Encounters with the New World: From Renaissance to Romanticism (New Haven, CT: Yale University Press, 1993).

[5] Thomas More, Utopia, trans. and ed. Robert M. Adams (2nd ed., New York: W. W. Norton & Co., 1992), p. 5.

[6] Mark Twain, Life on the Mississippi (1883; rpt. New York: New American Library, 1961), p.1. Michael Bright, Andes to Amazon: A Guide to Wild South America (London: BBC Worldwide, 2000), pp. 12, 57. The Cambridge Encyclopedia of Latin America and the Caribbean, ed. Simon Collier, Thomas E. Skidmore and Harold Blakemore (2nd. ed., Cambridge: Cambridge University Press, 1992), pp. 12-18.

[7] "Homer," The Iliad 3.189, 6.186, trans. Richmond Lattimore (1951; rpt. Chicago: University of Chicago Press, 1961), pp. 105, 158. Arthur Goldyng, Thabridgment of the Histories of Trogus Pompeius, collected and wrytten in the Laten tonge by the famous Historiographer Justine, and translated into English (London: T. Marshe, 1564). Arrian, The Campaigns of Alexander, trans. Aubrey de Selincourt, introd. J. R. Hamilton (1958; rpt. Harmondsworth, Middx.: Penguin, 1971), pp. 213, 356-357, 369. Diodorus of Sicily, The Library of History 53.1-4, trans. C. H. Oldfather (12 vols., Cambridge, MA: Harvard University Press, 1953), II, pp. 249, 251. John Boardman, Greek Art (2nd ed., London: Thames & Hudson, 1973), plates 129 and 167. See also Guy Cadogan Rothery, The Amazons in Antiquity and Modern Times (London: Griffiths, 1910); Truesdell S. Brown, "Euhemerus and the Historians,"

Harvard Theological Review 39 (October 1946), 267-269; Abby Wettan Kleinbaum, The War Against the Amazons (New York: McGraw-Hill, 1983); William B. Tyrrell, Amazons: a study in Athenian mythmaking (Baltimore: Johns Hopkins University Press, 1984); Josine H. Blok, The Early Amazons: Modern and Ancient Perspectives on a Persistent Myth (Leiden: Brill, 1995); and Lorna Hardwick, "Ancient Amazons: Heroes, Outsiders, or Women," Women in Antiquity, ed. Ian McAuslan and Peter Walcot (Oxford: Oxford University Press, 1996), pp.158–176.

[8] Jacob Burckhardt, The Greeks and Greek Civilization, trans. Sheila Stern, ed. Oswyn Murray (New York: St. Martin's Press, 1998), p. 22.

[9] The Greek Alexander Romance, trans. Richard Stoneman (Harmondsworth, Middx.: Penguin, 1991), pp. 143–146. Gautier de Châtillon, Alexandreis, trans. David Townsend (Philadelphia: University of Pennsylvania Press, 1996), Book 8, ll.9–57, pp. 131–133.

[10] Lodovico Ariosto, *Orlando Furioso*, trans. Sir John Harington, ed. Graham Hough (London: Centaur Press, 1962), p. 216.

[11] The Vinland Sagas, pp. 52, 100. On the patriarchal structure of Viking society, see Peter Foote and David M. Wilson, *The Viking Achievement* (London: Sidgwick & Jackson, 1970), pp. 108–111.

[12] The Travels of Sir John Mandeville, trans. and introd. C. W. R. D. Moseley (Harmondsworth, Middx.: Penguin, 1983), pp. 116–7.

[13] Felipe Fernandez-Armesto, Columbus (Oxford: Oxford University Press, 1991), p.34.

[14] Carlos Sanz, ed., *La carta de Colon, anunciando la llegada a las Indias y a la provincia de Catayo* [Madrid, 1958]. The Journal of Christopher Columbus, trans. Cecil Jane (London: Anthony Blond, 1968), pp. xv-xvi, xxi-xxii, 200–201.

[15] Eugenia W. Herbert, Red Gold of Africa: Copper in Precolonial History and Culture (Madison WI: University of Wisconsin Press, 1984), pp.125–127.

[16] Neil L. Whitehead, "The Historical Anthropology of Text: The Interpretation of Raleigh's Discoverie of Guiana," Current Anthropology 36 (1995), 53–74. The Journal of Christopher Columbus, trans. Jane, p. 191. See also Pagden, European Encounters with the New World, pp. 27–30.

[17] Petrus Martyr Anglerius, *Libretto de Tutta la nauigatione del Re de Spagna de le Isole et terreni noumente trouati* (Venice: Albertino Vercelle, 1504). Jose Toribio Medina, The Discovery of the Amazon, trans. Bertram T. Lee, ed. H. C. Heaton (New York: American Geographical Society, 1934), pp. 153–154. William Brooks

Greenlee, "Introduction" to The Voyage of Pedro Alvares Cabral to Brazil and India, trans. Greenlee (London: Hakluyt Society, 1938), pp. lxi-lxiv.

[18] Robert Southey, (3 vols., London: Longman, Hurst, Rees, and Orme, 1810), I, p. 6. Exodus 15:23. Medina, The Discovery of the Amazon, pp. 155–163. See also Stephen Minta, Aguirre: The Re-Creation of a Sixteenth-Century Journey Across South America (London: Jonathan Cape, 1993), p. 79.

[19] Garci Rodriguez de Montalvo, The Labors of the Very Brave Knight Esplandian, trans. William T. Little (Binghamton NY: Medieval and Renaissance Texts & Studies, 1992), pp. 456–458. See also Irving A. Leonard, "Conquerors and Amazons in Mexico," The Hispanic American Historical Review 24 (1944) 561–579; and Jennifer R. Goodman, Chivalry and Exploration, 1298–1630 (Woodbridge: Boydell Press, 1998), pp. 62, 66, 70.

[20] Gaspar de Carvajal, "Account," in Medina, The Discovery of the Amazon, pp. 177, 213–214, 234.

[21] Gonzalo Fernandez de Oviedo y Valdes, La historia general de las indias, in Medina, The Discovery of the Amazon, p. 399. Antonio Herrera y Tordesillas, Historia General de las Indias, Sixth Decade, trans. Clements Markham, in Markham: Expeditions into the Valley of the Amazons, 1539, 1540, 1639 (London: Hakluyt Society, 1859), p. 34. Lopez de Gómara, Historia de las Indias, quoted in Medina, The Discovery of the Amazon, p. 26.

[22] Odoardo Lopez, A Report of the Kingdome of Congo, trans. Abraham Hartwell (1598; rpt. Amsterdam: Da Capo Press, 1970), p.195. Samuel Purchas, Hakluytus Posthumous, or Purchas his Pilgrimes (20 vols., Glasgow: James MacLehose, 1905–7), VI, p. 508.

[23] Joyce Lorimer, English and Irish Settlement on the River Amazon 1550-1646 (London: The Hakluyt Society, 1989), pp. 1–9. Sir Walter Raleigh, "The English Voyages of the Sixteenth Century," in Richard Hakluyt, The Principal Navigations Voyages Traffiques & Discoveries of the English Nation (12 vols., Glasgow: James MacLehose and Sons, 1905) XII, p. 35. On the question of English translations, see Gesa Mackenthun, Metaphors of Dispossession: American Beginnings and the Translation of Empire, 1492–1637 (Norman OK: University of Oklahoma Press, 1997).

[24] Richard Eden, A Treatyse of the New India (London: Edward Sutton, 1553), sig. H.I.i.v. Eden, The Decades of the newe worlde or west India (London: William Powell, 1555), fo. 6r-6v.

[25] Purchas, Hakluytus Posthumous, XVII, p. 33.

[26] Raleigh, The History of the World in The Works of Sir Walter Raleigh (8 vols., 1829; rpt. New York: Burt Franklin, 1967), V, pp. 350–353.

[27] Winfried Schleiner, "Divina Virago: Queen Elizabeth as an Amazon," Studies in Philology 75 (1978), 163-180. Celeste Turner Wright, "The Amazons in Elizabethan Literature," Studies in Philology 37 (1940), 433-456.

[28] [James Aske,] Elizabetha Triumphans, Conteyning The Damned practizes, that the diuelish Popes of Rome have vsed euer sithence her Highnesse first comming to the Crowne . . . (London: Thomas Gubbin and Thomas Newman, 1588), pp. 23–24.

[29] See Louis Montrose's sensitive discussion in "The Work of Gender in the Discourse of Discovery," representations 33 (1991), 1–41.

[30] Raleigh, The Discoverie of the Large, Rich and Bewtiful Empyre of Guiana, ed. and introd. Neil L. Whitehead (Manchester: Manchester University Press, 1997), pp. 134, 165, 196, 146, 138, 199.

[31] "The admirable adventures and strange fortunes of Master Antonie Knivet," in Purchas, Hakluytus Posthumous, XVI, p. 225. Acuña, A New Discovery of the Great River of the Amazons, trans. Clements Markham, in Markham, Expeditions into the Valley of the Amazons, pp. 122–123.

Sealing Anuses and Devouring Men:
Utopia, Gender and Incorporation in the Early Image of America*

Mario Klarer
National Humanities Center
Research Triangle Park, NC

With the discovery of the new continent in the 15th century, a number of older literary traditions contributed to the creation of the early image of America. In particular, utopian features and cannibalism were projected onto the *terra incognita* and formed an integral part of what constituted the earliest conceptions of America. The equation of the New World with the Earthly Paradise and the Promised Land placed America in the tradition of ancient and medieval utopian texts, stylizing America as the indirect continuation of an ambivalent gendered view of the world predominant in most classical utopias and pastorals. The majority of early modern accounts of discovery and travel narratives about America reflect a peculiar fusion of a feminized utopian and paradise-like idyll of the new continent with cruel canni-balistic practices of the natives. This apparently paradoxical side-by-side of a benevolent, female Nature and obvious horror, which dates back to ancient and medieval texts, can be traced as a *leitmotif* in the travelogues of Columbus and Vespucci, as well as in many of the eyewitness accounts of the 16th century, not to mention literary adaptations in 18th- and 19th-century novels. The following analysis juxtaposes illustrative textual and pictorial examples of 16th-century travel narratives with ancient, medieval and early modern texts, thus attempting to provide an explanation for the striking interdependence of cannibalism and female utopian con-cepts in the first images of America.

For an analysis of the early image of America, it is crucial to place it in the context of ancient and medieval utopian visions, since these foreshadow and predetermine the European colonial image of this new continent to a considerable degree. Ancient sources frequently situate utopian communities in the West, i.e. the Atlantic. Plato's account of the mythological Atlantis in his *Timaios,* the manifold references to the so-called *insulae fortunatarum* or the Hesperidian Islands, and the fantastic report of an idealized island in the Atlantic by the sixth century Irish abbot St. Brendan are only some of these famous projections. Parallel to this myth of a utopian West, a number of medieval texts stylized the East as the location of the earthly paradise. Marco Polo's travelogue and Sir John Mandeville's geographic fantasies sketched a picture of the Far East which was eagerly absorbed by 14th century Europe. With the first Atlantic crossings, the two utopian traditions coin-cided and were thus projected onto the newly discovered territories. Columbus, for example, expresses this indirect fusion of Eastern and Western mythological concepts in his reflections on the earthly paradise. "The theologians and philosophers are probably right when they locate the terrestrial paradise in the far East, since it enjoys a very temperate climate. And the islands which I have discovered are the very end of the East" (Log-Book, 21 February 1493). Columbus's westward bound voyage, which was supposed to lead to the Far East, made it possible to project both Eastern and Western utopian traditions onto the newly discovered America.

Notions of a primordial Golden Age, as described by Hesiod, Horace and Ovid, prevail in many of the early accounts of America. Columbus and Vespucci, for example, describe the fertility of these islands in terms very reminiscent of ancient idylls, especially Homer's Phaiacian Island:

> [T]he other islands of this region, too, are as fertile as they can be. This one is surrounded by harbors, numerous, very safe and broad, and not to be compared with any others that I have seen anywhere; many large wholesome rivers flow through this land; . . . All these islands are most beautiful and distinguished by various forms; one can travel through them, and they are full of trees of the greatest variety, which . . . never lose their foliage. At any rate, I found them as green and beautiful as they usually are in the month of May in Spain.

In his description of a paradisiacal Cuba, Columbus emphasizes the fact that the use of iron is completely unknown on these West Indian islands. "There are also remarkable pines, vast fields and meadows, many kinds of birds, many kinds of honey, and many kinds of metals, except iron." The stress on specific metals, i.e. the lack of iron, together with the utopian exuberance of nature on this island, invokes classical notions of the Golden Age as well as traditional concepts of nature. These ancient utopian visions, in which a benevolent Mother Earth provides everything man needs, are obviously based on highly gendered principles.

Most ancient and early modern utopias depict nature as a caring organic whole. Both utopian and scientific discourses view nature as a benevolent nurturing *alma mater*, which provides everything necessary for life. Contemporary feminist philosophy of science has shown that this gendered conception of the earth is the underlying principle of western science and metaphysics. Parallel to this highly gendered world view there exists a contrary, and equally female, picture of a wild and uncontrollable nature, one which causes violent storms, draughts, floods and general chaos. Both aspects, positive and negative, are projected onto a world that is connoted feminine, thus becoming a leitmotif of scientific discourse and early travel narratives.

Most of the ancient pastorals, the above-mentioned accounts of discovery and the English Arcadia-idylls of the 16th century can be only be understood in the light of these first organic concepts. This view of nature as a well-meaning female is epitomized in Philip Sidney's Arcadia (1590) and Edmund Spenser's The Shepheard's Calendar (1579). These idylls depict Nature and women as generally passive and lacking any active means of control and power. The Renaissance pastorals, like their ancient precursors, react to urban and mechanistic trends by advocating a return to a simple life in an ideal natural environment. This world view of a passive benevolence invites the exploitation or manipulation of both nature and the feminine.

It is therefore not unusual that Christopher Columbus, in describing the earthly paradise, draws on overtly gendered metaphors deriving from utopias and pastorals:

> I have always read, that the world comprising the land and water was spherical . . . . But I have now seen so much irregularity, as I have already described, that I have come to another conclusion respecting the earth, namely, that it is not round as they describe, but of the form of a pear, which is very round except where the stalk grows, at which part it is most prominent; or like a round ball, upon one part of which is a prominence like a woman's nipple, this protrusion being the highest and nearest to the sky, situated under the equinoctial line, and at the eastern extremity of this sea, —I call that the eastern extremity, where the land and the islands end. ("Third Voyage of Columbus", 129)

This reference to a "woman's nipple" to depict the earthly paradise is repeated almost verbatim later in this account (see p. 131). Columbus not only invokes notions of an "alma mater"—a nourishing mother—which is a common topos in pastorals and idylls, but also creates a highly sexual context for his visionary paradise.

It is not surprising that after these descriptions of the 'American Paradise' many of the early illustrations of Columbus's and Vespucci's accounts highlight the inherent gender patterns in these visions of the terrestrial paradise. America is frequently allegorized as a female figure. Amerigo Vespucci, for example, visualizes the new continent as a naked, full-blooded woman, who idly reposes in a hammock. A vast number of pictorial representations show America as a female figure holding a cornucopia, thereby obviously invoking gendered concepts of Nature in the Golden Age or terrestrial paradise. Besides these paradisiacal notions, a number of other gendered utopian visions can be extrapolated from these early descriptions of the New World.

The second major textual models for a feminization of America—besides the recourses to notions of the 'Golden Age'—are a number of ancient and medieval sources that describe all-women's communities, such as the independent 'Islands of Women' frequently mentioned in Old Irish *Echtrae*. The so-called *Echtrae Conli*, for example, describes a land where "no other sex lives . . . save only women and maidens." During his various adventures the protagonist of the *Immram Curaig Duin* reaches an island of ladies whose queen offers him and his companions everlasting youth. After a lengthy description of a utopian island, the female narrator in the Old Irish "The Isle of the Happy" (7th/8th century) urges Bran and his men to continue their journey. "Let not thine intoxication overcome thee! / Begin your voyage across the clear sea, / If perchance thou mayest reach the Land of Women!" "The Sea-God's Address to Bran" ends in a similar way with an account of a utopian island and a reference to women. "It is not far to the Land of Women: Evna with manifold boun-teousness / he will reach before the sun is set." Many of these medieval invocations of an 'Island of Women' echo the widely-read *De Chorographia* by the ancient geographer Pomponius Mela. He writes about an island inhabited by nine virgins who possess supernatural powers. They can divine, heal and change the winds and the weather:

> Sena in the Britannic Sea, opposite the Osismician shore, is characterized by an oracle of a Gallic divinity whose nine priestesses are holy by virtue of their perpetual virginity. They are called Gallicenas and are thought to be endowed with unique powers: They move seas and winds with songs, change themselves into different animals and heal what is considered incurable for others.

This text might have influenced Geoffrey of Monmouth's account of the mythological island Avalon in his <u>Vita Merlini</u>: "Nine sisters rule over this island according to pleasant laws . . .. The first among them [Morgan] knows most about the art of healing and outdoes her sisters in beauty and stature." It is, of course, difficult to prove a direct influence of these ancient and medieval texts on the writings of explorers like Columbus and Vespucci. But even if these explorers were not familiar with specific textual sources, they must have known about some of these popular beliefs of women's communities on far away islands. One of the most prominent traditions of independent female communities is that of the Amazons, which was made known to a wide audience through Sir John Mandeville's <u>Travels</u>.

Mandeville, for example, devotes an entire section to the so-called 'insula amazonia': "After the lande of Caldee is the lande of Amazony that is a land where ther is no man but all women as men say, for they will suffer no men to lyve among them nor to haue lordshippe over them . . . . this lande is all environed with water." Mandeville's book is one of the first travel narratives which was available in vernacular French. Translations into a number of languages added to its popularity. These visions of Amazon tribes without men originally go back to Homer, Herodotus, Strabo and Diodorus Siculus. Common features of these ancient counter-cultures are the warlike nature of these women and their complete independence from men. Amazon communities have been a central topos in utopian thinking from the earliest Greek texts to contemporary feminist fiction. The 'masculinization of the female', which lies at the heart of this phenomenon, reflects this general bipolar quality of the feminine and seems to be very appealing to visions of the perfect state.

Because Columbus and Vespucci, like most of their contemporaries, believed in the existence of mythological beings like Cyclops and Sirens, they readily projected Amazons or Amazon-like women onto the newly-discovered islands. The description of female Indians in Columbus's *Epistola de Insulis Nuper Inventis* (February-March 1493) is very reminiscent of ancient images of Amazons: "These women moreover, do not occupy themselves with any work that properly belongs to their sex, for they use bows and arrows just as I related of their husbands." Amerigo Vespucci, too, stresses the military qualities of female Indians: "In some places also the women are very skillful with the bow and arrow."

In Columbus's writing, as the example of the terrestrial paradise has shown, gender issues can only be extrapolated via metaphors and subliminal discursive structures. With Amerigo Vespuicci, however, gender relations surface and can be traced in a number of instances. In his account of the four voyages, Vespucci dedicates extensive passages to the description of Amazon-like women, echoing the ambivalent attitude of the ancients toward this myth of a masculinized female community. Herodotus was the first to elaborate on the political aspects of the traditional Amazon-myth, highlighting the inherent warlike nature of this community as a potential basis for masculine offspring. Herodotus referred to a battle between the Scyths and a group of young warriors who eventually turn out to be women. The Scyths soon realize the eugenic potential of these masculine women and take the Amazons as their wives. The women agree to marry only if they can retain their unconventional social behavior, which does not conform to traditional gender roles. "We cannot live together with your women, because we do not have the same customs. We shoot with arrows and spears and live on horseback; women's tasks we have never learned. . . . Your women, however, do none of the things we mentioned, but rather do women's works." (Hdt. 4, 114; my translation). The Amazons refuse to accept the traditional roles of women in a patriarchal society and force the young Scyths to found a new community with utopian modes of coexistence: "Since then the Sauromats have preserved their old way of life. They hunt alone or together with men, go to war and wear the same clothing as men" (4, 114).

In his account of the first voyage, Vespucci writes about the Indians in a way that parallels Herodotus's description of the Amazons in many respects. The female islanders are warlike and physically equal to men; they also engage in masculine activities:

> When they go forth to battle, they take their wives with them, not that they too may participate in the fight, but that they may carry behind the fighting men all the necessary provisions. For, as we ourselves have often seen, any woman among them can place on her back, and carry for thirty or forty leagues, a greater burden than a man (and even a strong man) can lift from the ground. (Vespucci 94)

Vespucci mixes myths of Amazons with utopian legends of the masculinity of women in ancient Sparta. Many different mythological and textual traditions have contributed to the utopian picture of the Spartan community in classical Greece. Plato and many of the later theoreticians considered Sparta a pseudo-utopian model for their own visionary states. The military bias of the Spartan constitution indirectly determined its social and political life in terms of gender roles. The first century A.D. writer, Plutarch, delineates these topoi in a very vivid manner. His biography of the mythological Spartan emperor Lycurgus abounds with gendered features of Spartan life:

> He [Lycurgus] made the maidens exercise their bodies in running, wrestling, casting the discus, and hurling the javelin, in order that the fruit of their wombs might have vigorous root in vigorous bodies and come to better maturity, and that they themselves might come with vigour and the fullness of their times, and struggle successfully and easily with the pangs of childbirth. (Plut. Lyc. 14, 2)

Vespucci reiterates this physical equality of the sexes in regard to bodily strain when he describes the female islanders as being as vigorous as men. "All of them, both men and women, are graceful in walking and swift in running. Indeed, even their women (as we have often witnessed) think nothing of running a league or two, wherein they greatly excel us Christians. . . . and the women are far better swimmers than the men, a statement which I can make with authority, for we frequently saw them swim in the sea for two leagues without assistance whatsoever" (Vespucci, First Voyage, 93). Just like the Spartan women, Vespucci's Indians are also very efficient when giving birth. Even in this exclusively female activity they seem to supersede normal women:

> They are very prolific in bearing children, and do not omit performing their usual labors and tasks during the period of pregnancy. They are delivered with very little pain,—so true is this that on the very next day they are completely recovered and move about everywhere with perfect ease. In fact, immediately after the delivery they go to some stream to wash, and then come out of the water as whole and as clean as fishes. (Vespucci, First Voyage, 96)

The warlike nature, strength and vigor of these female natives represents the traditional wish for a 'masculinization' of the female that can be traced through utopian writing from antiquity to the present. Hand in hand with this positive projection of stereotypically male qualities onto utopian females goes an implicit fear of this very process. Most male utopian visions of a female community vacillate between these two extremes. On the one hand, a masculine female is a tempting idea; on the other hand, these very concepts undermine male power structures and turn into a vision of horror and subliminal fear.

Many ancient and medieval sources therefore connect cruel practices with all-women's communities, mentioning dismemberment, castration and decapitation of men as common practices. The masculinization of the female consequently results in fear of castration and bodily mutilation. Herodotus, for example, alludes to this when he tries to give an etymological explanation: "The Scyths call the Amazons *Oiorpata*; This name means 'man-killer' in the Greek language: *Oior* means 'man', *pata* means 'to kill'" (Hdt. 4, 110; my translation). There are similarities in a number of epithets of the Amazons. The Iliad (3, 189; 4, 186) calls them *ajntiavneirai*, which according to ancient interpretation can mean both "man-hating" and "man-like". Herodotus (3, 189; 4, 186) calls them *ajndroktovnoi*—"man-killing". Other sources try to show that the name Amazon (*a*—without, and *mazos*—breast) derives from the women's cruel practice of cutting off their breasts in order to better handle bow and arrow. Traditional descriptions of the Amazons point out that these women either meet with the men of a neighboring tribe for procreation once a year, or keep male slaves for this purpose. These slaves are mutilated to prevent them from using weapons. Male offspring are killed, maimed, or immediately sent back to the tribes of their physical fathers.

Another age-old gendered feature which early commentators on the New World include in their picture of America is the topos of 'female communism'. A number of ancient texts replace traditional monogamy with general promiscuity. Herodotus considers the absence of monogamy as a means of strengthening the tribal structures. He notes, "They live in a women's communism so that they are related to one another by kinship or marriage and so that there is no jealousy or disorder among them" (Hdt. 4, 104; my translation). The most famous example of this abolition of monogamous family structures is in Plato's *Politeia*. He dissolves the nuclear family, so that "all these women . . . belong to all these men . . . , so that no father knows his child, nor does any child know his father" (Plat. rep. 457d). Attic comedy also takes up this theme and turns it into the grotesque. Aristophanes's comedy *Ekklesiazousai* is the best example of this subversion of utopian topoi. Hellenistic utopias re-introduce this issue in a stoic disguise. Diodorus Siculus, for example, provides a picture of a promiscuous utopian tribe on the so-called Island of the Sun:

> They do not marry, we are told, but possess their children in common, and maintaining the children who are born as if they belonged to all, they love them equally; and while the children are infants those who suckle the babes often change them around in order that not even the mothers may know their own offspring. Consequently, since there is no rivalry among them, they never experience civil disorders and they never cease placing the highest value upon internal harmony. (Diod. 2, 58, 1)

These ancient notions of a utopian interaction between the sexes surface in Amerigo Vespucci's texts. He deliberately draws on the otherness of the Indians in respect to legal practices, political organization, private property and trade, but above all emphasizes their sexual behavior. A great deal of Vespucci's popularity derives from his vivid descriptions of exotic peculiarities, many of which center around the gender roles of these natives. The male fantasy of overt promiscuity, which can be traced as a leitmotif in ancient utopias, is eagerly projected onto these islanders, who are apparently only following their natural urges. Vespucci's voyeuristic accounts of female Indians and their sexual practices definitely appealed to his 16th century audience. The otherness of the exotic natives was increased by adding descriptions of women, who in the Western tradition already functioned as the 'cultural other'. Vespucci describes these female islanders as being naturally beautiful and libidinous: "We were surprised to see no women among them with sagging breasts and that the stomachs of those who had given birth did not differ in form and tone from those of virgins. The same can be said about the other parts of their bodies, which I will leave out for decency's sake." Vespucci also points out that their exaggerated libido results in rather cruel practices. He observes: "Since their women are libidinous, they make their husbands' penises swell to such a degree that it appears disproportionate and monstrous; this is is achieved with technique that makes use of food that had been poisoned through bites of special animals." Their sexual abnormality is also reflected in their promiscuous inclinations.

The passages in which Vespucci writes about their sexual behavior are particularly reminiscent of ancient visions of female communism in texts by Herodotus, Plato, Diodorus and Strabo.

> In their sexual intercourse they have no legal obligations. In fact, each man has as many wives as he covets, and can repudiate them later whenever he pleases, without its being considered an injustice or disgrace, and the women enjoy the same rights as the men. The men are not very jealous; they are, however, very sensual. The women are even more so than the men. I have deemed it best (in the name of decency) to pass over in silence their many arts to gratify their insatiable lust. (Vespucci, First Voyage, 96)

Their sexual liberty even includes men outside the tribal community. Vespucci describes sexuality among these islanders in terms of a social tool or ascribes to it the function of a gift. "The greatest and surest seal of their friendship is this: that they place at the disposal of their friends their own wives and daughters, both parents considering themselves highly honored if any one deigns to lead their daughter (even though yet a maiden) into concubinage. In this way (as I have said) they seal the bond of their friendship" (Vespucci 98-99). It comes as no surprise that Vespucci and the rest of the crew are eventually able to enjoy the same privilege: "Here we rested for the night, and the natives most generously offered us their wives" (Vespucci 108).

The last two references to the sexual liberty of the female islanders once again contain the most prominent features of the early image of America that has been perpetuated in its very ambiguity in various discourses over the past 500 years. America becomes a continuation of traditional pastoral idylls of a Golden Age in which a female Nature eagerly provides everything that is necessary for life. The accounts of the early explorations project these subliminally gendered concepts onto a more overt sexual level. Like the scientific or theological discourses of Christopher Columbus which describe America's flora and fauna as a passive alma mater, Vespucci's attempts at ethnographic descriptions subordinate the sexuality of the native women to this particular world view. As passive providers of sexual space, the female natives personify or parallel these concepts in utopian and scientific discourses, both of which submit nature to man's domination.

The early documents also incorporate the second traditionally feminized concept of nature, in which femininity without male control—as the examples of the libidinous females or Amazonian women have shown—causes general chaos. This second set of gendered features, which prevails in most of the early documents and runs contrary to the first cluster of female stereotypes projected onto the new continent, centers around the feminine as disorder. The extrapolation of the chaotic, destructive and vicious aspects of the *terra incognita* via the female islanders is once more a reiteration of the negative images of nature that traditionally connote the feminine.

The utopian territory of promiscuity, of masculinization, or of a gendered paradise, which America as a myth promotes, reflects the ambiguous attitude towards nature in general as being both order and chaos, or benevolence and viciousness. Both seemingly contradictory principles, however, enable the discoverers and conquistadors to exploit and abuse the continent on the grounds of these diametrically opposed, though both feminine, principles. On the one hand, the passive benevolence lends itself to active exploitation and abuse; on the other, the chaotic and intimidating projections legitimize conquest and subjugation. Both principles thus lie at the heart of colonization in general, but are most obvious in the specific case of America. No other instance of discovery and invention of a territorial myth is so well documented as that of America, coinciding with the advent of a most efficient means of reproduction of texts and illustrations through the printing press in the early 16th century. The Myth of America, as it manifests itself for the first time in Columbus and Vespucci, therefore, becomes a paradigm for the gendered deep structures of colonial discourses in general. The textual and visual indirect allegorizations thus provide a basis for numerous subsequent discourses on America that consciously or unconsciously employ these gendered themes, ranging from subliminal literary metaphors to contemporary images of popular culture.

The uses of these ancient and medieval utopias in texts which make America appear as a real manifestation of diverse temporal and geographical utopian projections in the here and now of the Renaissance, marks a decisive counterpoint to the repulsive cannibalistic practices attributed to the natives. Originating in the texts of Columbus and Vespucci, cannibalism not only serves as a leitmotif in all major subsequent travel narratives, but also functions as a seemingly irreconcilable counterpart to the utopian setting of the continent. Interestingly enough, many of these cannibalistic scenes in the early travel narratives involve women, thus intricately intertwining gendered utopianism with cannibalism as a trademark of the early image of the New World. Columbus and Vespucci frequently report instances of cannibalism and dismemberment of human bodies on these islands. Vespucci's descriptions are very detailed in these matters, consciously or unconsciously linking cannibalism and dismemberment with Amazon-like women.

It is common knowledge that cannibalism is closely connected to the newly discovered continent in a number of ways. Famous misconceptions in the context of the discovery of America include erroneously calling the natives "Indians" as well as "cannibals", a term which also derives from semantic shortcomings indirectly expressed by Columbus in the following passage:

> All the people I have encountered up until this time greatly fear the people of Caniba. The Indians with me continued to show great fear, insisting that the people of Bohio had only one eye and a face of a dog, and they fear being eaten. I do not believe any of this. I feel that the Indians they fear belong to the domain of the Great Khan. (Log, Monday, 26 Nov. 1492)

Christopher Columbus, who interpreted the name of the tribe of the "Canibe"—due to the first syllable *can*—as subjects of the Great Khan or man-eaters with dog-like snouts (from the Latin *canis*—dog), provided the basis for subsequent treatments of these "cannibals" in the texts of the 16th century. (See illustration 3: Cannibals with dogs' snouts in Lorenz Fries, *Uslegung Der Carthen,* Strassbourg, 1525). Columbus and his successors project a number of ancient and medieval topoi of anthropophagy onto the newly-discovered continent. The early travel narratives—especially the ethnographic *curiosa* of Amerigo Vespucci—employ the exotic motif of man-eaters and expand it as a popular feature. As early as the 16th century, the term "cannibal" replaced the older "androphage" or "anthropophage." The neologism thus changed from an ethnographic-geographical term into a general technical term for man-eater, and simultaneously serves as a *pars pro toto* for the new continent and its native inhabitants.

In a short passage from Vespucci's account of his second voyage, some of the above-mentioned contradictory elements in the image of America coincide in a very graphic manner. Vespucci's detailed description in this example consciously or unconsciously combines cannibalism with notions of femininity, i.e. Nature, subliminally interwoven with the new continent:

> The young man advanced and mingled among the women; they all stood around him, and touched and stroked him, wondering greatly at him. At this point a woman came down from the hill carrying a big club. When she reached the place where the young man was standing, she struck him such a heavy blow from behind that he immediately fell to the ground dead. The rest of the women at once seized him and dragged him by the feet up the mountain. There the women, who had killed the youth before our eyes, were now cutting him in pieces, showing us the pieces, roasting them at a large fire. (Vespucci 138-139)

The depiction of these cruel practices is a good example of the paradoxical nature of the image of America. Shortly after having gently touched the young sailor, the female Indians murder, dismember and devour him. The structure of the passage is paradigmatic for a majority of concepts of cannibalism in early travel narratives. A benevolent, feminine setting as familiar from the *alma mater* tradition suddenly turns into a cannibalistic monster. (See illustration 4: This woodcut from 1505 is regarded as one of the earliest depictions of Brazilian Indians. It juxtaposes a nursing mother with cannibalistic images). The notion of a tempting but devouring Amazon is a very popular motif which is increasingly expanded in the iconography of the travel narratives. In many of these allegorizations, America is rendered as a voluptuous temptress and/or an Amazon-like monster in a background of dismembered, mostly male human bodies, which are often in the process of being prepared for consumption.

This apparently contradictory combination of a utopian nature with anthropophagy is by no means an invention of early modern texts. It stems from a long-standing tradition in ancient and medieval sources. The most famous classical example of cannibalistic practices in the utopian context of a travel narrative is the description of the Island of the Cyclops in Book IX of The Odyssey. The fact that Columbus depicts cannibals as "men with one eye ... who eat men" (Log Sunday 4 Nov. 1492) corroborates the theory that the one-eyed Cyclops served as a model for his man-eaters. Interestingly enough, in both the Homeric Isle of the Cyclops as well as the narratives on America, the descriptions of an idyllic nature with an abundance of food coincide with anthropophagy:

> Thence we sailed on, grieved at heart, and we came to the land of the Cyclopes, an overweening and lawless folk, who, trusting in the immortal

gods, plant nothing with their hands nor plough; but all these things spring up for them without sowing or ploughing, wheat, and barley, and vines, which bear the rich clusters of wine, and the rain of Zeus gives them increase. Neither assemblies for council have they, nor appointed laws, but they dwell on the peaks of lofty mountains in hollow caves, and each one is lawgiver to his children and his wives, and they reck nothing one of another. (Od. IX, 105-115)

As in passages from the early accounts of America, the idyllic description of nature as a benevolent giver permits the Cyclops to remain in a pre-agrarian state of being including cannibalism. Thus: "Two of them at once he [Polyphem] seized and dashed to the earth like puppies, and the brain flowed forth upon the ground and wetted the earth. Then he cut them limb from limb and made ready his supper, and ate them as a mountain-nurtured lion, leaving naught—ate the entrails, and the flesh, and the marrowy bones" (288-293). The concept of pre-agrarian, pre-civilization cannibalism is intricately interwoven with ancient theories of cultural evolution. The Neolithic revolution, i.e. the transition of man from hunter-gatherer to peasant, was generally explained as a substitution of anthropophagy for agriculture. This concept does not end in antiquity but continues in various forms in modern cultural history.

For example, a passage about man-eaters in John Mandeville's 14th-century fantastic travelogue, which combines a utopian idyll with anthropophagy, appears to be a model for 16th-century accounts of cannibalistic American Indians:

From this country men go through the Great Sea Ocean by way of many isles and different countries, which would be tedious to relate. At last, after fifty-two days' journey, men come to a large country called Lamory [Sumatra]. In that land it is extremely hot; the custom there is for men and women to go completely naked and they are not ashamed to show themselves as God made them, for they say that God made Adam and Eve naked, for nothing natural is ugly.

After establishing the traditional topoi of paradisiacal conditions on the island, Mandeville introduces some motifs of classical utopias such as communal property (including women and children), as well as an abundance of gold, silver and other natural resources. The description ends with a reference to cannibalism among this people: "Merchants bring children there to sell, and the people of the country buy them. Those that are plump they eat; those that are not plump they feed up and fatten, and then kill and eat them. And they say it is the best and sweetest flesh in the world" (Mandeville 127).

An illustrative example of how these concepts of anthropophagy are adapted for religious purposes is the anonymous Andreas. This Old-English text in the Vercelli manuscript (10th century), which goes back to an ancient Latin or Greek source, shows a number of the features of the cannibalistic text mentioned above. Although these topoi are present in Andreas they are employed in a highly stylized form. Again the setting is that of a travel narrative; again a non-barbarian is confronted with a cannibalistic people; again the plot is situated in a utopian setting. As in most other texts, <u>Andreas</u> superficially condemns cannibalism and places this phenomenon in opposition to the utopian setting. While many texts on cannibalism introduce the utopian element as a descriptive Cockayne-idyll with a benevolent Nature out of the Golden Age, the utopian features in <u>Andreas</u> manifest themselves indirectly through the Christian hope of redemption. The texts starts with a description of the island Mermedonia where God had sent his disciple Matthew as a missionary to the Androphagoi:

> There was no bread in the place to feed men, nor a drink of water to enjoy, but throughout the land they feasted on the blood and flesh, on the bodies of men, of those who came from afar. Such was their custom, that when they lacked meat they made food of all the strangers who sought that island from elsewhere. Such was the savage nature of the people.

God sends his disciple Andreas, whose cruel martyr's death at the hands of the androphagoi saves the condemned Matthew. An interesting feature of this text is the fusion of ancient notions of anthropophagy with the Christian doctrine of salvation, which also makes use of a cannibalistic form of incorporation. Already with the fall of Adam and Eve incorporation as the eating of the forbidden fruit functions as a central motif later taken up in the Eucharist, although with new valences. Utopia and anthropophagy coincide as apparently irreconcilable principles constituting an integral part of the Eucharist. Incorporation of the Other thus serves as a prerequisite for the restitution of a pre-lapsarian unity or utopia.

Like a number of early accounts of America, <u>Andreas</u> executes the equation of Christian communion and anthropophagy in an indirect and encoded manner. The Christian concept of salvation superficially opposes cannibalistic primitivism as uncivilized atrocity, although both phenomena function according to analogous structures of incorporation. While cannibals devour strangers to re-establish the unity of subject and object, Christians eat the "body" of Jesus as guarantor for a utopian unity or oneness with their God. <u>Andreas</u> and the early accounts of America thus work with a utopian hope which is deeply entrenched in western cultural tradition and manifests itself in more or less stylized forms of incorporation of the Other.

Most of the ancient and medieval texts and the modern travel narratives set cannibalism in opposition to utopian imagery of the territories described by employing anthropophagy as a sign of primordial savagery. Michel de Montaigne in his famous essay *"Des Cannibales"* (1580) was the first to analyze these two apparently contradictory images of utopia and cannibalism as interdependent mechanisms. He places the new continent in the ancient tradition of utopian thought like the Platonic Atlantis-myth and other westward geographical projections. These geographical utopian extrapolations in *"Des Cannibales"* are followed by examples of ancient temporal re-projections into a utopian past of a Golden Age, which Montaigne also links with the American continent. "I think that what we have seen of these people [Indians] with our own eyes surpasses not only the pictures with which poets have illustrated the golden age, and all their attempts to draw mankind in the state of happiness, but the ideas and the very aspirations of philosophers as well" (110). The following description of the idyllic fertility of America's nature is reminiscent of Homer's utopian island of the Phaiacians in <u>The Odyssey</u>, Diodorus' depiction of the Jambulian Sun Island or Christopher Columbus's newly discovered islands in the Caribbean. "For the rest, they live in a land with a very pleasant and temperate climate, and consequently, as my witnesses inform me, a sick person is a rare sight; and they assure me that they never saw anyone palsied or blear-eyed, toothless or bent with age. They have a great abundance of fish and meat" (Montaigne 110). Like most of the ancient and medieval descriptive utopias, Montaigne's image of America is characterized by a benevolent nature and a lack of law as well as civilisatory achievements:

> This is a nation, I should say to Plato, in which there is no kind of commerce, no knowledge of letters, no science of numbers, no title of magistrate or of political superior, no habit of service, riches or poverty, no contracts, no inheritance, no division of property, only leisurely occupations, no respect for any kinship but the common ties, no clothes, no agriculture, no metals, no use of corn or wine. The very words denoting lying, treason, deceit, greed, envy, slander, and forgiveness have never been heard. How far from such perfection would he find the republic that he [Plato] imagined: 'men fresh from the hands of the gods'. (Montaigne 110)

Montaigne's long list of various "things" can be explained as a general lack of *difference.* Neither figures, letters, clothes, property or kinship, which could oppose a total *unity,* disturb this pre-lapsarian wholeness. Montaigne continues in his enumerations by stressing conventions of the native Americans that bear likeness to ancient notions of a communism of women and children which is generally introduced into utopian visions in order to do away with differentiating family ties. This is also a very common topos in early accounts of America; here it is employed to emphasize the symbiotic wholeness of the inhabitants of the New World. The absence of separating difference, which Montaigne depicts on various levels, is epitomized in his interpretation of cannibalism. It marks the abolition of the ultimate difference—the division of subject from object, i.e. interior from exterior. Montaigne's noble savages—just like Andreas in the apocryphal gospel—want to be devoured, since they comprehend incorporation as the necessary consequence of a view of the world based on total unity. The savages do not eat their prisoners immediately but give them the opportunity to beg the victorious party to feed on them. Montaigne uses an Indian condemned to die as a mouthpiece for a ballad which expresses the desire for this utopian wholeness:

> I have a ballad made by one prisoner in which he tauntingly invites his captors to come boldly forward, every one of them, and dine off him, for they will then be eating their own fathers and grandfathers, who have served as food and nourishment to his body. "These muscles", he says, "this flesh, and these veins are yours, poor fools that you are! Can you not see that the

substance of your ancestors' limbs is still in them? Taste them carefully, and you will find the flavour is that of your own flesh." (Montaigne 117)

(Illustration 5: De Bry uses this engraving of a proud prisoner speaking before his execution twice, as an illustration for Hans Staden's and Jean de Léry's accounts. Both texts most probably influenced Montaigne).

Montaigne's essay, like a number of other early travel narratives, belongs to an age of drastic changes in the interaction of men with animate and inanimate nature. The year 1600 marks a turning point in Western philosophy of science which can be described in simplistic terms as a process of replacing an organic-holistic concept of nature with an overall mechanistic view of the world. Holism considers nature as an organic whole, very much resembling a living creature as a self-contained unit. Implicit in this organicist notion is a nature connoted as being feminine: like a nourishing mother, she provides everything men need. Most of the descriptive utopias in ancient, medieval and early modern texts are part of this tradition. The lack of agriculture and a general abundance of natural gifts are signs of a feminine deep-structure manifesting itself in notions of an *alma mater* or Mother Earth. The younger mechanistic concept explains nature as a conglomerate of supposedly feminine elements which achieve form and structure through a masculine spirit. Nature is primarily chaotic, lacking any kind of organization without the structuring male principle. These contradictory positions within the philosophy of science in the early modern period are not only present in scientific discourses but also dominate the literary utopias of that age. Francis Bacon's <u>Nova Atlantis</u> (1627) and Tommaso Campanella's <u>Civitas Solis</u> (1602) represent these two opposing traditions in an overt way. In <u>Civitas Solis</u>, all human actions are part of a cosmic wholeness. Stellar configurations, seasons and the plan of the city mirror a holistic world view into which man is integrated as one of many members. In Francis Bacon's technocratic vision, male scientists can combine matter in almost limitless variety. Thus the male spirit opposes nature, exploiting it for the benefit of mankind.

Montaigne subliminally refers to these two traditions by equating the culture of the discoverers with mechanism and by describing the concept of nature found with the Cannibals in holistic-organicist terms:

> These people [cannibals] are wild in the same as we say that fruits are wild, when nature has produced them by herself and in her ordinary way; whereas, in fact, it is those that we have artificially modified, and removed from the common order, that we ought to call wild. In the former, the true, most useful, and natural virtues and properties are alive and vigorous; in the latter we have bastardized them, and adapted them only to the gratification of our corrupt taste. (Montaigne 109).

Montaigne seems to foreshadow Francis Bacon's mechanist concepts when referring to the "modern" practice in European science of imitating nature's living creatures. As the former writes, "With all our efforts we cannot imitate the nest of the very smallest bird, its structure, its beauty, or the suitability of its form, nor even the web of the lowly spider" (Montaigne 109). The cannibals of America, however, "are still governed by natural laws and very little corrupted by our own" (Montaigne, 109). While Montaigne, and with him the proponents of an organic concept of nature, argue for man's integration into a cosmic whole, the advocates of the new mechanistic world view aim at the subjugation of nature, or as Francis Bacon puts it: "The end of our foundation is the knowledge of causes, and secret motions of things; and the enlarging of the bounds of human empire, to the effecting of all things possible."

Montaigne's natural-theological interpretation of trans-Atlantic cannibalism, in which a human being offers his body for a "Communion" with the cosmic whole, is definitely the most obvious convergence of the two poles of utopia and anthropophagy in the context of the Christian doctrine of salvation. Most travel accounts of the 16th century subliminally reflect this religious-ritual component, but superficially present it with utter disgust or in obvious conflict with the Christian ethic of love for others.

A striking example of the interdependence of Christian belief in salvation and cannibalism is the 1557 account of the German Hans Staden entitled The True History and Description of a Land of the Wild, Naked, Grimm Man-Eaters, Situated in the New World America. Like most authors of 16th-century accounts of America, Staden juxtaposes the "grimm man-eaters" with Christians, who are deeply rooted in their faith. In continuous variation he comments on the deeds of the cannibals with recourse to Christian doctrines. The similarities to Andreas are striking, especially when Hans Staden soothes his fellow-Christians who are about to be devoured by the cannibals with Christian hope of salvation. "They asked me whether they will also be eaten; and I said that they have to leave that decision to the will of the heavenly Father and his dear son Jesus Christ, who was crucified for our sins" (Staden, 94; my trans.). In his detailed depictions Staden clearly situates the rituals revolving around the devouring of the Christians in the vicinity of liturgical practice. Concepts of fertility and death are intertwined when, for example, a woman of the victorious tribe attending to a prisoner even has sexual intercourse with him. "If she conceives a child from him, they raise it until it is grown, then slay and eat it" (Staden 138; my trans.). The prisoner, who is subjected to various ritual practices all reflecting sexual and fertility symbolisms, is ultimately killed with a phallus-like club. They take egg shells, "crush them to powder and cover the club with it" (Staden, 139, my trans.). After a woman has drawn something in the powder of the egg shells, the club is subject to a night-long ritual. Then it is stuck between the legs of the executor—again stressing the sexual connotation of the ritual action: "The chief of the hut takes the club and sticks it once between his legs. This is considered an honor among them" (Staden, 143; my trans.). The following detailed description of the killing, preparation and eating of the prisoner is quoted in its full length here since it will later serve as major example in the discussion of the connection between Renaissance folk-culture and images of cannibalism in the early image of America. Staden writes:

> Then he hits the prisoner on the back of his head, making the brain gush out; and immediately the women take the dead man and drag him

across the fire, scratch off his skin, make him completely white and seal his anus with a piece of wood to make sure that nothing goes to waste.

When his skin is scraped off, a man takes him, cuts off his legs above the knees as well as the arms close to the body. Then four women take the four pieces and run around the huts screaming joyously. Then they separate the back with the buttocks from the front. That they share among them. The women keep the entrails. They boil them, and with the broth they make a thin pulp, called ming·u, which they and the children lap up. They eat the entrails as well as the meat of the head. The children devour the brain, the tongue and anything else from the head that is edible. When everything has been distributed, they return home taking with them what is their share. (Staden, 146; my trans.)

(See illustration 6: Woodcut from Staden's printed text of 1557; as well as illustration 7: Engraving in Theodor de Bry's monumental work based on Staden's woodcut). Hans Staden's account fusing culinary preparation and anatomical medical discourse is not only representative of numerous other travel narratives but also reflects a topos of grotesque literature in the 16th century. The revival of cannibalism in the modern travel narratives has its counterpart in the folk culture and literature of the late Middle Ages and early Renaissance. The most striking example of this fusion of utopian and cannibalistic imagery can be found in carnival practices of the time. These carnal motives in literature and travelogues coincide temporarily with the strengthening of the carnival in Europe, which sees itself as an inversion of current hierarchical order of European social reality.

The carnivalesque traits of Rabelais's <u>Gargantua and Pantagruel</u>, as discussed by Michael Bachtin, show obvious formal parallels to early travel literature, which incorporated structural features of the carnivalesque into the descriptions of the New World. Both phenomena—the European carnival and the imagery of the new continent—are characterized by utopian features which turn current conditions upside down. E.R. Leach describes this utopian inversion as follows:

> we find an extreme form of revelry in which the participants play-act at being precisely the opposite of what they really are; men act as women, women as men, Kings as beggars, servants as masters, acolytes as Bishops. In such situations of true orgy, normal life is played in reverse, with all manners of sins such as incest, adultery, transvestitism, sacrilege, and lÈse-majesté treated as the order of the day.

Leach's characterization of the carnival as an upside-down state of affairs could also serve as a summary of the proto-ethnographic depictions in the early travel narratives. They are full of these carnivalesque inversions of European perspectives. Masculinizations of women or feminizations of men in the contexts of Amazon myths, role reversals, and above all grotesque corporeality and anthropophagy are central motives in the early image of America that largely correspond to elements of the carnival (see Illustration 6 from Theodor de Bry's illustration of Staden's account, which, through its emphasis on costumes and masks, is very reminiscent of carinvalesque images).

Michael Bachtin tries to find a common denominator for carnivalesque Renaissance culture when using the cosmic human body as the center "uniting all the varied patterns of the universe" (Bachtin 365). In his focus on the human body, Bachtin draws a direct link between carnivalesque folk culture and utopian hope as reflected in concepts of the Golden Age, the ancient Staurnalia cult and Christian visions of salvation: "Even more, certain carnival forms parody the Church's cult. The tradition of the Saturnalias remained unbroken and alive in the medieval carnival, which expressed this universal renewal and was vividly felt as an escape from the usual official way of life" (Bachtin 7-8). The "carne vale" of "farewell meat", despite its superficial negation of the consumption of meat, ultimately leads to the Last Supper as the "cannibalisitic" part of the Christian ritual. The cannibalistic deep-structure in Christian tradition is thus indirectly reflected in the carnival of early modern times.

The analogy to the New World can hardly be overlooked. America becomes, even more than the European carnival, "the potentiality of a friendly world, of the golden age, of carnival truth" (Bachtin 48). While the European carnival represents a temporary, though cyclical, enclave of utopian conditions in the course of the year, its basic elements are permanently transferred to the new continent. Grotesque motifs, which are part of the ritual renewal of the old world in the carnival, are realistically projected onto America. Bachtin coins the term "grotesque realism" (21) for these basic features in the European carnival, which characterize both the structure of grotesque physical disfiguring and the cannibalisitic elements in the early image of America. In other words, the concepts of a continually regenerating world derived from folk rites are transported onto the newly-discovered continent, thus making America an expression of these subliminally regenerative deep-structures, or as Bachtin put is in his characterization of the carnival: "People were, so to speak, reborn for new, purely human relations. These truly human relations were not only a fruit of imagination or abstract thought; they were experienced. The utopian ideal and the realistic merged in this carnival experience, unique of its kind" (Bachtin 10). What Bachtin says here about the carnival characterizes to an even greater degree the conceptions of America in the 16th century. The New World across the Atlantic materialized as the carnivalesque—a world whose main features include the utopian inversion of social, political and personal structures, all indirectly reflected in anthropophagy. A number of my examples from pre-modern periods have already illustrated the interrelation of carnal motifs with utopian topoi. This is especially true of the works of Rabelais, which are roughly contemporaneous with many of the travel narratives and also treat the motif of incorporation or introjection in a very similar way. Rabelais's texts are full of references to dismembered human bodies, and their diction indirectly reflects the language of anatomy as well as the butcher's craft:

> He beat out the brains of some, broke the arms and legs of others, disjointed the neck-bones, demolished the kidneys, slit the noses, blackened the eyes, smashed the jaws, knocked the teeth down the throats, shattered the

shoulder-blades, crushed the shins, dislocated the thigh-bones, and cracked the fore-arms of yet others. Others he smote so fiercely through the navel that he made their bowels gush out. Others he struck on the ballocks and pierced their bum-gut. (Rabelais I, 27 or p. 99-100).

Rabelais not only describes dismemberment and bodily mutilation in culinary metaphors, but also depicts the preparation of food and eating in a way that makes them seem almost cannibalistic: "So they made their prisoner their turnspit, and at the fire in which the knights were burning they set their venison to roast" (Rabelais II, 26 or p. 252). In another episode in Turkey, Panurge is covered with lard in order to be roasted over the fire: "The rascally Turks had put me on a spit, all larded like a rabbit" (Rabelais II, 24 or p. 214).

Even the most detailed account of the cannibalistic practices of Brazilian man-eaters refers to this very passage about the cannibalistic Turks by Rabelais. Jean de Léry's Histoire d'un voyage fait en la terre du Brésil, auterment dite Amérique (1578) is—despite its overt distancing from Rabelais—very much rooted in the same grotesque and carnivalesque tradition. Léry argues that the cannibals of the New World always dismember their victims before they roast them on grids over the fire. Despite this negation of Rabelais, Léry's text abounds in imagery reminiscent of culinary language hardly different from that used in Gargantua and Pantagruel. The prisoners are "being fattened like pigs at the trough" (Léry XV or p. 122); "[The cannibals] come forward with hot water that they have ready, and scald and rub the dead body to remove its outer skin, and blanch it the way our cooks over here do when they prepare a suckling pig for roasting" (Léry XV or p. 126).

Like Staden, Léry also introduces the motif of woman as a tempting and devouring monster, when relating the tribe's practice of giving the prisoners to their own women. "[A]fter the woman has made some or another lamentation, and shed a few feigned tears over her dead husband, she will, if she can, be the first to eat of him" (Léry XV or p. 125-126). Many passages in travel narratives, including Vespucci's account of the cannibalistic Amazons (quoted above) and Léry's devouring women, fit perfectly into Bachtin's explanation of the carnival. Here is the latter:

> Earth is an element that devours, swallows up (the grave, the womb) and at the same time an element of birth, of renascence (the maternal breasts). Degradation here means coming down to earth, the contact with earth as an element that swallows up and gives birth at the same time. To degrade also means to concern oneself with the lower stratum of the body, the life of the belly and the reproductive organs; it therefore relates to acts of defecation and copulation, conception, pregnancy, and birth. (Bachtin 21)

The passage from Hans Staden about the cannibals which was quoted above contains all the same elements that Bachtin includes in his characterization of the carnivalesque. Regeneration through conception and birth is directly linked with incorporation. Even Staden's peculiar reference to the sealing of the anus "to make sure that nothing goes to waste" (Staden 146), fits into the overall concept in which excrement is regarded as an integral part of the pan-corporal universe. Or as Bachtin puts it, "Dung and urine lend a bodily character to matter, to the world, to the cosmic elements. It transforms cosmic terror into a gay carnival monster" (Bachtin 335). (See illustration 9: This engraving by de Bry accompanying Staden's account shows how the women prepare the dead body). In these quasi-historical discourses, incorporation and regeneration manifest themselves in a form Bachtin labels as "grotesque realism", which transfers all latent ritual-theological aspects of the European tradition of cults onto a material level by grounding then in the New World.

One can therefore trace a common denominator among traditional concepts of anthropophagy in classical myths, medieval religious texts, early travel narratives, grotesque and carnivalesque literature of the Renaissance and the philosophical notions of holism in Montaigne, always linking utopian hope with motives of incorporation regarding the human body. All the various manifestations of the canni-balisitic, despite their rather divergent appearances, share a utopian longing for unity through the sublation of difference, or as Bachtin summarizes this latent wish for completeness:

> These traits are most fully and concretely revealed in the act of eating; the body transgresses here its own limits: it swallows, devours, rends the world apart, is enriched and grows at the world's expense. The encounter of man with the world, which takes place inside the open, biting, rending, chewing mouth, is one of the most ancient, and most important objects of human thought and imagery. Here man tastes the world, introduces it into his body, makes it part of himself. Man's encounter with the world in the act of eating is joyful, triumphant; he triumphs over the world, devours it without being devoured himself. The limits between man and the world are erased, to man's advantage. (Bachtin 281)

To explain the fusion of utopia and cannibalism by recourse to Bachtin's notion of the carnivalesque is both fashionable and at the same time under attack for various reasons. Bachtin's entire reading of the carnival in general and Rabelais in particular have been severely criticized for not being sufficiently grounded in textual and historical evidence. Dietz-Rödiger Moser, for example, attacks Bachtin's approach by accusing him of utopian projections:

> Much more did he [Bachtin] turn his attention to the west, since he thought to be able to find there—in the carnival—two things, which he missed in the all so progressive new socialist society: The freedom of the people and the liberation of the pressure resting on many of them. (91-92)

The structure is not to be overlooked. In both cases, in the utopian descriptions of America and in Bachtin's utopian delineation of the carnival, a westward projection tries to ground a utopian wholeness in a spatial manner. Bachtin's procedure of extrapolating his utopian carnivalesque from medieval Europe thus parallels

Renaissance discursive practices that also inscribe carnivalesque motives into the territories of the West in order to make utopian notions materialize in a spatial manner.

This utopian urge for the restitution of a lost unity with the world or the Other, which Bachtin places among the "most ancient objects of human thought" (281), also serves as the basis for psychoanalytic theories of identity. All major theoretical movements in the 20th century ground their arguments on binary oppositions or difference. Signifier and signified in linguistics, the raw and the cooked in structural anthropology, as well as subject and object in psychoanalysis are only a few of the numerous manifestations of basic dichotomies which (if one wants to go that far) ultimately boil down to the opposition between inside and outside, i.e. edible and inedible. The constitution of the subject in Freudian Oedipal theory is directly linked to incorporation or introjection. As Freud writes: "The original pleasure-ego tries to introject into itself everything that is good and to reject everything that is bad. From its point of view, what is bad, what is alien to the ego, and what is external are, to begin with, identical." The subject-object dichotomy can thus be traced back to the opposition of the edible and inedible. The pre-lapsarian—or in this case pre-oedipal—wholeness of man, which was lost through eating and not-eating is consequently ritually restored through various forms of incorporation or introjection.

In conclusion, this also sheds light on the causal relationship between utopia and cannibalism ranging from the earliest ancient theories of cultural evolution and theological discourses, to the grotesque-realistic materialization in the image of America propagated by the early travel narratives. Rites, myths and historiography, which link cannibalistic incorporation with utopian spaces, reflect this subliminal human drive for a restitution of primordial oneness through an incorporation of the Other. In the early modern image of America, these two very contradictory concepts—the utopia of a feminized Golden Age or terrestrial Paradise and anthropophagy—seem to fuse and take form through a realistic and material projection of stylized utopian rituals of incorporation onto the New World.

*All scholars surely fear the loss of their documentation or portions of their research—whether this material is left on a train or lost in the ether. Unfortunately during several intercontinental moves, Prof. Klarer experienced this very loss. The editors had decided to include his significant essay here despite incomplete scholarly citations. We share the conviction that what bibliographical and critical apparatus is here maps both the terrain Prof. Klarer did cover, and possible directions and sources his readers can follow on their own.

John R. Leo

Illustrations:

Illustration 1: Amerigo Vespucci "discovers" America; late 16th century; Theodor Galle.

Illustration 2: <u>America</u>: (1581-1600); Philippe Galle; Honour, 88.

Illustration 3: Cannibals with dogs' snouts in Lorenz Fries, *Uslegung Der Carthen*, Strasbourg, 1525. John Carter Brown Library.

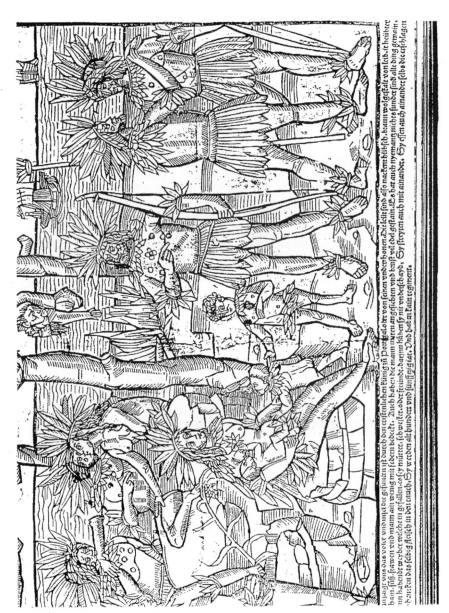

Illustration 4: This woodcut from 1505 is regarded as one of the earliest depictions of Brazilian Indians. It juxtaposes a **nursing** mother with cannibalistic images. *Bayrische Staatsbibliothek München.*

Illustration 5: De Bry uses this engraving of a proud prisoner speaking before his
execution twice, as an illustration for Hans Staden's and Jean de
Léry's accounts. Both texts most probably influenced Montaigne.
Americae Tertia Pars, The Getty Center for the History of Art and
the Humanities.

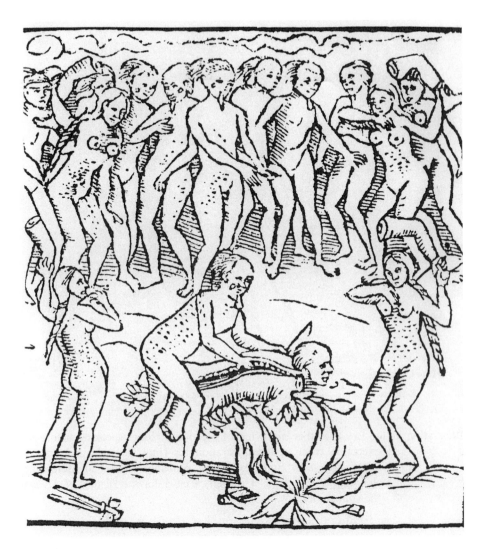

Illustration 6: Woodcut from Staden's printed text of 1557. Herzog August Bibliothek Wolfenbüttel.

Illustration 7: Engraving in Theodor de Bry's *Americae Tertia Pars* based on
Staden's woodcut. The Getty Center for the History of Art and the
Humanities.

Illustration 8: Theodor de Bry's illustration of Staden's account, which, through its emphasis on costumes and masks, is very reminiscent of carinvalesque images. *Americae Tertia Pars,* The Getty Center for the History of Art and the Humanities.

Illustration 9: This engraving by de Bry which accompanies Staden's account shows how the cannibal women prepare the dead body. *Americae Tertia Pars*, The Getty Center for the History of Art and the Humanities.

Landscape of Consuming Passion: Thomas Moran's "Mountain of the Holy Cross" and the Signifying of Perspectives

John R. Leo
University of Rhode Island

The space under . . . view from out standpoint . . .is thronged with
a great multitude of objects so vast in size, so bold yet majestic
in form, so infinite in their details, that as the truth gradually reveals
itself to the perceptions it arouses the strongest emotions.

Capt. Clarence E. Dutton

If religion is to mean anything definite for us, it seems to me
that we ought to take it as meaning this added dimension of
emotion, this enthusiastic temper of espousal, in regions where
morality strictly so called can at best but bow its head and acquiesce.
It ought to mean nothing short of this new reach of freedom for us,
with the struggle over, the keynote of the universe sounding
in our ears, and everlasting possession before our eyes.

William James

"The Mountain of the Holy Cross is in some respects the most remarkable peak on the American continent," writes Ferdinand Vandeveer Hayden, chief geologist for the US Geological and Geographical Survey of the Territories, 1869-1878, and employer and promoter of William Henry Jackson and Thomas Moran. "The distinguishing feature of the mountain, which may be seen by the naked eye as far away as the summit of Gray's Peak in the Colorado or Front Range, a distance of from 80 to 100 miles, is the cross on its south side. This cross . . . one of the most attractive and most conspicuous landmarks in the west, is produced by snow lying in two intersecting seams of gneiss or granite [. . . .] Under what circumstances, or at what time, the mountain received its exceedingly appropriate name is not now known. But it may be excusable to suppose that the words 'Monte Santa Cruz' came almost spontaneously to the lips of some early, long forgotten Catholic missionary, as . . . the uplifted symbol of his faith suddenly appeared before his wondering eyes." Hayden's mixture of scientific description and pop romanticizing glosses Moran's engraving of the mountain (Hayden and Moran, Plate 10 and commentary). He also

Thomas Moran, "The Mountain of the Holy Cross," (engraving of a painting), in William Cullen Bryant, ed., Picturesque America (1874). Reproduced by permission of the Huntington Library, San Marino, California.

tells us how good the fishing is at the peak's base. Their collaboration, *The Yellowstone National Park, and the Mountain Regions of Idaho, Nevada, Colorado and Utah*, was published by Louis Prang with his chromolithographs based on Moran's art (Hayden 1876; cf. Jackson in Fryxell 1958). While this edition was limited—the plates were destroyed to guarantee its value—the image of America's holy mountain already enjoyed widespread popularity and circulation in the public's *musée imaginaire*. In the post-bellum period western topics in general were commercialized by scores of photographers besides such notables as Carleton E. Watkins, Timothy H. O'Sullivan, and Jackson, and by painters such as Bierstadt, printmakers and engravers, and by "local color" writers such as Bret Harte (cf. Mitchell 1996, 56–93; Naef; Dippie, 688–689, 697–698; Jackson). Jackson's collodion photograph of the Holy Cross, which established its iconic status, appeared almost literally out of the blue in late 1873 to rapturous receptions. While Moran painted a number of watercolors and made other studies of the subject, his oil painting of the peak, exhibited at the Centennial Exposition in Philadelphia in 1876, was heaped with honors and emerged as the most famous landscape of the century (see Fisch; Clark; Moran, Appendix). Moran's engraving of the subject was published in 1874 in the acclaimed series *Picturesque America*, an illustrated travelogue edited by William Cullen Bryant (Bryant 1874). It is this representation I focus on below.

Like other contemporary reproductions of vistas, for example of Niagara Falls, the Delaware Water Gap, Yosemite and numerous Western landscapes, the representation (or "imagetext") of this Colorado peak does extraordinary popular cultural work (the term is Mitchell's [1994, 83–84] and already folds narration into the pictorial). Foremost is the integration, through media and literacy, of American nationalist and religious ideologies with the *similitude* of national cultural and geographical unity—the very economy of an assimilating "frontier." Such a preliminary commodification of "nature" or of otherness is achieved by making the unfamiliar *legible* by the encroaching culture's media (Anderson chaps. 1–3; Baird; Jameson; Mitchell 1981; Pratt). The conversion of the "unique" (other) place into a "unique" image and thence into widely circulated copies, that is, the mechanical leveling of heterogeneous geographical spaces to a geoculturally homogenous set, Walter Benjamin calls

> "the contemporary decay of the aura," which rests on two circumstances, both of which are related to the increasing significance of the masses in contemporary life. Namely, the desire of contemporary masses to bring things "closer" spatially and humanly, which is just as ardent as their bent toward overcoming the uniqueness of every reality by accepting its reproduction. Every day the urge grows stronger to get hold of an object at very close range by way of its likeness, its reproduction [. . . .] To pry an object from its shell, to destroy its aura, is the mark of a perception whose "sense of the universal equality of things" has increased to such a degree

that it extracts it even from a unique object by means of reproduction [. . . .] The adjustment of reality to the masses and of the masses to reality is a process of unlimited scope. . . . (Benjamin 223)

But Benjamin's analysis here lends itself to a tempting possible inversion, one predicated on his insight that because reproductions may succeed and repeat each other they affirm the "truth" of their contents. What I would like to suggest is how "intangibles" including discourses may also become paradoxically "auratic," for example the *nation-state, nationality* and *nationalism, divinity,* and the *citizen-subject* (all macro-identities however mobile, fluid, and "singular" their instantiations may be). These discursive formations, that is, also become thingly and reified by means of their investment and correlation with, and their "embodiment" within, *the products and means of mechanical reproduction*. These include not only "aesthetic" print-making and commercial photographs of the American West imbricated with biblical texts and popular mythemes and ideologemes of Manifest Destiny and westward expansion. They include as well popular magazines and newspapers (e.g. *Illustrated Police News, New York Daily Graphic*) and their stories and illustrations on these and related topics (Dippie 674–680). According to Benjamin to "bring [a thing] 'closer' spatially" by grasping its "likeness, its reproduction" would seem to "destroy its aura" by "overcoming [its] uniqueness." But can we counter-argue that the recycling of selected reproductions into a discourse celebrating national "uniqueness" also *re-illumines* them—"re-aureates" them—just as they "re-vision" the landscape? Nineteenth-century American "exceptionalism" inheres to a Chosen People. On this view some reproductions acquire paradoxical "auras" activated, as Taussig puts it splendidly in another context, by the same performance that would seem to destroy them: "the eye acting as a conduit for our very bodies . . . the eye grasping . . . at what the hand cannot reach" (146). It is the impulse within nationalism and nation that posits uniqueness, an irreproducible difference that "articulates the nation as a spirit-in-dwelling [giving] it legitimacy" (Miller 28). The continent, re-viewed, is "performative," or as William Cullen Bryant holds, America offers a "unity of effect" for artists and beholders: it is "fresh" from God's hand (1830, i-iv). By some optics "America" is all "aura."

If modern nationhood is culturally and historically achieved, as Benedict Anderson and Toby Miller argue, through the spread of print (and visual) media and literacy—especially popular novels and newspapers—then media make "it possible to imagine a nation through the invention of *meanwhile*, a term to describe action taking place elsewhere, but also now; part of our world as connected individuals looking at a text, but not available to us as connected at a single site" (Miller 29; Anderson 22–36). As Miller puts the issue:

The expressive interiority attached to national sentiment legitimizes public education's displacement of oral language through writing that spans distance and difference, in the very way popular culture binds people who have never met and do not expect to do so. Identity becomes transferable through literacy and a formal method of educating people [. . . .] Industrial culture divides even as it rationalizes, creating diffuse collective identities as well as officially endorsed ones. . . . (Miller 29-30; cf. Fluck)

Anderson and Miller both see in modern nationhoods an "iconographic change" and a departure from the "sacred languages" of medieval European national imaginings—languages and visualizations representing "the foundational Christian myth" at odds with the modern "chronotropic logic" of "simultaneity" (Miller 29). Yet nineteenth-century American popular prints and travel literature suggest an anachronistic if complex reenactment of this myth, or more pointedly, an "expressive interiority" of "national sentiment" legitimized by Manifest Destiny. While the Christian myth for medieval Europeans was "a spectacle that was always contemporary and local" (Miller 29), so too is the myth of Manifest Destiny as it plays itself out in popular scenic writing and landscape art, notably reproductions. On this view the Christian fable may be regrasped less as a *typology* pre-authorizing a view of landscape or a method in literary and art criticism, and more as an aesthetic reworking of nineteenth-century *spectacle*—an alternative aesthetic norm in popular culture—intimately tied up with fantasies of nationhood and technologies of citizenship (Jenkins 102–108).

The Word and its Double
    The issues of popular consumption of an imagetext and its power effects on viewers conjoin, particularly when an "original" work becomes a circulated "copy" in a reproductive medium. What was handcrafted but once or had small coterie audiences now has recurrences constituting even more "worlds." Moran's engraving of the Holy Cross peak in *Picturesque America* problematizes key critical categories such as ideology, representation, reception and perception, and it raises questions regarding the displacement of biblical narrative and of "historical" pictorialization onto landscape. These in turn invite reassessment of related (and especially art historical) concepts and of critical method, especially those of viewpoint, spectator, iconography, and most emphatically, perspective.
    It is in the coincidence of writing, visualization, and the reproducibility of the image that we find (after Benjamin) the "Messianic" moment, in the America of the 1870s, at its grandest, its most self-congratulatory, at its most self-blinding and imperial, in the sense that the reproducibility and spreading out of frontier and culture contributed to an increasingly institutional—*normative*—version of otherness which, once domesticated and standardized by books, illustrations, and patterns of circulation and consumption, became another part of a totalizing immanence (see Slotkin 1998, Part One). Just as early cinema would shortly do well before 1915, late nineteenth century American popular cultural institutions would rapidly stitch together discourses, genres, and innovations on the basis of what Jenkins calls "historical poetics" or "aesthetic norms"—shared expectations (cultural literacies) among producers and consumers (cf. Miller, 2–32; Ulricchio and Pearson; Mitchell 1994, 417–425).[1] Landscapes (mountains, redwoods, geysers), Native Americans, as

well as explorers and settlers, are reinscribed and recirculated into media as the contemporary "picturesque" or vestiges of a "mythic" past, at once telegraphic shorthand celebrating inevitable national expansion and a sense that "we are already there." The land and its creatures are the utterance of God—the word as both story and discourse, *parole* and *langue*—and therefore participants in a moment at once eternal and synchronic, temporal or diachronic. The ahistorical displacement of human subjects into transcendence, into divine subjects, is in brief a utopian transfiguration of the here and now of experience into its redeeming other. As Louis Marin puts the problem in another context, "the Kingdom of God is here, but outside of space, present outside of space, not connected to a 'word' of space and even less of time to a name. In short it is a utopia, which is at the same time present and absent, a presence which is 'the other' of space" (Marin 1980, 68; Marin 1973). The worldly—experiential, historical—referent is dissolved within—filtered, screened through—its specular and divine double. This "haunting" of the American landscape also shadows its pictorializations, for as we will see more critically, a representation or "reproduction" makes its claim to legitimacy precisely on the basis that it is a *substitute* for the "real," i.e. the representation is *presence*.

Iconographical analysis holds that not only is America God's book (a memory and a typography of possible forms), it is his garden (an impossible plentitude, the Edenic origin) and yet paradoxically the modern promised land (an impossible copy of the origin and yet its return and future) (cf. Novak). On this view American cultural typologies are divinely ordained to organize phenomena they are always already immanental to: frontier expansion as well as metaphysics are totally "natural," that is, from nature (the limit of the given) and therefore outside of history. That the Rockies in the 1870s should have inscribed on a single lofty peak ("on this Rock") the emblem of the Law and passion was, for an "enthused" seeing, final evidence of God's everlasting signature—the Word—on the righteousness of Westward expansion and all that it implied. Even within a scheme of iconographical or typological adumbration it is hard to imagine the figure of Jesus and the passion narrative so popular, so sedimented within secular myths, that the biblical story could underwrite and redeem so much new space and forgive, or repress, the toll of colonial acquisition. Once more, albeit in an era secularly removed from Cotton Mather's *Magnalia Christi Americana* (1702), the biblical text "emanated" and "miraculated" from a land legible and figurable to a chosen people; once again the land objectified a collective metaphysical fantasy and after Althusser an imaginary set of beliefs and relations to the real (Deleuze and Guattari; Althusser; Kroes 7–13).

It is precisely at this juncture that we may sense the limits of iconographical method and turn instead to cultural and semiotic critique. Now we may ask: what are the mechanisms of signifying, and how do they accomplish cultural work? Iconography (to which we may add iconology and typology) issues *from* a textually preconceived notion of an image's content "which predates the reading, and has been elaborated externally to it," and *to* which the method appeals for its hermeneutical authority. It closes interpretation of visual meanings by grounding them in textual meanings. Iconography "attempts essentially to state what the images represent, to 'declare' their meaning [whereas] semiotics [strips] down the mechanisms of signifying [and brings] to light the mainsprings of the signifying process, of which the work of art is, at the same time, the locus and the possible outcome" (Damisch 29).

So: let us establish a homology between the aesthetic goal of graphic reproduction and nineteenth-century America's peculiarly religio-nationalist self-configuration: to reduce or obliterate the distance between the original and the copy, Eden and promise, in the (present) production of the double, the model, the simulacrum. It is instructive to recall Asher Durand's statements on reproduction in the first issue of *The American Landscape* (1830), suggesting as they do early stirrings of a cultural movement toward mass representation and the simulation of presence as an avowedly desirable aesthetic effect. Noting that the "numerous productions" of European scenes have been "multiplied" by engravings to the extent that just about everything has been seen and rendered, Durand claims both "charms" and monetary "reward" for those portraying the relatively untouched American landscape. He promises in his advertisement "fidelity and accuracy" of representation in any engraving using some original work for its model, stressing *"that its characteristic features will, in all cases, be truly and correctly copied"* (Durand's emphases, 3-4). The ploy here is that the "truth" of a reproduction lies in its status as a *re*-presentation of some original, itself a faithful *copy* (true to nature) of an *anterior* (original) landscape, the *real*. The "truth," then, of a representation, is representation, a discontinuous process of advocacy, delegation, and substitution: the persuasive *substitution* of a tacit *same* for an exchangeable *other*. The "truth" of representation, which is to say "the effect of its power" (e.g. to persuade), is our acquiescence (or our negation, or the process of sublimation) to a chain of represented "equivalences" we see (produce).[2] Now let us consider how corridors and networks within Moran's engraving of the Mountain of the Holy Cross open onto social and cultural space.

Extending the Solitary Gaze
Moran repeatedly worked a number of Western landscape subjects before 1900, notably vistas of the Grand Canyon and of the Yellowstone (which became a middle nickname) (see Wilkins; Jackson; Moran). Specialization became a way of appropriating, whether by style or locale, and Moran, Bierstadt, and Thomas Hill steered clear of each other's turf (Arkelian; Mitchell 1996, 56–93). Hill, for example, turned out paintings by the score of Yosemite and had work lithographed by Prang, although it was Moran who was commissioned in 1872 by John Muir to etch the frontispiece, "The Half Dome—View from Moran Point," for his celebrated *Picturesque California*, published in 1887 with texts and illustrations by Joaquin Miller, Ernest Ingersoll, Hill, Remington, and others. Moran first drew the Holy Cross from Jackson's photograph in late 1873 or early 1874, finally seeing and sketching the "splendid peak" in August 1874 while with a Hayden survey party under the guidance of James Stevenson. The view was "one of the grandest he [had] ever seen" (Wilkins 99). It was the first rendition—a copy from a mechanical reproduction—that appeared as a full-page engraving in *Picturesque America*.

Moran's large oil painting of the peak (82.75" x 63.75"; approximately 2.3m x 1.4m), finished in 1875 and exhibited in New York and Boston before the Centennial Exhibition, was, as I have indicated, a critical, popular, and a financial success. Two out of four known watercolors of the peak survive, and one of the lost versions, whose provenance is Louis Prang, presumably provided the basis for the chromo-lithograph published in *The Yellowstone National Park* (Clark). An etching of the mountain from 1888 survives, as do several woodcut proofs. All these different versions share basic features, including a vertical composition appropriate to the "height" of the subject; a deviance from strict topographical criteria (e.g. the placements of the cascades are fictions dictated by the compositions and changed from work to work); and a traditional illusionistic disposition of the scene according to the visual pyramid (with subsequent elimination of detail and of high tonal contrast in the move from foreground to background). One significant difference is found in the engraved—and the only widely reproduced—rendition, which portrays the walking figure of the Spectator or Solitary, that conventional isolated wanderer or aesthetic beholder found so abundantly in European and American baroque and romantic visual art. In nineteenth-century American versions of pastoral, he appears in the familiar declensions of Indian, mountain man or frontiersman, or scout, and after 1870 increasingly in the poses of the sportsman, tourist, *flâneur*, and cowboy (Westermeir; Meigs; Curry; and Pratt, esp. part III).

Let us examine the space of the Spectator in Moran's engraving. He produces a distinct sort of human space. As we have observed, he is our delegate to the viewing and consuming process and the product of it, and he is the collective representation or symbol of American expansion and the souvenir of Moran's and Rideing's actual, that is, editorial, collaboration. The figure's disposition articulates and makes meaningful the formal division of space within the engraving. Because this engraving appears in *Picturesque America*, the figure of the isolated viewer does not signal exclusively the human dimension in the representation. He performs a semiotic function that comments on and links the elements of the scene in order to reach and move a viewing readership. Moreover, as a figure in a representative space depicting the very process of looking—at the least, making representations to himself—and bounded by a textual process concerned with tourism and sightseeing, the gazing Solitary is redoubled. His activity constitutes him as a representative of the process of representation within an image pretending to be a "window" open to us (a mass viewing public). Thus the image at once reverses outside and inside, "there" and "here," and mediates to the reading viewer (the armchair and increasingly the Pullman tourist), who itinerant ambassador he is and whom he reflects, a properly specular role. Finally the Spectator is, like the Moran who illustrates the accompanying travel piece "The Rocky Mountains" and like the journalist W. H. Rideing who writes it, both the recording "mirror" and the souvenir of visiting, drawing and writing (cf. Guillén; Pratt).

Whatever conventional meanings and symbolic dimensions the solitary con-veys, he also signifies a *recording* (the transcript of imaginary or actual tours, the working of the steel engraving plate), an *invitation* to see as well as the object seen, and at the level of content an *imitation* of what we would most likely do if we were to be "there" in the same scene: look, be absorbed by and yet appropriate the landscape (Taussig 1993). Whether as fantasmatic representation and actor glimpsed through a cultural window, or as mimetic representation reflecting the ambient world, the figure of the Spectator produces the scene and is produced by it even as the gesture of his inclusion comments on and signifies meanings to others. To alter Susan Sontag's description of the photograph, the reproduction "makes everyone a tourist in other people's reality, and eventually in one's own" (Sontag 57; cf. Pomeroy). While he is distinguishing among contrasting styles of painting the better to train his readership in "how to" view high art, influential pundit and critic James Jackson Jarves's remarks are premised on the power of illusion to reduce the distance between an absent source and the copy, an evoked real and its scenic substitution. "But the effect of high art is to sink the artist and the spectator alike into the scene," he intones conventionally, adding: "It becomes the real, and, in that sense, true realistic art, because it realizes to the mind the essential truths of what is pictorially disclosed to the eye. The spectator is no longer a looker on, as in other ['idealist,' painterly] styles, but an inhabitant of the landscape" (Jarves II, 254). The aesthetic goals and power effects of representation are an indistinguishable consumption and entangling: the specular appropriation of the beholding subject by the subject of representation, the willing suspension of disbelief and thrill of *being there*.

Let's once more reposition the Bible as an immanental culture force, but with the purpose of linking it to other signifying functions and rhetorical operations in Moran's representation of the sacred peak. The prominence given to the viewing of a full-page engraving of an ostensible biblical imagetext certainly depends upon and reinforces the prior inscription of the Word, no matter what the secular displacements and rewritings. Virtually all the essays in *Picturesque America* and similar travel literature and autobiography have, as their subtext or partial motivation, some version or other of a divine mandate to remake the land and put it into a special view of history. The once purely religious gaze will aestheticize its own fascination with the sheer power of its inscriptions to remake—re-totalize—"nature." *Picturesque America*, then, is a figural spectrum graphing and glossing the Testaments in the projection, in the screening and reflecting, of the nationalist eye into land and life. Within such immanence an anointed people can see and read profitable and provident signs of their historical privileging *because* they regard, mark, and graph phenomena: "selfhood" is a "anemic inscription" (cf. Irwin 220– 221). Manifest Destiny is the possibility and the outcome of literacy as such. If the Bible and the land "represent" at the same time the once-for-all-origin/presentation of divine discourse and yet its historical unfolding, then the "miming" of this textualization—a people's recording and representing of events—recodes both literacy and history as always already infused with divinity and divine sanction (cf. Taussig 1993). "Nature" exists as the screen/mirror and the window/stage on and through which the "real" is seen, constituted, and enacted. Thus it is that the mimetic plane of the "Mountain of the Holy Cross" is a mirror with a realistic superimposition or traced representation of a "natural event," and thereby a dissimulator; and yet this plane also signals a stage with an ongoing performance of the land's story and history, and is thereby an assimilator (cf. Lyotard; Marin 1977).

Such miming on another level, of course, also produces the nostalgic evocation or representation of a disappearing wilderness, the storyteller's tale of the disappearing or diminishing deity. The creation of the California School of Design in San Francisco by 1874, the Geological Surveys, the emergence and rapid spread of landscape photography, the popularity of panoramic paintings, dioramas, and atmospheric landscapes (with too much "trash-literature of the brush," according to Jarves, including a "virulent epidemic of sunsets"), the creation of Yellowstone as the world's first national park, tourism: these post-bellum events help index the growth of "nature" as finally *the* image—a consummate representation, a very big *thing* in the nascent industrial commodity system.[3]

Space—whether conceived of as locale, topos, site, or sight—must be understood as a *set* of actions, which occur in some *places* of that space. In art and life space is unavoidably heterogeneous, shaped, oriented; it is never neutral or "empty." Its very nature is defined by the actions, gestures, things, representations, and imaginings which *take place in* it and give it flux and directionality. Thus in art, representative space is not merely the (iconographical) surface or container for the relational construction of thematic or ornamental figures, *topoi*, and the like; rather it is the disposition of the figural as such which unfolds—vectorizes—representative space and gives us a basis in the first place for any discussion of other *extensive* meanings. As I have mentioned, "truth" in a representation is its effect, and it follows that the "truth" of representability is that someone is always self-representing, self-narrating, within the spaces of social configuration. Indeed, it is the work of representational devices such as narration or visual perspective to realize the rhetorical potential of an image—to install its "truth" as its own fullness of meaning, as presence.

Truisms from nineteenth-century discourses on artistic practices and intended effects on viewers are helpful here. Here's Moran: "I never painted a picture that was not the representation of a distinct impression from Nature," he is quoted as saying, but he qualifies just what he offers back as "representation" and "truth":

> I place no value upon literal transcripts from Nature. My general scope is not realistic; all my tendencies are toward idealization. Of course, all art must come through Nature; I do not mean to depreciate Nature or naturalism; but I believe that a place, as a place, has no value in itself for the artist only so far as it furnishes the material from which to construct a picture. Topography in art is valueless [. . . .] [In "The Grand Canyon of the Yellowstone"] forms are extremely wonderful and pictorial, and while I desired to tell truely [sic] of Nature, I did not wish to realize the scene literally, but to preserve and to convey its true impression. Every form introduced into the picture is within view from a given point, but the relations of the separate parts to one another are not always preserved. For instance, the precipitous rocks on the right were really at my back when I stood at that point, yet in their present position they are strictly true to

pictorial Nature; and so correct in the whole representation that every
member of the expedition with which I was connected, declared, when he
saw the painting, that he knew the exact spot which had been reproduced.
The rocks in the foreground are so carefully drawn that a geologist could
determine their precise nature. (Sheldon 124–126)

In the same interview Moran praises Turner because "his landscapes are false"
and sacrifice "the literal truth of the parts to the higher truth of the whole." Moran's
aesthetics here are conventional and orthodox: composition or the "idealization" of a
scene is played off against the requirements for a rigorous mimetic realism within a
governing organicism harmoniously distributing parts and wholes. But while he
expresses himself in the languages of nineteenth-century art discourse and
psychology (pictorial nature, the true impression), Moran makes it plain that truth in
a scene, for artist and viewer alike, is the "impression" or rhetorical effect. Truth in
"pictorial Nature" is the sense datum or "distinct impression"; truth in the
representation is the power "to convey its true impression"; *truth is representation.*
In this sort of economy of oppositions the "literal" is reduced to the "topographical,"
and the natural "place" is important only as an archive of potential images and
rearranged compositions. The very idea of the referent is curiously banished as an
artistic standard and authority when it suggests the origin or phenomenal "place," yet
it is invoked to explain the persuasive seduction of the representation as a substitute
for an absent actuality. In an important way Moran's comments here are institutional,
they are part of a pervasive and increasingly "autonomous" art discourse whose
assumptions are shared by major artists such as Washington Allston, Jarves, Bryant,
and Bierstadt, and as such they show that "true art" is whatever dominant art
discourse says it is (cf. Hewitt 55–56). If referentiality is the scripted science of
topography at the discursive level of the geological surveys—with the schematized
referent the map and related graphing systems—in art it is the isomorph of the "true
impression" (cf. Mitchell 1996, 56–93).

This textualization of aesthetics and of lived experience is a reminder that for
the scriptural attitude the New World is the profane and holy Book. But divinity
inhabits the land unevenly, its more-or-less presence reflecting ambivalent attitudes
toward settlement and a shrinking wilderness, and suggesting a recognition that the
land provides both accelerating and diminishing returns. One set sees divine
presence, as when Christian creation and American history are felt to be mutually
implicated in a process of transfiguration. Continent, nation, and godhead are
indistinct. This view underwrites romantic landscape art, now partially grasped as the
conversion and the representation of a seemingly inexhaustible "surplus" land into a
picturesque garden or benign wild. For artists like Moran the West is the source and
the occasion for an abundance of Wordsworthian returns, just as for entrepreneurial
settlers and the War Department it is an extendable resource with an alterable
frontier. On the other hand this utopian romance of the Western landscape points to
the historical reality of its own undoing, as when the once vast West is no longer its
own excess. Space thickens and crowds into peculiarly human places: the sublimity

of "God's land" becomes the domesticity of the cottage. If for the more secular minded history is the Fall from the Garden, it uses the languages of exploration, settlement, and tourism alike. California, the Cascades in the Oregon Territory, Utah, and other Western regions invariably appear as new Edens, settlement at one point a new Fall, and the land's fecundity and seeming endlessness appear as the oft-stated advertisement or promotion as much as any act of wondrous faith (cf. Franklin; Pratt).

The Shaping of Dimensions

How do other spaces in Moran's engraving unfold and signify? How does the use of perspective distribute the biblical narrative into the rendered landscape and recode two intersecting ravines on a slope in the Rockies (the vertical approximately 400 meters, the transverse about 130 meters), cruciform when snowfilled, so that they seemingly manifest themselves as not only the signs of the divine but also its incarnation? And interpellate a nation? Our task is to describe the body of the print, including its habitat—the page—and to examine how a preliminary reading of perspectival apparatuses connects and modifies the mainly metaphorical operations we have so far considered.

The Spectator's height is 7/8" (2.22cm) in an engraving 9" x 6 ¼" (22.9cm x 15.9cm), appropriate for his pilgrim tourist status and Adamic connotations. He is walking left to right on a small ledge, his immediate staging area. This ledge is coincidental with the boulders forming a bank of the Holy Cross stream, and because of the stream's represented direction the ledge intersects the bottom edge (margin) of the representational space pretty exactly at the center. The matrix of a purely human set of significations within this landscape is confined to a small corner in the foreground locale, which is the horizontal register from left to right rising 3" (7.6cm) from the bottom margin. Traditionally the foreground in mimetic works offers the most detailed expositions, and Moran here is traditional if not strictly mimetic or topographical. (For this engraving Moran has traced the peak's contours directly from Jackson's photograph, but he has constructed the rest of the scene imaginatively if also "strictly true to Nature"; the stream and other mountains are not actually "there" from this angle of viewing.) The middle ground is also about 3" (7.6cm) and phases its illusory depth more radically into recession than the foreground. Its nearer zone overlaps with the foreground and holds its share of dead trees and boulders—the *roches moutenées* Moran dreaded to climb but liked to draw—whereas the distant middle ground recedes by planes (cf. *coulisse*, a theatrical backdrop) marked by foothills and gulches (cf. *couloir*, coulee) and bounded by clouds. The upper third register is traversed by steep slopes which also act as dramatic *coulisses* for the middle ground foothills profiled against them, but in the engraving's vertical schematization of content the background is dominated by the isolated summit of the Holy Cross.

Moran's variation of a traditional formalist composition may first be considered in its conventional setting as a page (recto) in *Picturesque America*. The engraving is labeled outside the bottom margin of the image proper; it has a title that entitles the viewing reader to narrate the text and episodes of Christ's passion. The title,

"Mountain of the Holy Cross," as print already processes some of our attention and spaces it within its own power of regulation (syntactical linearity, proper naming, "authoritative" referencing). The imagetext ensemble, including its title, names the cross as word to Word, as text to the visual ideogram or hieroglyph formed by the cruciform ravines (cf. Mitchell 1994, 98; Marin 1977). The left-to-right movement in the reading of the title reflects a series of left-to-right pictorially coded movements that orient—which create the effect of an orientation—in the depth of the representation. The solitary Spectator walks, as we have noticed, toward the viewer's right, but also towards us as positioned spectators, however indirectly. The stream follows in parallel movement, and its last represented cataract falls "out" of the picture plane and "below" the right hand corner frame. The left half of the print articulates space by diagonals representing the foothills and mountain slopes and "pushes" the ponderous geological mass toward the division formed by valley and stream, the effect being "as if" the right bank and right half of the engraving were being crowded out (or "falling out") of the field of representation. The engraving also seems to put itself in motion giving the static categories of hierarchy and elevation (fig. 1) a torque (fig. 2).

These combined effects already imply their own potential for anamorphosis, which postulates at least two physical viewpoints which a beholder must occupy if s/he is to narrate the signs within the scene and complete its story (cf. Guillén; and Osborne under "Perspective"; Marin 1971, 1973, and 1977; Preziosi; Jay). Indeed, the engraving has several sliding points of view. The reader's position is doubly elevated, for example, since the engraving's illusory depth locates us "above" the foreground and looking "down" on the stage or screen (note the Spectator's path and his shadow relative to our angle of viewing). Second, we are "above" the page by virtue of the usual physical position we have holding and reading a book. Of course this first elevated viewpoint is also a specialized use of perspective, in this instance what is known as three-point and also inclined plane perspective, which employs three vanishing points beyond the right, left, and bottom margins (i.e. beyond the page). To the economy of an inclined plane perspective Moran adds another, usually labeled single point or central convergence perspective, albeit with rhetorical rather than mathematical rigor. This rhetorically dominant perspectival system directs our gaze to the mountain and to the intersection of the ravines containing its vanishing point. And in his gradated use of tonalities to suggest distance and depth, achieved by finely hatching the steel plate, Moran uses aerial perspective in the simulation of mountain gloom and glory.

We may diagram the engraving's content and composition I have discussed to see how these schemata signify other spatializing functions.

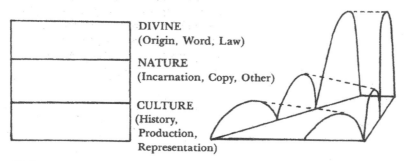

DIVINE
(Origin, Word, Law)

NATURE
(Incarnation, Copy, Other)

CULTURE
(History,
Production,
Representation)

Fig. 1:
The picture plane.

Fig. 2:
Projection of scene's illusory depth.

At their most general, figures 1 and 2 graph widely disseminated cultural categories which are biblically derived textualizations or figural readings of American landscape, history, and national identity. They mark at the same time Moran's deployment of conventional codes of pictorial composition to produce an idealized hierarchical organization of representational space appropriate to his subject. Experience so imagined in its totality is the fantasm of its ordering categories or epistemes, and this sort of conjugation of space and time into culture, nature, and the divine derives from related religio-historical configurations such as the chain of being, models and metaphors of correspondence, and the like, all with complex genealogies. (The "stylistic" play of multiple perspectives, which I have alluded to and partly outlined in figure 2, poses problems I deal with shortly.) The diagrams also graph the received wisdom—evident in the discursive overlapping of religion, nationalism, and Manifest Destiny as American "exceptionalism"—that would see these categorical oppositions as critically, religiously, and philosophically universal and valid for all time. These are the same ways of seeing, furthermore, that ground the sort of bourgeois apologetics and aesthetic pedagogics in Jarves's *The Art-Idea*, that underwrite the pictorial and critical lingua franca of the art market (e.g. conoisseurship, a purchasing public for Moran, Hill, Bierstadt and other popular landscapers), and finally that help account for the vast popularity of landscape reproductions.

The tripartite registers of the engraving also overlap; each is contingent on the others; and all play their differences against each other. These registers signifying space and time, which seem to produce a pious and binding hierarchy, are *produced by* (the power of) representation and negated by it, and any failure to recognize this is simply to be entrapped within the immanence portrayed, that is, within the ideological structures freighted by the imagetext and its networks. The viewing subject, in this instance a reader of *Picturesque America*, and the subject of representation, here a peak whose many cultural connotations are ratified by a strolling delegate of the viewing process, are both positioned—produced—by the full rhetoric of the engraving, including its perspective effects. What is less apparent and yet important to consider in a culture where nascent mass media are already technologies of knowing, is the proposition that the reading subject and the rendered subject are both dismissed by the representational process as functions of its power in the public sphere (cf. Hewitt 178–184; Warner). The objectified *autonomy* of the image already binds the seeming autonomous (and even anonymous) specularity of the citizen to a world of simulacra and totalizing (if also unpredictable) representation. This is immanence, or the conjoining of representation, theatricality, and power. (Thus "Mountain of the Holy Cross" inscribes within itself the implication of blasphemy, for even the divine is contained within and by the hegemony of the image.) In this sort of representational irreality history is arguably without a subject, for history's visualized and narrated authority, for much of a mass spectatorial public, is a mythologized metaphysics whose signs are natural—and nationalized—phenomena, the scene of "nature," and whose immanental workings and providential summonses are the self-miraculating productions of "culture." Where "nature" is, there already "America" shall be.

The aesthetic impulse to create the "true impression," to conflate the original with the copy in the production of the double and the autonomous simulacrum, certainly indicates a profound secular tendency toward the consumption of reproduction and of the commodity at the expense of any religion of *identity* (cf. McKenna on "biblioclasm"). The condition of immanence, in addition to structuring its secular and theological meanings within the metaphysics of presence, inverts and decenters the hierarchy of the sacred over the natural and cultural categories it ostensibly authorizes and lends fixed identities (positions) to, but not because the divine is recuperated and diffused through all things (the comfortable pantheism D. H. Lawrence finds in Ben Franklin), and not because the order of culture is moving "up" to and overcoming in some Nietzschean sense the sacred. Rather the process of representation—the representability of everything or anything—so ambiguates the notion of the referent as to replace it. Thus we may claim that in Moran's engraving the portrayal of a venerated and privileged center, the Cross and the Christian holy as such, also posits the structural equivalence of the viewpoint and of the vanishing point. As the religious and ideological beginning and end of all "perspective" (speculating/looking through, behind, toward) and of all history, the divine is the source of everything: it is the production point for all that we see and similarly the horizon, the limit, for all that we mean and make. But what of the beholder and the viewpoint?

"What We See Is Where We Are"

The division of space in the "Mountain of the Holy Cross" is necessarily entangled with the narrative of Christian redemption. Our task now is to consider the tripartite registrations of hierarchical space and the uses of perspective as deictic signs, as directionals or "shifters" within the imagetext guaranteeing that a dialogical relation with a viewer becomes a part of the image's story. The narrative problem in the imagetext is to order signs and codes enabling the viewer to self-narrate its story, that is, to begin it, grasp the significance of the (central) represented moment, and to finish (see Marin 1971, "Elements pour une sémiologie picturale," 17–43). The critical problem is to understand how these signs and codes are open to interpretive activity displaying the workings of representational systems in culture. The icon of the cross, the vertical emphasis of the engraving, and multiple uses of perspective to create effects of depth and divine presence, are pictorial signs warranting the story-telling sequences we have discussed in part. These are the co-presence of Jesus and the American continent, the destined rightness of the chosen people to appropriate this continent, and nationhood as the reconciliation of culture, nature, and divinity.

What facilitates and substantiates this otherwise problematic narrativizing is the textualization of history and of experience, which here takes the form of the displacement of the historical narrative into the genre of landscape. Our critical reading of these same pictorial signs as signifying functions within cultural immanence and as elements of mechanical (and early "mass") reproduction, however, extends cultural critique. By giving themselves to the Word and taking a continent, by invoking one "origin" and legitimating another, and by crafting a national identity in multiple public spheres by visual media, Americans (to rewrite Gertrude Stein) showed themselves to be the oldest of contemporary civilizations by inventing the *modern*. The abandonment of history resulted in its reinvention in and through media, and by allegorizing (reterritorializing) the land in purely Christian tales of redemption, some nineteenth-century American cultural products take giant steps, however utopian, toward the unchecked *afflatus* of pure ideology (cf. Warner; Wawrzyczek; Hewitt 93–101).

Moran's simulation of a "present moment" in the Colorado Rockies for the viewer to see intersects the biblical texts, reorders their thematics, and sends to the consuming viewer—the cultural subject—other signifying functions. The figure of the Solitary, for example, fulfills several narrative semiotic functions. In the context of the travelogue and the ongoing exploration and settlement of a land with endless natural wonders, he invites a narrativization that the represented moment is the present one, the moment of viewing (and thus the force of the picture plane as mirror or window). But this paradoxical presentness of both the newly viewed and the re-presentation of the already seen is configurated by biblical events that are even more distant. The discursiveness of the Christian fable opens up gaps at the level of the textual and visual referentiality of its icons.

Let us effect a displacement, in spatial terms, of viewing and reading the truth/power effects of the "Mountain of the Holy Cross" the better to diagram the correlate structures of the representational and perspectival apparatuses and the formal structures of the visualized Christian story. We may then trace the signifying of representation as such as it works perspective to shift different elements of meaning. The power of perspective to operate viewpoints and the simulation of presence is remarkable for its *scope* (cf. Tagg, 8–16).

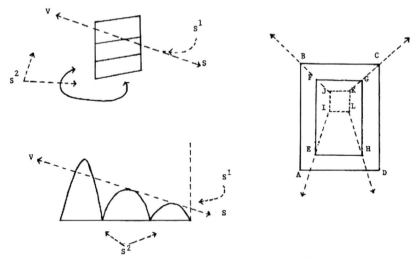

Fig. 3:
Lateralization of representational
and perspectival apparatuses.

Fig. 4:
Scenographic cube.

Figure 3 above lateralizes the engraving and the spectator/reader's viewpoint in order to display the binding of representational methods and the imagetext's content to the narrative they enact. Figure 4 elaborates the visual pyramid into the "scenographic cube" (after Marin), but maintains the viewer's frontal vantage point. This procedure shows the relations between the picture plane as window and mimetic screen, the space of viewing, and the "interior" and "exterior" limits of the scenographic cube, that is, the functions of the viewpoint and the dominant vanishing point. Figure 3, by effecting a dramatic side projection, as it were, of the engraving, and repositioning us with regard to the mountain and the Spectator, reveals the shifting "ascent" and "descent" of multiple meanings and the interweaving of interpretive codes within the print's hierarchical space. Figures 3 and 4 both indicate the forceful signifying activity of the viewpoint and the central vanishing point. The vanishing point is necessarily the sign or locus marking the limit of represented space: in a visual work it is the sign signifying there is nothing more to see beyond itself. As I mentioned, this point or locus can also be grasped as the active source producing the spectacle or representation before us (and in Moran's engraving this point by default is the ubiquity of the Christian deity). Similarly, the consuming viewer's position before the represented scene is also a vanishing point and a locus of production (minimally the seer's self-narration and the represented story; and finally the unconscious). The viewer's position and the representation's limit of space are structurally equivalent points which operate reversible functions, including the production and dissemination of cultural codes, the organization of different symbolic spaces, and the move from one signifier to another. The perspectival system, in short, works much like the representational: it regulates, disperses, and transforms meanings; it allows for their replication and consumption; it also helps secure certain kinds of visual literacies through popular cultural technologies (cf. Miller, Part 1).

In figure 3 we have one version of the narrative potential of the view-point/vanishing point equivalence. If we understand their connection as a theoretical line SV (and $SV1 \ldots SV$ n+1) to take into account different perspectives and anamorphoses), a line not present nor indicated as such in the engraving but instead one posited by the power of the perspectival code and its production of illusory depth, then that line occupies the same space as storytelling: it marks the narrative beginning, middle, and end—the "present moment" of viewing *and* of self-narrating the imagetext's content. This line, which is a lateralization of the viewing axis in the scheme of representation, also presents itself as the production-consumption axis for the national narrative of continental expansion with divine sanction. It diagrams the shifting of story elements, their "polyphonic organization with each voice at a different level of reading [. . . .] The importance of this notion of shifter is that it accounts for the process of configuration, rather than for objects and functions. It accounts for the symbolic aspect of exchange. It provides an insight into the problem of the mode of operation of ideology within the built world. It allows us to enter into a mechanism of production of sense that corresponds to an ideology of exchange" (Agrest and Gandelsonas 115–116). In sum, a critical explanation of the engraving's signifying elements allows us to generate counter-critiques of immanence in the service of colonial power. Once more (*pace* Benjamin) we may, in Mitchell's sense, "de-reify" representation, in short, rethink it "as relationship, as process, as the relay mechanism in exchanges of power, value, and publicity"; representation finally "suggests an inherently unstable, reversible, and dialectical structure," one without ordained "directionality" (Mitchell 1994, 420).

Figure 4 offers further metacriticism of perspectival regulation by diagramming the system's limits and exclusions in the production of representation. The first limit is the plane *ABCD*, which is the *page* of *Picturesque America* and the physical precondition for the scenographic cube holding the imagetext. This plane has its framing margins that mark off the space of representation, the plane *EFGH*; this is the image proper with the proper name of its title visualized. The margins also formally announce and invite the act of seeing; they separate off and privilege a place within the page's space and inaugurate the aesthetic attitude. The second limit is the inner (farthermost) plane *IJKL* of represented space, which we must imagine as the plane suspending the dominant vanishing point, the icon of Holy Cross and symbolic center of the engraving. Finally, the third limit is the outer limit of the scenographic cube, indicated by broken lines to underscore the multiple "planes" and multiple public spheres for (mis)understanding, beholding, responding, and re-fashioning (cf. Robbins). What you *see* is what you *get*. The power effects of perspective are real and they are open to critical analysis. If the second limit of representation connotes the mimetic screen, which reflects and reproduces, then the third limit implies the window which opens onto the world's spaces. The first limit shows the effects of dissimulation in representation, the second reveals the workings of assimilation. Both figures 3 and 4 are concerned with how limits are not "part" of the represented subject or narrative but rather annunciatory *signifiers of representation* to a seer: "Look here, there is something worthy of viewing." Lastly, both diagrams show how viewers and imagetexts are themselves crisscrossed by re-combinative codes and symbolic sets and work together in the (re)production of representation and of the codes and sets themselves.

The Manifesting Text

Moran made several engravings to illustrate Rideing's travel piece on the Rockies for *Picturesque America* just as he illustrated essays on travel and scenery by other contributors. Other artists are also included in the volumes. Despite the resulting variety—prose descriptions of the Native American, for example, invoking the typology of the noble savage by locating him as yet subhuman in a framework of Darwinian evolution—we still have the characteristic tropes, subtexts, and concerns over issues of representation. Text and visualization complement each other within the same problematic: together they form the instructive program of *Picturesque America* to replace the unseen phenomenon with the witnessing representation, absence with simulated presence, "nature" (the not-yet-human) with "culture," and untutored or unknown desire by a civic virtue and good citizenship. As an anthology of optics, styles, and testimonials, the book establishes its own veracity as a substitution, as a representation of a real, by the power of discourse itself. The book is authoritative because it is the scene of autobiographical writing, "faithful" reproductions, and the intertextual locus for other discourses and authorities, such as geology and governmental surveys. The anthology affords the reading viewer a passage beyond the frontiers of the known and the unknown through the very means of representation. In his "Preface," for example, Bryant declares that the purpose of *Picturesque America* is to bring to the public familiar yet "strange, picturesque, and charming scenes . . . places which attract curiosity by their interesting associations" (I, iv). H. E. Colburn's "The Cañons of the Colorado," commissioned for the anthology and illustrated by Moran from Hiller's Powell Survey photographs, seemingly undercuts the authority of its visual descriptions with the conventional aside that Western scenery can be equivocated only by a "large canvas, and by the use of the many-tinted brush" (II, 506), yet the effect of this platitude is to legitimize further the visualizing discourses surrounding it. So it is that space becomes "unified" in the sense that representational processes make it "ever more identical with itself" (Debord 165). Different "places" (including that of the reader) are organized as exchangeable "equivalences" through the mediating powers of the discourses of art, tourism, and the sublime.

Where Moran's engravings for "The Rocky Mountains" invest the panoramas or conventionally grand scene with repose ("Chicago Lake" [II, 491]; "Long's Peak, from Estes Park" [II, 483]), Rideing's text draws out, in his words, the "latent grief" and "morbid brooding" inspired by the "inanimate" sublimity of the scene. He fills with familiar words and tropes both the empty landscape and the always potentially empty representative space of language. His is an instance of the domestic sublime, the practical imagination of settlement, for it is only within the act of representation that strange voices and feelings are reprojected into the possibility of cultivated apples. For Rideing, silence and mountains are not necessarily golden; his text simultaneously registers and shifts objects in its anxious and relentless naturalizing. A self-conscious aestheticizing becomes a necessary defense against raids from the landscape or from his unpredictably moody interior. It is a spring evening in Estes Park at the base of Long's Peak:

> A void is filled. A man on the heights, looking into the valley, would be conscious of a change in the sentiment of the scene. The presence of humanity infused itself into the inanimate. . . . Our sympathies find vent, but not in hysterical adulation. Our admiration and wonder are mingled with a degree of awe that restrains expression. (II, 488)

Letting go is to travel too far toward the estranging otherness of the "void" or into the overwhelming plentitude "hysterical adulation." A metonymical infusion of human "presence" into the "inanimate" is the enabling fantasy and act of writing unifying space and transforming things and experiences into representational equivalences: we get Rideing's "copy" (in all senses).[4] The energies and charges of geographic otherness are assimilated also by the pervasiveness of Rideing's evocative generalizations, which signal the discourses of aesthetics and the travelogue in a shared situation of looking. "The heart of man is not felt; we gaze at the varied forms, all of them massive, most of them beautiful, feeling ourselves in a strange world" (II, 488). Such strangeness affiliates with darker emotions, and to keep them distant the acts of scoping and recording are never far from imagining cultural replication and the plantation of communities: "And so our white tents, erected on the fertile acres of the Estes Park, throw a gleam of warmth among the snowy slopes, and impart to the scene that something without which the noblest country appears dreary, and awakens whatever latent grief there is in our nature" (II, 488).

Grief in Rideing's prosaic regime might well be an indication of the anxiety brought on by the very nature of the pressure-filled historical moment, which finds him standing in a pre-capitalist space about to disappear even as he writes his copy. He looks about him and prepares the ways for others, and otherwise performs his function as the delegate of the viewing and consuming process. "Roundabout are wonderful 'bits' of nature" (II, 492), he writes, decomposing what he sees into specialized fragments, and all around him he observes other specialists replicating his own additive activity: "The photographers and naturalists [are] working with exemplary zeal in adding to their collections." Collecting things not only fills the void of Eastern ignorance of the West. It serves to "prove" a later reconstruction of events and permits things to enter into other representational schema, classifications, and collections.

But if Rideing and his colleagues are in a wilderness, others are not far behind; in fact, it is being settled and converted into other scenarios. Rideing himself can look and admire with the right optics. At Twin Lakes he confesses to having "no more occasion for morbid brooding, but a chance to go into healthy raptures, and to admire some tender, almost pastural [sic] scenery." He sees too the very *type* of Moran's Solitary: "And not the least charming object to be met on the banks is an absorbed, contemplative man, seated on some glacier-thrown bowlder [sic], with his tender rod poised and bending gracefully . . . ready for the gleaming fish that flaunts his gorgeous colors in the steadily-lapping waters" (II, 498). The contemporary advertising copy ring to this description is a just reminder that in the nineteenth century the popular images of tall and proud mountain men and of scouts such as Kit Carson, Zenas Leonard, and James "Ohio" Pattie, were the structural bases for the emerging images of the sportsman and gentleman hunter. Like Moran's engravings, Rideing's text has its windows and mirrors for the world, even as its own representational activity subsumes the world by its metaphoricity; description cannot help but to act—to represent—American dreams. Rideing, no less than the fisherman, has stepped into a mediating image and discovered there—captured—his own gaze. The "absorbed, contemplative" sportsman is the votary of the landscape performing sacramental acts, which is to say that he self-narrates his ideal reflection, Adamic and romanticized as it is, in his performance of ideally heroic acts mediated by popular myth and artistic representation. Rideing, in turn, sees the real thing and is "charmed." Rideing's perceptions merge with popular myths and stories, and they slip finally into a fantasy of plantation: gazing at the land of the Rockies, Rideing yearns for framing hedges, a farmhouse, ploughed earth, an orchard, for these "might change the sentiment of the thing, but would not make it less beautiful" (II, 492).

Rideing's dream of reification, his impulse to aestheticize vistas as real estate, is to dematerialize landscapes by symbolic exchange, a process ironically not very different from the conversion of natural signs into transcendental signifieds, "God's land." If the discourse of the sublime suggests an affinity (recognition) between a surplus and wild land and an unruly, terrified and grief-stricken subject, then ownership of that scene is the instrumental means to a fulfilled and practical citizenship. We may relocate the sublime's tensions and oppositions in Rideing's and others' travelogues, those shifts in mood and utopian wishes for a socialization of the wildness they edgily encounter, as instances of a phenomenological reduction entailing splits between material signifiers and signifieds as the latter emerge as signifiers in their own right. (Husserl's "natural standpoint" may be understood as a culturally sedimented aesthetic "framing.") Terms such as *noble, strange, vague, feeling, dreary, grief,* and *contemplative,* while coming from a century-old discourse on the sublime in a context of travel literature and public art, turn into mass-mediated signifiers of representation ("see, look here") whose effect is the production of simulacra and codes similar to those discussed regarding the "Holy Cross." Estes Park is certainly there, but it undergoes a "haunting": its "meanings" are both self-miraculating and dissolved in transcendence. And so too the beholding subject, whose feelings are seemingly being written and drawn by the landscape and dissolved in the unrepresentable. The sublime's discursive terms, then, may be construed as performing analogical operations with the viewpoint and the vanishing point we discovered in Moran's engraving of the mountain. As detached and floating terms, words like *noble* and *strange* are the deictic sources (signifiers, production points) for the very meanings they shuttle, dissolve, and cause to vanish or reappear within a welter of aesthetic (and transcendental) signifieds. The fissures in Rideing's essay are exemplary here, for the various episodes and narrative descriptions project a sense of movement which in turn is arrested by prolonged moments of viewing; the eye is arrested by a scene over which it casts a veiling film of familiarity and utopian wish. This suspension of the eye is the work of representation in the simulation of presence, or more precisely the separation of perception from representation by the spectatorial citizen subject's alignment with nationalist fantasies indistinguishable from the aesthetic act (cf. Hewitt 161–194). This tendency, this process writ large, shows how some collective fantasies, in a cultural milieu predisposed toward simulacra, *become* or *replace* history.

"The present banishes the past so quickly in the busy continent that to the younger generation of to-day it already seems a very dreamy and distant heroic age when men went out upon the great prairies of the West as upon a dreaded kind of unknown sea," laments E. L. Burlingame in his travel essay, "The Plains and the Sierras," illustrated by Moran for *Picturesque America*. He continues: "How remote the day seems when men tightened their pistol-belts and looked to their horses, and throbbed (if they were young) with something of the proud consciousness of explorers" (II, 168–169). Burlingame's nostalgia regrets the annihilation of aboriginal space even as it heroicizes pioneers as the representatives of a new and admirable people. Even those early settlers who are caricatured, such as the Mormons, are nevertheless delegates of an infused divine and secular will and recipients of sacred texts. Burlingame's fanciful reconstruction of the Mormons hearing Brigham Young's "first sermon in the 'Promised Land'" displays a number of issues we have examined. The writer is "literally" looking at a gorge near Hanging Rock through a train window and visualizing the occasion of the sermon as a picture—a vivid document "for us"—and at the same time representing in his textual copy a version of "history," the event of the sermon, now recast as a publicly circulated piece of aesthetic (and ekphrastic) travel writing (cf. Schivelbusch; Lalvani 177–184). He writes:

> Full of all that is wild and strange, as is this rocky valley, seen even from the prosaic window of a whirling railway-car, what must it have been with the multitude of fanatics, stranger than all its strangeness, standing on its varied floor and looking up at the speaking prophet, whom they half-believed, half-feared? The weary multitude of half-excited, half-stolid faces turned toward the preacher; the coarse, strong, wild words of the leader echoing from the silent rocks—why has no one ever pictured for us all of the scene that could be so pictured? (II, 180)

The text here effects its own displacements of figural narrative onto its own version of a representational screen and window, for the deixis of the present moment of a "rail-way car" and its mobile viewing ("this rocky valley . . . from the prosaic window") gives way before another representational moment with another viewing, one whose features are *supra*-organizational, redemptive, Messianic ("faces turned toward the preacher . . .wild words . . .echoing from the silent rocks"). The description also becomes a question, with the question a deixis and a "frame" around the passage constituting it now as the domain of aesthetics ("why has no one ever pictured . . .all the scene that could be pictured?"). The question erases the very picture just limned and converts the passenger window into a blank screen for yet other representations.

Brigham Young's archaic and Old Testamentary prophetic mode is brought up and yet repressed in a complex recognition of its alien belonging in American experience, its kinship "for us." But of singular interest here is Burlingame's textual strategy which simulates and doubles presence, which copies binocular vision and doubles a representation within a representation. Young's sermon works as a perspectival system (viewpoint, vanishing point, their reversibility as sources of representational production), a system which then generates the "depth," the dimensions and proportions, for the figural articulation of "actual" and "imagined" space. The question shifts a putative historical description to a (haunted) topos for visual reproduction and effectively lateralizes the text. That Young is evoked in the first place shows clearly the *practice* of investing the land with transcendental signifieds that are then contemplated and consumed as self-ratifying, autonomous cultural realities. Not only is Young the paradigmatic American holy man whose words descend from the Word and whose mission is to plant a nation, he is also a redemptive fulfillment of history who ought to be both memorialized and yet restored by reproductions and their "truths."

Not that the American landscape remains a permanent repository for dreams and representations of divine transcendence. The Mountain of the Holy Cross was disestablished as a national monument in another secular spell, in the early 1950s; its cruciform ravines were eroding into something else. Burlingame knew the need in the 1870s for flexible attitudes and practical adjustments. Leaving the Sierra for Oakland, the Pullman viewer confronts "the prosaic rail-way peddlers come back again with their hated wares; for us, the picturesque is over; and already the hum of the still distant city seems almost to reach our ears" (II, 203).

Much of the original research for this essay was carried out at The Huntington Library, San Marino; the Oregon Historical Society, Portland; and the Rockefeller Library, Brown University, Providence. An earlier version appeared in <u>SubStance</u> 42 (1983). I wish to thank Lee Clark Mitchell, Donald Preziosi, and David Wyatt for their help and insights on all things visual and Western. My greatest debt is to the late Louis Marin, teacher and mentor, whose rigor sparkled with his grace, his wit, and his generosity.

NOTES

[1] "But suppose we thought of representation, not as a homogeneous field or grid of relationships governed by a single principle, but as a multidimensional and heterogeneous terrain, a collage or patchwork quilt assembled over time out of fragments. Suppose further that this quilt was torn, folded, wrinkled, covered with accidental stains, traces of the bodies it has enfolded. This model . . . would make materially visible the structure of representation as a trace of temporality and exchange, the fragments as mementos, as 'presents' re-presented in the ongoing process of assemblage [. . . .] It might explain why representation seems to 'cover' so many diverse things without revealing any image of totality [. . . .] It might help us to see why the 'wrinkles' and differences in representation, its suturing together of politics, economics, semiotics, and aesthetics, its ragged, improvised transitions between codes and conventions, between media and genres, between sensory channels and imagined experiences are constitutive of its totality" (Mitchell 1994, 419). Cf. Jenkins and Ulricchio and Pearson, who argue that cinema works and inhabits the social similarly; Ulricchio and Pearson in particular argue that early film draws from and assumes multiple literacies and competencies—e.g. familiarity with popular novels, urban viewing formations, "attractions"—which "fill in" what later film generations see as narrative gaps in any specific film.

[2] One of the more intriguing popular culture items here is the stereoscope. Some works, like Charles Quincey Turner's do-it-yourself package Yosemite Valley through the Stereoscope (1902) came complete with stereographs of Carleton E. Watkin's photographs, a guidebook, map, and a set of directions for simulating an outing in the park. Turner was a former editor of the magazine Outing. Parlor illusions were also popular; see Castle.

[3] See the following for documentation on some of these developments: Weston et al.; Goetzman, 1959 and 1966; Pomeroy; Runte; Starr; Abbeele; Pratt. On the politics of ecology, land rehabilitation and re-inhabitation, see Kemmis and Davis. On the "postmodern West" with "hyperdevelopment and plugged-in modernity," see Riebsame and Trobb. Naef et al. and Prown et al. offer exceptional exhibition catalogues.

[4] Compare the arguments that social metonymies are reflected in the proto-abstractionism of Luminim: see Conron 1980.

WORKS CITED

Abbeele, Georges van den. "Sightseers: The Tourist as Theorist," <u>Diacritics</u> 10 (1980): 3–14.

Agrest, Diana and Mario Gandelsonas. "Semiotics and the Limits of Architecture," in <u>A Perfusion of Signs</u>, ed. Thomas Sebeok. Bloomington: Indiana Univ. Press, 1977. pp. 96–123.

Althusser, Louis. "Ideology and Ideological State Apparatuses," in <u>Lenin & Philosophy</u>. New York: Monthly Review Press, 1971. pp. 127–186.

Anderson, Benedict. <u>Imagined Communities: Reflections on the Origin and Spread of Nationalism</u>. Rev. edn. London: Verso, 1991.

Arkelian, Marjorie Dakin. "Artists in Yosemite," <u>The American West</u> 15 (1978): 34–47.

Baird, Joseph A., Jr., comp. <u>The West Remembered: Artists and Images, 1837–1973</u>. San Francisco and San Marino: California Historical Society, 1973.

Bryant, William Cullen. "Preface," <u>The American Landscape</u>, No. 1. New York: Elam Bliss, 1830. pp. i-iv.

Bryant, William Cullen, ed. <u>Picturesque America; or, The Land We Live In. A Delineation by Pen and Pencil</u>. New York: D. Appleton, 1874. 2 vols.

Castle, Terry. "Phantasmagoria: Spectral Technology and the Metaphorics of Modern Reverie," <u>Critical Inquiry</u> 15.1 (Autumn 1988): 26–61.

Clark, Carol, ed. <u>Thomas Moran: Watercolors of the American West</u>. Austin: Univ. of Texas, 1980.

Conron, John. "'Bright American Rivers': The Luminist Landscapes of Thoreau's <u>A Week on the Concord and Merrimack Rivers</u>," <u>AQ</u> 32 (1980): 144–166.

Curry, Larry. <u>The American West: Painters from Catlin to Russell</u>. New York: Viking, 1972.

Damisch, Hubert. "Semiotics and Iconography," in Thomas A. Sebeok, ed., <u>The Tell-Tale Sign</u>. Lisse, Netherlands: Peter de Ridder, 1975.

Davis, Mike. <u>Ecology of Fear: Los Angeles and the Imagination of Disaster</u>. New York: Vintage, 1998.

Debord, Guy. <u>Society of the Spectacle</u>. Detroit: Red and Black, 1977.

Deleuze, Gilles and Felix Guattari. Anti-Oedipus: Capitalism and Schizophrenia, rev. edn. New York: Viking, 1977.

Dippie, Brian W. "The Visual West," in Clyde A. Milner II, et al., eds. The Oxford History of the American West. New York: Oxford Univ. Press, 1994. pp. 674–705.

Durand, Asher. "Prospectus of the American Landscape," The American Landscape, No. 1. New York: Elam Bliss, 1830.

Fisch, Mathias S. "The Quest for the Mount of the Holy Cross," The American West 16 (1979): 32–37, 57–58.

Fluck, Winfried. "The Americanization of Modern Culture," in Agata Preis-Smith and Piotr Skurowski, Cultural Policy, Or the Politics of Culture? Proceedings of the 7th International Conference of the Polish Association for American Studies, Serock, November 1997. Warszawa: Univ. of Warsaw Press, 1999.

Franklin, Wayne. Discovers, Explorers, Settlers: The Diligent Writers of Early America. Chicago: Univ. of Chicago Press, 1979.

Goetzman, William H. Army Exploration in the American West, 1803-1863. New Haven: Yale Univ. Press, 1959.

___. Exploration and Empire: The Explorer and the Scientist in the Winning of the American West. New York: Knopf, 1966.

Guillén, Claudio. "On the Concept and Metaphor of Perspective," Literature as System: Essays Toward the Theory of Literary History. Princeton: Princeton Univ. Press, 1971. pp. 283–371.

Hayden, Ferdinand Vandeveer and Thomas Moran. The Yellowstone National Park, and the Mountain Regions of Idaho, Nevada, Colorado and Utah. Boston: Louis Prang & Co., 1876.

Hewitt, Andrew. Fascist Modernism: Aesthetics, Politics, and the Avant-Garde. Stanford: Stanford Univ. Press, 1993.

Irwin, John T. American Hieroglyphics. New Haven: Yale Univ. Press, 1980.

Jackson, William Henry. "With Moran in the Yellowstone," in Fritioff Fryxell, ed., Thomas Moran: Explorer in Search of Beauty. East Hampton, NY: East Hampton Free Library, 1958. pp. 49–61.

Jarves, James Jackson. The Art-Idea, Fourth edn. 3 vols. New York: Hurd and Houghton, 1877.

Jay, Martin. Downcast Eyes: The Denigration of Vision in Twentieth-Century French Thought. Berkeley: Univ. of California Press, 1993.

Jenkins, Henry. "Historical Poetics," in Joanne Hollows and Mark Jancovich, eds. Approaches to Popular Film. Manchester and New York: Manchester Univ. Press, 1995. pp. 99–122.

Kemmis, Daniel. Community and the Politics of Place. Norman: Univ. of Oklahoma Press, 1990.

Kroes, Rob. If You've Seen One You've Seen the Mall: Europeans and American Mass Culture. Urbana: Univ. of Illinois Press, 1996.

Lalvani, Suren. Photography, Vision, and the Production of Modern Bodies. Albany: SUNY Press, 1996.

Lyotard, Jean-François. "Considerations on Certain Partition-Walls as the Potentially Bachelor Elements of a Few Simple Machines," in Le Macchine Celibi/The Bachelor Machines. New York: Rizzoli, 1975. pp. 98–109.

McKenna, Andrew J. "Biblioclasm: Derrida and his Precursors," Visible Language 12 (1979): 289–304.

Marin, Louis. Études sémiologiques: Écritures, peintures. Paris: Klincksieck, 1971.

_____. Utopiques: Jeux d'espace. Paris: Minuit, 1973.

_____. "An American Event on the French Stage: Notes on an Eighteenth-Century Engraving," Glyph 3. Baltimore: Johns Hopkins Univ. Press, 1977. pp. 1–17.

_____. Semiotics of the Passion Narrative: Topics and Figures. Pittsburgh: Pickwick, 1980.

Meigs, John, ed. The Cowboy in American Prints. Chicago: Swallow, 1972.

Miller, Toby. Technologies of Truth: Cultural Citizenship and the Popular Media. Minneapolis: Univ. of Minnesota Press, 1998.

Mitchell, Lee Clark. Witnesses to a Vanishing America: The Nineteenth-Century Response. Princeton: Princeton Univ. Press, 1981.

_____. Westerns: Making the Man in Fiction and Film. Chicago: Univ. of Chicago Press, 1996.

Mitchell, W. J. T. Picture Theory: Essays on Verbal and Visual Representation.
    Chicago: Univ. of Chicago Press, 1994.

Moran, Thomas. Home-Thoughts from Afar: Letters of Thomas Moran to Mary
    Nimmo Moran, ed. Amy O. Bassford. East Hampton, NY: East Hampton
    Free Library, 1967.

Naef, Weston J., James M. Wood, Therese Thau Heyman, eds. Era of Exploration:
    The Rise of Landscape Photography in the American West, 1860-1885. Boston:
    New York Graphic Society, 1975.

Novak, Barbara. Nature and Culture: American Landscape and Painting, 1825-1875.
    New York: Oxford Univ. Press, 1980.

Osborne, Harold, ed. The Oxford Companion to Art. New York:
    Oxford Univ. Press, 1970.

Pomeroy, Earl Spencer. In Search of the Golden West: The Tourist in Western
    America. New York: Knopf, 1957.

Pratt, Mary Louise. Imperial Eyes: Travel Writing and Transculturation.
    New York: Routledge, 1992.

Preziosi, Donald. Rethinking Art History. New Haven: Yale Univ. Press, 1989.

Prown, Jules et al., eds. Discovered Lands, Invented Pasts: Transforming Visions of
    the American West. Exhibition catalogue sponsored by the Gilcrease Institute
    and Yale Art Gallery. New Haven: Yale Univ. Press, 1992.

Riebsame, William E. and James J. Trobb, eds. Atlas of the New West: Portrait of a
    Changing Region. Center of the American West, Univ. of Colorado.
    New York: Norton, 1997.

Robbins, Bruce, ed. (for the Social Text Collective). The Phantom Public Sphere.
    Minneapolis: Univ. of Minnesota Press, 1993.

Runte, Alfred. National Parks: The American Experience, Second edn. Lincoln:
    Univ. of Nebraska Press, 1987.

Sheldon, George. American Painters: With One Hundred and Four Examples of their
    Work Engraved on Wood, enlg. edn. New York: D. Appleton, 1881.

Slotkin, Richard. Regeneration Through Violence: The Mythology of the American
    Frontier, 1600–1860. Middletown, CT: Wesleyan Univ. Press, 1973.

_____. Gunfighter Nation: The Myth of the Frontier in Twentieth-Century America. Norman: Univ. of Oklahoma Press, 1998.

Sontag, Susan. On Photography. New York: Farrar, Straus & Giroux, 1977.

Starr, Kevin. Americans and the California Dream, 1850-1915. New York: Oxford Univ. Press, 1973.

Tagg, John. Grounds of Dispute: Art History and the Politics of the Discursive Field. Minneapolis: Univ. of Minnesota Press, 1992.

Taussig, Michael. Mimesis and Alterity: A Particular History of the Senses. New York: Routledge, 1993.

_____. The Nervous System. New York: Routledge, 1992.

Turner, Charles Quincey. Yosemite Valley through the Stereoscope. With stereographs of C. E. Watkins's photographs, guidebook, map, and set of directions. New York and London: Underwood and Underwood, 1902.

Uricchio, William and Roberta E. Pearson. Reframing Culture: The Case of the Vitagraph Quality Films. Princeton: Princeton Univ. Press, 1993.

Warner, Michael. "The Mass Public and the Mass Subject," in Robbins (1993). pp. 234–256.

Wawrzyczek, Irmina. "Studying Early America and the Extended Epistemological Crisis in American Historiography," in Piotr Skurowski, ed., American Studies 15. American Studies Center, Univ. of Warsaw. Warszawa: Univ. of Warsaw Press, 1997. pp. 23–30.

Westermeier, Clifford P. "The Modern Cowboy—An Image," in The American West: An Appraisal. Santa Fe: Museum of New Mexico Press, 1963. pp. 25–34.

Wilkins, Thurman. Thomas Moran, Artist of the Mountains. Norman: Univ. of Oklahoma Press, 1966.

Nature in Ruin:
The Rephotographic Survey Project as a View of History and a Study of Site

Anthony Marasco
University of California at Berkeley

No one can answer the question of what nature is unless he knows what history is.
R. G. Collingwood.[1]

A Venture in Repeat Photography

In 1867, the forced relocation of the Arapaho, Comanche, and Cheyenne tribes west of the 100th meridian lifted the last major obstacle to the 'opening' of the Far West. The final push to occupy the last 'empty' tract of the nation's territory had initiated during the Civil War with the passage of the Homestead Act of 1862. The new instrument made 160 acres of surveyed public land available at a nominal fee to any farming family willing to occupy uncultivated land for more than five years. Stalled during the first stages of the war effort, the drive to western colonization regained momentum with the speculative pressures that followed the granting of public-domain land to those railroad corporations willing to develop routes into the new territories. As the Union Pacific and the Central Pacific railroads advanced toward each other to join their spikes somewhere in the Utah territory—claiming their share of public domain as they went along—the Federal Government decided to further aid the industrial development of the region by prospecting the geography, geology, and natural resources of the newly opened of land. Before being consolidated under the United States Geological Survey in 1879, four independent operations amassed a formidable inventory of data on the territories that were to become Colorado (1876), Wyoming (1890), Utah (1896), and Arizona (1912), among others. On the data collected, these lands were 'opened' and connected to the burgeoning industrial economies of the eastern seaboard. These areas that would later be known as the New West, the now famous 'last frontier' the Census 'closed' with its 1890 annual report.[2]

Among the data collected by the four survey operations were hundreds of photographic images of the newly opened territories.[3] Often catalogued as mere data, these images were later fully appreciated as art and canonized in the 1930s as one of the earliest vernacular traditions in American landscape photography.[4] As such, Survey photography enjoyed a veritable revival in the 1970s when a whole new generation of art photographers decided to 'return' to the expressive restraint of those early topographic images in reaction to the counter-culture's far-flung subjectivism in photography.[5] During those years one of the most fervent acts of homage paid to nineteenth-century photography was the Rephotographic Survey Project.[6] Between 1977 and 1979, that group of photographers and curators of photography retraced and rephotographed 122 views made during the great western surveys. Aided by trigonometry and Polaroid trials, the Project paired some of the old prints almost to perfection. In the process, the rephotographers also collected data of their own. Exposure after exposure, the Project recorded changes in the land that were the consequence of the opening of the New West. What the rephotographers learned from their experience in repeat photography was published in 1984 as <u>Second View: The Rephotographic Survey Project</u>. As edited, the book was intended to be 'a report in rephotography,' a catalogue of findings pertaining both to photographs and landscape. Yet, only a few, key instances of rephotography were commented upon and explained in the apparatus itself. In all other respects, the geographically arranged catalogue of images stood as a body of evidence awaiting further interpretation.

In what follows, I try to argue primarily three things. First, in reading the Project's work we may follow two paths: one more concerned with the artistic value of the photographs repeated, the other more interested in their documentary content. Second, the first path is bound by necessity to mine only the semantic flank of rephotography (the ways in which this type of image suggests meaning), leaving its pragmatic side largely unattended. (By pragmatics I allude here to the recovery of the local patterns of discourse that gave specific meanings to given images). Third, by integrating the first approach with the second, two of the most obvious strategies of semantic play that the Project seems to elicit—'revision' and 'reinscription'—find in the pragmatics of site-analysis a prudential locus of historiographic mediation. Approached that way, rephotography seems to be not only available, but also peculiarly suited to help excavating those intricate networks of discursive events that endowed certain places with historic meaning.

Rephotography as a Type of Revision

Introducing a book of photographs published in 1992 by the former Chief Rephotographer, Mark Klett, Patricia Nelson Limerick offered a historian's interpretation of the evidence collected by the Rephotographic Survey Project.[7] A pioneer of 'New Western History,' Limerick identified rephotography as a 'revisionist' view of history similar to her own. Like the work of Elliot West, William Robins, Donald Worster, and Richard White, the Project's photography understood that the West could no longer be depicted as a sequence of discontinuous advances into a 'void.'[8] Unlike the work of other 'New Western Historians' such as William Cronon, John Mark Faragher, Walter Nugent, and David Weber, rephotography restored the landscape of the American West to its proper regional status by rephotographing a body of images that showed the regional continuity of its history. In other terms, if the Project agreed with both groups when they claimed that the 'West' could no longer be depicted according to the 'Frontier thesis' advanced by Frederick Jackson Turner in 1893, rephotography agreed more with those who renounced even the last remnants of a 'process' view of its history, and upheld the value of seeing the west as just another 'place' among places.[9] (Foner 12). To catch the subtlety of that distinction, it is necessary to recall once more how Turner came to his conclusions. Standing high on a podium within the precincts of the Chicago Columbian Exposition in 1893, Turner used the Census's 1890 annual report to declare two things at once: the frontier experience had been the site upon which the

American experience was born; regrettably, the frontier was now gone. Thus from the very start, the frontier thesis had a double edge: it decoupled national and Anglo-Saxon identity, opposing historians such as Herbert Baxter Adams when they connected the American experience to the genetics of the Anglo-Saxon folkways; but it did not surrender the anxieties caused by the non-Anglo-Saxon character of recent immigration. Now that the frontier was no longer there to 'Americanize' new immigrants, what would become of America?

Among the many things that revisionist historians like Limerick wanted to do away with was a lingering tendency of reading the history of the western sections of North America as a surrogate way of defining the character and the mission of the American nation. The West had its own regional character, and its history spanned centuries of multiracial development before being forced within the gridiron Thomas Jefferson originally drew on to organize the Northwest Territory in 1784. If the last phases of its development manifested the traces of a process of 'advance,' it was because the East had 'conquered' the West by imposing its own interests and cultural hegemony. No wonder archaeology had never fully supported the frontier thesis: the evidence needed was simply not there. Far from being the site on which the North and the South were dialectically reconciled after the disruptive events of the Civil War—a plot Owen Wister popularized into that most successful of American genres, the western—the West had its own character and its own autonomy.

One of the most resilient narratives the Turner thesis left behind was that of predicating the history of the Western regions of the United States on a romantic paradigm of depletion: the West had once been a beautiful, if vacant land; by occupying it Americans spoiled it. "Built into the first movements of Europeans into this 'New' World was a future regret, regret patterned on Adam and Eve's departure from Eden. The process of migration, colonization, invasion, and conquest lent itself to the most stark before-and-after pictures."[10] It is precisely this narrative that Limerick thought the Project was intent on revising. If the Turnerian narrative had pictured the West on a before-and-after sequence that emphasized not change but loss, the rephotographic pair showed that even before the 'opening' of the 'last frontier' the landscape was already fully inhabited. In fact, the history of the American West did not divide into two, as in the opposition:

Before: The West, pristine and astonishing, peopled by colorful and heroic giants.
After: The West, tainted and reduced, peopled by dull pygmies.

On the contrary, the history of the western regions had always been an uneasy compound of beauty and use: not all had been romance in the era of the covered wagon; not all was in utter disarray in the age of strip mining. "Dreariness and romance occupied the same territory then, and occupy the same territory now."[11] Like true revisionists, the rephotographers understood that the West had never been a depopulated Eden awaiting civilization.[12] Their before-and-after pairings of the same view did not return an Eden on the left side and a wasteland on the right. Both sides had their Edens and their wastelands; and looking at them with hindsight, it is possible to reconstruct a better, if ironic history of the conquest of the West.

To recover the data contained in these pairs, Limerick proposed that historians adopt an interpretative grid she called 'hindsight without smugness.' Keeping smugness at bay, the possessor of hindsight could finally hope to regain sight of the unpredictability of a past's future.[13] Once that insight is regained, the viewer can begin to question the very notion of 'process' we still apply to the history of the American West by default. A few examples will better underscore the plausibility of Limerick's argument. Looking at a repeat photograph made near Virginia City, Nevada, Limerick writes:

> Engaged in rephotography, Klett and his colleagues saw, and recorded, the physical outcome of the conquest of the American West. If the mid-nineteenth century posed the question, "What will Anglo-Americans make of this distinctive place?" the RSP pictures offered one set of answers, and, as in the case of the Virginia City mill, the answers often carried a considerable freight of irony. With just a slight tone of smugness, it would be easy to give that irony a heaviness that would turn it into a battering ram aimed at the viewer's mind. "Look at this," the smugness would say; "they went to an enormous amount of trouble to build this industrial site; they thought they were empire-builders and they thought this was progress. Now it's all gone. Some progress. Some empire."[14]

Like our own future today, the past's future was also unpredictable. To understand this is liberating because we can have a better sense that no domination is inevitable, and that the power our adversaries hold over us is not without limits. So the temptation to be smug on the past is sometimes insuppressible: it shows our awareness of the way ideology works on behalf of domination.

Consider the temptations to smugness presented by what the rephotographers learned about the practices of the nineteenth-century photographers. The classic western landscape proved, in many cases, to be artistic creations, artifacts of craft and technique. At Hanging Rock in Echo Canyon, in northern Utah, what was in Andrew J. Russell's 1868 photograph a looming, overhanging rock now proved to be a slightly recessed cave, its drama primarily a product of the photographer's skill. Hindsight with smugness would be a perfectly natural response to these revelations: "Those old fellows tried to fool us, but we found them out."[15]

Limerick, however, recognized that the rephotographers did not introduce such a strong element of disdain in their rephotographic recovery of old images. On the contrary, in select cases the rephotographers had chosen to dialogue with the past by presenting new ideas and possibilities.

William Henry Jackson's original image shows a man confidently measuring the interior of a geyser. Returning for his photograph, Klett found the geyser,

matched the vantage point, and then, in the veritable mood of the geyser, confronted a puzzle. "Jackson's photograph," as Klett wrote, "shows the geyser being 'plumbed in its depths' by an inquisitive survey geologist." The rephotographers, Klett and Gordon Bushaw, then faced a choice. They could show the geyser erupting or not erupting. Very consciously, they chose to use the photograph with the active geyser "as a counterpoint both in composition and viewpoint" to Jackson's vision of "man's equality with or domination over nature." The rephotographer chose, instead, to "return a natural autonomy to the geyser," and thereby to respect and record their own second thoughts about "man's control over natural resources."[16]

As Limerick remarked, the fact that the historian and the photographer were beginning to share a similar view of the region signaled that "a fundamental re-envisioning of the West" had taken place.[17] As younger historians in the field were learning to do, the rephotographers used a given past's unpredictable outcome—their present situation—to cleanse the West of what was left of the past's ideological make-up. As a form of revision, or better of 're-envisioning'—as Limerick called it—, rephotography repeated exactly 'the way people saw in the past' in order to show the arbitrary nature of the limits it imposed on the gazing of the present. Looked at side by side, the rephotographic pair allowed a process of cognitive revision that demystified the ideological constructs of the past, making room for radical change.

Given the political character of her reading method, smugness is actually very difficult to decouple from hindsight. What the constant emergence of irony and sarcasm may be signaling at the discursive level is the cognitive overlapping of contexts that are ordinarily kept separate. Words and deeds said and done in earnest may be received ironically only by an interpreter situated both inside and outside the speaker's context of reference. Since we know that the quartz mill outside Virginia City vanished, we can ironize on the nature of the 'empire' many Americans thought they were building in the West.

As Limerick herself admitted, however, the strategy the rephotographers used was not really meant to ironize over the past, but to dialogue with it. In fact, their rephotographic approach to the landscape of the American West is not inherently trans-contextual (ironic), but rather can be read as a form of reinscribing de-contextualization. By 'returning natural autonomy' to the geyser, the rephotographers erased the original text, rewriting it according to the rules of the new context's formation. In other words, instead of using the context of the present to ironize over the ideological contradictions of the past, the rephotographers used their practice to erase the surface of nature of all previous inscriptions in order to reinscribe it with new meaning.[18]

The Semantics of Reinscription

Playing with the trans- or de-contextualization of a set of historic images via a strategy of repetition, the Rephotographic Survey Project may be read as an act of revision or of reinscription, depending on the point of view. At the origin of such

ambiguity is the deceitfully neutral editing principle governing the compilation of the Project's report.

The structuring principle used to edit <u>Second View</u> emphasized landscape over art, culture over history. Instead of dividing their material according to author or survey operation, the rephotographers flatly arranged their repeated views on a map of the American West. Despite the presence of a few exemplary readings, the report's textual apparatus remained uncommitted to any particular interpretive aim. And yet, the editing principle the report adopted is far from being flatly neutral. If we take the rephotographic body to be a collection of data on the nature of change in the cultural landscape of the American West, we are not told why the rephoto-graphers decided to repeat only those photographs that were made during the great surveys of the 1870s. Was it because those images were later canonized as art photography? In that case, we are not told why the pairs were not arranged according to author. Or were the surveys the real focus of the Rephotographic Survey Project? In that case, we are not told why the material was not arranged by survey operation. As printed, the rephotographic corpus is 'evidence' of something never properly defined. The passing of historical time that so strongly characterizes these images is thus the expression of a view of history grounded on ambiguous evidence. Let us return for a moment to the vanished mill near Virginia City, Nevada. Did it simply vanish? Or was it rebuilt only a few inches beyond the image's margin? We are not told. Evidently, the history of the mill was not the type of history the rephotographers recovered. (We know from the autobiographical notes of William Henry Jackson that the quartz mine had almost already played itself out by the time O'Sullivan photographed it. Jackson also saw Chinese workers at the site, confirming once more the complex ethnic character of the 'Far West').

What conclusions can we draw from such evidence? If we are to reconstruct the Project's view of history, I do indeed believe we might profit by reading it not as a body of evidence, but as a palimpsest, a manuscript erased to be rewritten on. The difference between the two approaches is that by using the second reading strategy we do not need to raise unwarranted truth-claims about the nature of cultural change in the American West. The Rephotographic Survey Project is a close reading of a text, a text that is not the landscape of the American West, but an inscription about that landscape. It might be claimed that all human knowledge is but a palimpsest, and that all facts are but a formalized fiction of some kind. The Project's textualization of the landscape of nature is thus a very sophisticated move in the direction of plying the symbolic environments to our changing collective needs.[19] Unfortunately, such a reading cannot be sustained on the 'evidence' furnished by the Rephotographic Survey Project. Not only is the mimetic 'transparency' of the photographic medium never questioned by the rephotographers—making a few artful images paradigmatic of a whole landscape—but the very motives behind their rephotography seem to go in the opposite direction. Once the original print is exactly matched by its repeated image, the landscape is freed of previous inscriptions by showing the contingency of all inscription. Such a realization, however, is far from liberating. Quite the contrary, what is celebrated by rephotography is a better adherence to the truth of nature, almost as if the best of all possible landscapes is a landscape devoid of human presence:

> As our methodology developed, we discovered that each new picture, when combined with an earlier image, forms a mutually dependent pair with fresh potency. … The earlier pictures mark the starting point, but no one image, first or last in the series, represents a definitive statement. … The individual pictures are like single frames picked from a time-elapsed film; when they are viewed in succession they give the appearance of time in motion, of continuous change. However, in this case, they are perhaps the first two frames in a monumental film, one which will span thousands of years. [20]

As an opening into a dimension that is meaningless to the viewer's temporal experience, culture is turned into a passive receptacle (a film) that receives its meaning from without (the landscape). Far from being a pragmatic acceptance of the contingency of our human situation, the Project re-opens the doors to one of the most abiding principles of American identity, Nature. In bringing his introductory essay to a close, the Chief Rephotographer, Mark Klett, agreed with the quasi-mystical remarks of one the Project Photographers, Rick Dingus:

> Each series of photographs I took reminded me of a phenomenological exercise in perception—as if I were moving from vantage point to vantage point asking perceptual and conceptual questions about the place and receiving an appropriate response each time in the form of the resulting image. My experience at each site became an interaction, a king of double funnel: *a flood of awareness poured in from the site and my selected responses seemed to pour back onto it.* My experience was both an exchange and interchange, an engaging and a blending, an agreement and an affirmation. (Emphasis added).[21]

As the Absolute celebrated by Emerson is substituted by the machinical ubiquity of the filming apparatus, the camera supplies a 'transparent eyeball' with which to blend the subjective and objective dimensions of 'Nature.' It seems not at all implausible that such a depleted form of idealism should be at the origins of the Project's reinscriptive practice. What structures it is a desire to recapture that 'immediacy with nature' that many generations of Americans have considered representative of a certain national spirit. So if it can be argued that such a body of images calls attention to the regional status of the West, it can also be argued that within its spires the ancillary status of the West resurfaces again. In this regard, the West is forever linked to a vision of the American nation as a whole. Two converging and yet heterogeneous desires thus structure the rephotographic palimpsest: that of regaining an immediacy with nature and that of mediating the contact with nature via the exact, machinical repetition of aesthetically fulfilling images. The contradiction, however, is only apparent. Only a strong aesthetic drive may have the power to reenergize the depleted Romantic discourse reactivated by the repeat photographers. But what other discourses did they repeat by trying to reproduce such a select body of survey photographs? Those images were the product of a romantic notion about the landscape, but not exclusively and not intimately. As 'Romantic' images, the survey photographs are quite late. Did anything else come into the making of the original photographs that the rephotographers also repeated? In attempting to give an answer to that question, we will face once again the fundamental ambiguity lurking at the core of this body of images. As we shall see, in looking into the discourses repeated by the Project, we will find there are meanings and attitudes that go in the opposite direction of the revisionism Limerick read into them.

A Monument in Ruin

Limerick's revisionist interpretation of the Rephotographic Survey Project relied on a few examples to argue that no 'fall from Eden' is discernible in passing from the image on the left to the image on the right. In a broader analysis of the whole corpus, one may reach other conclusions. For example, it could be argued that at least one type of 'deterioration' occurs in *all* cases: all views go from the status of canonized art to the condition of tentative undertaking. It is that aesthetic incline that most often tilts the reading toward a temporality of decline rather than toward one of continuity.[22] Translating such a loss of aesthetic wholeness in historical terms, the reader also gets a sense of overall historical decline. But if that impression is correct, what exactly went into decline? To try to answer that question, we must depart from the views that were on average less affected by change once repeated: those monumentalized by National Park laws. What the invariance of such images shows in the midst of deterioration is that what were once monuments of a natural scenery had now become the ruins of one. But is this what the Project truly depicted? Before answering—negatively—this question, we must first analytically unfold what an affirmative answer would imply. To do so we need to answer yet another question. What symbolic action went into the monumentalization of nature in the 1870s?

The legal instruments that set aside scenic sites as national monuments were first deployed with the creation of the Yellowstone National Park in 1872. Those instruments donated to the public a large tract of the territories that were to become Montana, Idaho, and Wyoming. The purpose of the donation was to preserve the inspirational value of such scenes from the brute exploitation of land resources pursued by private capital. So a contradiction is nested at the core of the donation. With one hand the Federal Government was conceding land to railway companies free of charge, and with the other it was trying to save what an aesthetic sensibility thought should be preserved from the exploiting ventures of private capital. In other words, what was being monumentalized in the 1870s was a select portion of what was otherwise being depleted. Such contradiction allows the whole park movement to be contextualized within a wider international phenomenon. In roughly the same timeframe in Paris, wide portions of the medieval town were being razed to the ground to make room for the Boulevards of the Second Empire. As more and more portions of the old city underwent destruction, select medieval monuments were singled out and monumentalized to preserve a lasting memory of what was being otherwise demolished. What unites the two types of monuments—Nature, the vestige—is the role they both played in preserving at least a semblance of what 'progress' was destroying with its advance. Both played a strategic role in the tradition-building processes that tried to respond to the challenges of heavy industrialization during the nineteenth century. Both were deployed to tame the most disquieting aspects of the new situation by discursively connecting the advance of progress to the glory of the nation. Due to the uneasiness of the connection, which made private interests public in ways that were never fully rationalized, the palpable presence of tradition had to be reasserted in the midst of changes. The monumentalization of vestiges in Europe admirably fulfilled that function by publicly manifesting the nation's resolve in subjecting industrial modernity to the unquestionable, if vague authority of the past.

Ruins began to assume the new role of national signposts in England at the decline of neoclassicism. Whereas the Enlightenment had favored the cosmopolitan appreciation of the ruins of antiquity as mementos of history, English gardeners began to revalue and recreate Gothic ruins as visual markers of the *genus loci*. The re-appreciation of Gothic ruins in opposition to Classical ruins followed the valuation of the English landscaped garden in opposition to the geometrical layout of the Franco-Italian tradition. Both oppositions were justified discursively by the superiority of the British mentality over that of the Continent. Symmetry and clarity were now signs of Continental despotism, so much so that by the time of the rebuilding of the British parliament, the Gothic style had become the only and proper national style. During most of the Victorian Age, plastered Gothic moldings made outlandish iron-framed structures look tame and vernacular, somehow the products of abiding traditions. A similar, yet different strategy was followed in the rebuilding of Paris. There, vestiges were preserved to be reinserted in a diagram of power relations connecting tradition to the new monumental investment banks, railway stations, and sites of public spectacle such as the new Opera House. That was the intent clearly legible on the map of Paris Napoleon III sketched for the newly appointed prefect of the Seine, Baron Haussmann. In the network of ceremonial axes and diagonal crossings Haussmann built for the Emperor, lines of sight connected the nodes of communication and exchange to the vestiges of that very same medieval past that was being demolished to make room for the new. It is my claim that the same may be true of the United States, but with a twist: instead of taming industrial modernity by monumentalizing vestiges of the past, Americans strategically monumentalized an object outside time, Nature.[23]

Thomas Jefferson was one of the first intellectuals to unite the progress of the American nation to the prospect offered by an 'empty' continent. As Drew McCoy has argued, by wanting his federation of republics to expand in space, Jefferson sought to retard the degeneration that the Republican theory associated with the development of a pure market economy.[24] Unlike agriculture, commerce generated the accumulation of riches that had already afflicted all previous Republics in history. To retard the downfall associated with industry, Jefferson negotiated the purchase of Louisiana with Napoleon I. Such a reservoir of unspoiled agricultural land to the West would retard the degeneration of the new federation of American Republics perhaps for a few centuries more. Westward expansion and regeneration were thus one in the American republican imagination even before the coming of Romanticism. The new set of ideas added a tightening of the binds between national character and natural scenery. Unlike Europeans, the American people found its representative sense of identity not from the recapturing of the vestiges of a glorified past, but from the contemplation of a living being, Nature. The Romantic conception of nature was eclipsed by the Civil War and by the vogue for realism in the arts. And yet, books like The Red Badge of Courage (1895) and the logic behind the first suburban migration clearly testify to the resilience of the ideal of Nature well beyond the heyday of the American Renaissance. In Crane's novel, the unreality of killing is made even more poignant by the soothing qualities of the natural landscape—the very qualities used by Frederick Law Olmsted to design his urban parks and suburban parkways. No less a detractor of the Absolute than William James still found in the most pristine parts of the New England landscape the most intimate part of his sense of identity.[25]

We could then conclude that during the 1870s the preservation of the natural landscape of the West worked on many levels at once. It allowed many Americans to feel that there was a limit to be placed on the rising assertiveness of railroad corporations—even if that limit was still blurry in contours and hopelessly sentimental. It gave them a sense of belonging and a hope for the future expansion of democracy—even if the demolition work and the sheer exploitation it entailed hardly testified on behalf of its sustainability. Gaining monetarily, but wasting cultural capital in the process, the urban elites of the eastern seaboard took up conservationism as a gentleman's crusade in the 1870s.[26] Like many other aspects of the age of gilded surfaces, that surface, too, served its purpose in covering up and hiding what most people of distinction and wealth did not really care to see.

Photography played an important role in the monumentalization of nature in the post-Civil War era. Along with the campaign to map the Far West went a campaign to picture its beauties for the entire nation to see. So it was not by chance that photography assisted the birth of the first National Park in 1872. As Congressmen debated the proposal to turn the Yellowstone into a protected area, emblazoned prints of the valley were circulated by the Survey people to lobby in favor of the initiative. These images spoke eloquently of what was at issue. As their author, William Henry Jackson, later wrote in his autobiography, Time Exposure, published in 1940, "by the end of February [1872] I was back in Washington. The photographs, which I had prepared…, had helped do a fine piece of work: without a dissenting vote, Congress established the Yellowstone as a national park, to be forever set aside for the people. And on March 1, 1872, with the signature of President Grant, the bill became law."[27]

When the Rephotographic Survey Project repeated the images made during the great surveys of the 1870s, they also repeated those early monumentalizing attitudes by default. The different context, however, impressed a different sense of temporality upon the repeated views. Whereas those early images were expressive of a sense of spatial and temporal advance, the new ones expressed a sense of decline and damage. Partly physical and partly aesthetic, the impression of loss informed the act of rephotography. The fact that such a sense of dissolution is less evident inside the areas protected by National Parks legislation only adds to the overall sense of loss. Those protected areas are now like veritable ruins, fragments of a bygone era that time has dissolved. Should we then conclude that nature lay fully historicized before the rephotographer's camera? Has nature become what ruins were for Europeans, a memento of the past? To ask this question is not to indulge in mere curiosity. As often remarked, the drive to refuse its postlapsarian condition is not a marginal aspect in the history of Nature's nation.[28] Have nature-worshiping Americans finally understood the historical character of the monument they cling to? Can these Americans now join Henry Adams on the steps of the Ara Coeli and contemplate Nature as Adams contemplated Rome?[29] Now, is that the type of temporality the Rephotographic Survey Project responded to in assembling its rephotographic palimpsest?

As anticipated, I do not believe that to be the case. Like many Americans before and after him, Adams thought of the West as 'the land of the future.'[30] That view was still redolent of Jefferson's agrarian utopia, the vision of the future that had become the most widely shared vision of the country's future. Like a true Adams, however, Henry hid his contempt for the elegant symmetries of the Virginian only to make it more insidious and cutting. The outcome of the advance of progress into the West caused the sectional strife at the origins of the Civil War, a conflict that ushered one of the most corrupt ages in American history. 'The best and brightest man of his generation,' the Chief Surveyor Clarence King, not only did not profit personally from his deep knowledge of the area, but also went bankrupt in an attempt to extract profit from science. Not scientific knowledge, but speculation ruled in the trans-Mississippi West. Dreaming up his vision of the future from the Palladian symmetry of his hilltop abode, the sage of Monticello forgot the cautionary warnings on human nature issued by Adams's great-grandfather, the New England savant and President of the United States, John Adams.[31]

But the vision of history offered by the repeat photography of the West is not yet the view from Ara Coeli; rather, it is still the hilltop view from Monticello.[32] It was there that Jefferson pieced together one of the most enduring American traditions, the tending of one's lawn as a way of coming into middle contact with Nature. Unlike European royalties, the American yeoman farmer could enjoy the pleasure of the lawn not by plotting intricate palterres and exotic greenery. All he needed to do was to weed the grass that so abundantly grew on American soil. The rephotographers still did something close to that: they repeated the views that opened the West to exploitation by 'weeding out' all traces of the acquisitive attitudes that those images masked. By doing so, however, they did not rub off the residual make-up of the gilded age. They restored it, cleansing the surface of nature of all offending inscriptions and returning the monument of nature to its past grandeur in one monumental act of nostalgia. So it is not historicity that shines through the re-photographic palimpsest, but Nature regained. As the rephotographers put it, their couplings are but the first two frames of a 'monumental film' that will span the centuries. As that film unfolds, the idea that 'Nature' had been monumentalized in an attempt to limit the disquieting effects of instrumental rationality is forgotten and contradicted. The machinical triumph of the imaging apparatus will restore nature to its pedestal, as we too become dust. Instead of reminding us of the truth of Vico's dictum—*Verum et factum convertuntur*, only what Man made can be known by Man—the Rephotographic Survey project cleared the tablets once more in the vain hope that nature might want to reveal its truth to us *photographically*. Had the Project taken the very transparency of the medium to task, the Rephotographic Survey Project might have produced not a palimpsest rewritten with light, but one open to the prospect of our cognitive frailness. We know what we make, if we know at all. As to the meaning of 'Nature,' the only thing we can reasonably say is that like ancient Rome, nobody really knows what it meant. Perhaps Henry Adams was right, "perhaps it meant nothing."[33] But the only way to know for sure is to study what it meant to others in history. And that is why I believe that in the study of the American West, 'process-oriented' approaches are as useful sometimes as 'region-oriented' ones. Process history, with its stages and lines of development, does come dangerously close to thinking history from the top down, from abstract models to people on the ground. But at crucial junctures, it may also help us keep the motivational value of past ideas well in view. Those ideas were never 'true' in themselves, and sometimes they were indeed made up only with the purpose of deceiving. But to bypass their explicative power entirely is to come dangerously close to overlooking a crucial aspect of the past of that region. The frontier theory is not the 'truth' about the West. It is an inseparable part of its history.

What we may gain from looking at Survey photography from a 'process-oriented' standpoint is the productive complication of the notion of 'conquest' that is sometimes too flatly applied to the practices and attitudes that assisted the opening of the New West. What such an approach may help us recover (instead of erasing and reinscribing) is the uneasy sense of ambivalence and contradiction that ruled over the entire period. In fact, instead of being the testimony of an uncomplicated act of appropriation, Survey photographs are also proof of an early, if sentimental attempt to limit the power of corporations. That such images actually succeeded in lobbying forward restrictive park legislation is proof positive of their implications in the early steps that moved in the populist and progressive direction of using Federal legislation to curb the power of corporations.

The Pragmatics of Site Analysis

As I said at the beginning, the paired views assembled by the Rephotographic Survey Project seem to give way to two distinct strategies of interpretation. The first privileges the semantics of the images themselves and plays epistemic games with them; the second is more attentive to the pragmatics that went into the making of the original images. By avoiding the pragmatic aspects touched upon by the practice of rephotography, semantic approaches such as revision and reinscription may run the risk of losing their historic moorings. By committing both to the pragmatics of site-analysis, one might hope to reach a prudential point of mediation in which the epistemic games of the present meet the historicity of the epistemic games of the past. Approached this way, rephotography could then represent a formidable tool for excavating those networks of discourses that were used in the past to endow certain places of concrete historic meaning. To recover the conflicted character of Survey photography, *in situ* rephotography must be approached not as the means to form the building blocks of a wider palimpsest, but as a tool to excavate the tense discursive network connecting local camera placements to the printed view. The inclusion of the whole network in the excavation of the viewing site is crucial. Instead of relying solely on the photographic image to recover it's meaning, we must use the repeated viewing as a moment of contextualization. Avoiding at this stage both trans-contextualization (irony) and de-contextualization (reinscription), we must place the knowledge we gain from rephotographing a certain view on the body of discourses and practices that prompted the original camera placement. In most cases, the Project's report is silent on that topic. There is one image in the rephotographic catalogue, however, that I believe may help us enhance heuristic aspects of rephotography. As I said, that image is not a rephotograph proper, but a repetition of a repetition. By excavating the pragmatics that went into the making of such site, I believe we may begin to retrieve positive data on the nature and goals of Survey photography.[34]

Panorama of Mt. Lincoln 1a

Panorama of Mt. Lincoln 1b

Panorama of Mt. Lincoln 2a

Panorama of Mt. Lincoln 2b

Panorama of Mt. Lincoln 3a

Panorama of Mt. Lincoln 3b

Panorama of Mt. Lincoln 4

The image I am referring to is made of four individual prints collated to form part of the panoramic view available from the summit of what is today Mount Lincoln, Colorado. What is curious about the repetition of that particular set is that it was already a repetition to begin with. On August 10, 1873, Jackson was hard at work when bad news reached him. "Gimlet, the mule that carried my [glass] negatives," he wrote in his journal, "had tumbled down the hill above camp & many of my negatives were ruined & broken." In a later reminiscence, The Pioneer Photographer, published in 1929, Jackson re-narrated the smash up:

> I hurried after and found the situation fully as bad as reported. The Doctor
> had been the first to discover the mishap. It was a serious matter and he

evidently wanted to be severe with someone about it. At first he seemed
inclined to regard me as in some way responsible, but I was so distressed
and showed it so plainly, that he had nothing more to say.

The 'Doctor' whose reactions Jackson feared so much was Ferdinand Vandiveer
Hayden, the geologist in charge of operations. In his journal, Jackson wrote that "it
was agreed on the spot to make good the loss by replacement." But what exactly was
lost? We need to ponder over such a question because the set is hardly an act of
communion with the land or a pictorial sensation. In fact, it seems eminently
valueless. So why did Hayden order an exhausted Jackson to repeat the lost set? And
exactly what kind of information could be so easily repeated?

It is at the crossroads between these two questions that I believe the idea of
rephotography may begin to perform its heuristic function. On the issue of
repeatability, it must be pointed out that before the invention of instantaneous
cameras in the 1880s, all photography was easily available to rephotography. Before
shutter speed could capture motion on a fast enough emulsion, photography was
about the reproduction of the outside surfaces of stationary objects. Only after the
invention of hand-held apparatuses such as the Kodak did photography become
about unrepeatable events. It is important to note that since immobile objects could
be rephotographed easily and conveniently, a whole cottage industry developed on
the premises of photography's stationary status. In Rome, one photographer after the
other waited to re-occupy the same famous sites from which to make those
stereotypical views that sold so well on the tourist market. Discovered by engravers
and re-occupied by early photographers, these sites were still visited well into the
twentieth century to produce mass-marketed postcards. We may then conclude that
what rephotography rediscovered about early photography was that, in the case of
the representation of inanimate objects, the view made was a function of the site
found. So what view had Jackson made on the site Hayden ordered him to reoccupy
in order to 'make good the loss by replacement?'

Before 1973, the achievements of the Hayden surveys had been many, but not
in the field of topography.[35] In fact, many accused Hayden of being a mere
boosterist, a 'businessmen's geologist' interested only in finding resources in ore.[36]
To speed up the production of the data needed to compile scientifically acceptable
maps, Hayden put Jackson to work on the assumption that photographs would later
assist mapmakers in the filling-in of geological information. On this assumption,
Hayden sent Jackson to make views from all designated survey stations. It is now
very important to understand the logic behind such a choice. Introducing a book of
photographs in 1870, Sun Pictures of the Rocky Mountain Scenery, Hayden
maintained that photography constituted "the nearest approach to a truthful
delineation of nature."[37] On such an assumption he justified the use of a camera
operator for both scientific and illustrative tasks. As Hayden wrote in his 1873
annual report, "[t]he panoramic views of the mountain peaks have been of great
value to the topographer as well as the geologist, and have proved of much interest
to the public generally."[38] Hayden expanded on this very idea in the report of the
following year:

Especial attention has been paid, all the time, to make these views instructive as well as pleasing to the eye, and the system of panoramic views which has been carried out has been of very great assistance to the topographers in working up their notes and expressing the peculiarities of mountain-forms. To the geologist, also, they prove of great value in recalling to the mind the surface-features, inclination of strata, proportion of valley mountain land and of timber to the rocky summits lying above it.[39]

Let us now connect the two aspects of Survey photography we have excavated on Mount Lincoln via the rephotographic act. First, we have seen how before the Kodak, view and site were united in a relation of production: once the site was regained, the same picture could be made over and over again. Second, we have also seen how the site on which Jackson was ordered to place his tripod was often the very surveying site upon which the topographers had been ordered to place their theodolite. What made the two coincide was a belief in the delineating power of the camera—a belief Hayden and Jackson shared. Jackson's own description of his practice in his diaries reinforced the idea that the camera was capable of reproducing the view objectively, as if itself a sort of scientific instrument. He rarely called his activity 'picture-making' or even 'photography.' In his own words, the most used term is the 'making of views.' For example: "found a beautiful lake on top & made some fine views of the peak reflecting in it."[40]

> FRIDAY [July] 25th. [1873] Did not get up very early. All the rest pulled out & went up canyon. I have to wait until Harry returns from Oro with a box of stereo glass that should be there for me. Tried to do some *viewing* in the a.m. but my shield leaked light so badly that I had to give it up & spent the rest of the day in general repairing.[41] (Emphasis added).

View-ing is thus the toilsome activity he is practicing, and *views* are the pictures made. *View*, however, is used by Jackson both to designate the picture and the scene before his eyes. It is the context that gives the word its meaning:

> MONDAY [June] 2d. [1873]. Turned south thro' the woods and about noon camped in a pleasant little park where *I had a fair view* of [Long's] Peak. *Not able at all to make any view* of the range in p.m. Sun in wrong place for one thing and every afternoon so far has proved stormy. Great rolling masses of clouds coming up & giving us alternate spats of rain & hail.[42] (Emphasis added)

Even the toponyms seem to take part in this ambiguous game of designation: "stopped at Mountain called Belleview & made 3 views looking down towards Gothic Mtn."[43] On the widest possible scale, the photographer, like the topographer, seemed about to take in the entire landscape of the American West.

Now it must be noted that it was the easy equation between 'the view made' and 'the view seen' that the rephotographers dispelled with their camerawork. Picture after picture, they discovered conscious manipulations in points of view that gave drama to the scenes depicted. It then follows that hidden within the first two layers comprising the survey site was a third layer the other two were designed to reinforce. If the first stratum worked on the paradigm: 'the view made is a function of the site found;' and if the second stratum worked on the paradigm: 'the view made equals the view seen;' the third stratum used the other two to objectify beliefs into actualities. As it was practiced and cognized, photography was a 'purely objective' venture. Jackson knew Hayden would require from him some photos to publicize his discoveries, so he occasionally gave him grand, magniloquent views—views he thought were as objective as the views he had to take from the top of the topographic triangles. Such an ability to use and hide aesthetic, and even emotive, statements under the skin of the dispassionate photographic apparatus was rationalized with the notion that every scene offered the photographer at least an angle from which most, if not all, of its significant details could be fully seen. That belief ran parallel to the way the surveyors thought of their practice. In the words of one of the four survey heads, Clarence King, by gaining elevation, the surveyor "put everything in full view."[44] On such a principle, surveyor and photographer could agree that they were engaged in the same activity—even if one managed measuring instruments, and the other a picturing device. Both sought to find the site from which a certain object could be put in full view. Thus the viewing site was not arbitrary, but an inherent characteristic of the object to be viewed.

Survey photography then rested on an ambiguous foundation that could mask several contradicting attitudes in a way that is reminiscent of the era. Grounded on a productive relation that would allow Jackson to return in later years to the same scenes he had visited under government payroll to make views he could handsomely sell on the market, the photographic site was also a prospect point from which all could be dispassionately seen. As such, the photograph could be considered a scientific collection, a scientific collection so eloquent that it could be easily used to prove the worth of protecting the Yellowstone valley—while lobbing for more appropriations. Produced as a re-producible commodity, but made as an objective statement, the photograph abstracted the view in a way that symbolically prepared it for parcellization and exchange on the market.[45] At the same time, encoded in those views were contemplative attitudes that communicated to the viewer a sense of nature's grandeur.

The conflicted nature of the whole Survey attitude can be spotted in a passage of Hayden's fifth annual report.

> We caught the first glimpse of the great basin of the Yellowstone, with the lake . . . which reminded one much, from its bays, indentations, and sur-rounding mountains, of Great Salt Lake. To the south are the Tetons, rising above the rest, *the monarchs of all they survey*, with their summit covered with perpetual snow.[46] (Emphasis added)

The recourse to the magniloquent hides a most interesting displacement. Having come to 'survey' the Yellowstone valley, the surveyor in chief rhetorically surrendered authority over the landscape *below* to nature *above*. By shifting to the side of that axis, the surveyor becomes a mere spectator allowing him to reveal the conflicted attitude encoded in his daily practice of surveying. 'To survey,' the Oxford English Dictionary reminds us, is "the, or an, act of looking at something as a whole, or from a commanding position; a general or comprehensive view or look." As a substantive, 'survey' is also 'that which is thus viewed; a view, prospect, scene: a delineation of this, a 'view,' picture (*obs*).[47] As we have seen, that is precisely the outlook repeated by many Survey photographs. Coined from the French *sur-veoir*, to survey literally means 'to view from above.' Now Hayden's displacement of the viewing subject allowed him to express in full a cultural attitude attached to that act of viewing: to look down onto one's possessions as a monarch/proprietor would do. As some 'New Western Historians' would say, that was an act of 'conquest' conducted at the cognitive level. At the same time, however, the fact that it was a mountain that dominates the scene can also be read as the intuition that a limit should have been placed to exploitation. In the passage, it is nature that surveys over nature in a moment of sheer beauty that deserves to be preserved in perpetuity, perhaps even by law. Photographs could also save such redeeming moments of clarity by encoding a sense of unease within the very act of symbolic appropriation they performed. Their reluctance to picture the railroad tracks that brought them there, however, would come back to haunt their views a century later when their masterful compositions no longer held.

Conclusion

By reoccupying the stations marked by survey teams at the opening of the New West, and by repeating the photographs Survey photographers made from those stations, the Rephotographic Survey Project revealed changes in the land that were largely the consequence of that opening. At the same time, however, the very act of rephotography allowed the landscape to be reinscribed with new meaning—new meaning that was not too distant from the original strategic act of displacement that allowed unresolved attitudes to be dissimulated as simple acts of observation. Vast historical differences exist between the two contexts of observation—differences that blurred themselves out as the two acts adhered to each other in an attempt to re-capitalize nature into Nature.

And yet, the practice of rephotography is not bound by necessity to function as a symbolic act of revision or recapitalization. Approached outside the confines of the Project's report, rephotography does seem to be available to the discourse of site analysis. As a type of cultural pragmatics, site analysis seems to be strategically placed to limit the semantic free-play of both revisionism and reinscription. In particular, I believe that reinscriptive approaches may gain in solidity by dialoguing with the results of that type of historical analysis.[48] Human knowledge may be indeed a constantly revised palimpsest. Yet its revision must be plotted carefully—for what is too easily erased may as easily return to blur the legibility of what is being reinscribed.*

NOTES

[1] R. G. Collingwood, The Idea of Nature (Oxford: Oxford University Press, 1945), 177. Collingwood's book on the philosophy of nature was published one year before his book on the philosophy of history: The Idea of History (Oxford: Oxford University Press, 1946).

[2] Two of the four surveys were led by military men, Lt. George M. Wheeler and Maj. John W. Powell. The other two surveys were put in the hands of two civilians, Ferdinand V. Hayden and Clarence King. When the surveys were finally incorporated in 1879, King became the head geologist. Two classics on the 'Great American Surveys' are: Richard A. Bartlett, The Great Surveys of the American West (Norman: University of Oklahoma Press, 1962), and William Goetzmann, Exploration and Empire: The Explorer and the Scientist in the Winning of the American West (New York: Alfred Knopf, 1966).

[3] Schmeckebier, L.F. "Catalogue and Index of the Publications of the Hayden, King, Powell, and Wheeler Surveys." U.S. Geological Survey Bullettin, No 222, 1904.

[4] Early survey photography was included in the show that opened the Photography Department at the MoMA, show that was later to constitute the backbone of the seminal: Beaumont Newhall, History of Photography, 1839–1987, (New York, NY: The Museum of Modern Art, 1937). In 1942 Ansel Adams, then curator at the MoMA, canonized the whole period in the show "Photographs of the Civil War and the American Frontier."

[5] One of the most influential 'schools' of landscape photography of the 1970s was directly inspired by the topographic attitude they embodied. See: William Jenkins, The New Topographics: Photographs of a Man-Altered Landscape, (Rochester, NY: International Museum of Photography at George Eastman House, 1975). As the historian of photography Jonathan Green remarked, "in the seventies straight photography moved away from documentation of the outcast, bizarre, and the freak and turned back to the most basic source of American myth and symbol: The American land." Jonathan Green, A Critical History of American Photography: 1945 to the Present: (New York, N.Y.: Harry N. Abrams, 1984), 163. As an example of that shift, Green used the Rephotographic Survey Project.

[6] Klett, Mark, Ellen Manchester, JoAnn Verburg, Gordon Bushaw, Rick Dingus. Second View: The Rephotographic Survey Project. (Albuquerque, NM: New Mexico University Press, 1984).

[7] Patricia Nelson Limerick, "Second Views & Second Thoughts: Mark Klett and the Re-exploration of the American West," in: Mark Klett, Revealing Territory (Albuquerque, NM: New Mexico University Press,1992), 7–110.

[8] In plotting the distinctions inside the New Western History group I am following Richard Write's survey piece "Western History," in Eric Foner, Ed., The New American History Philadelphia, PA: Temple University Press, 1997), 203–230.

[9] "Perhaps most important to me and my colleagues in western American history, the Rephotographic Survey project rested on the idea that western American history was a continuous, running story. For decades, western historians had taken the discontinuity of the past for granted. The history of the nineteenth-century *West* was the history of the *frontier*. The West was no particular place; it was simply a transitory condition at the edge of Anglo-American settlement. Thus, when the frontier ended, somewhere around 1890, western history broke in half, or stopped on its tracks," *Ibid.*, 12.

[10] Limerick, 8.

[11] *Ibid.*

[12] "Intentionally or not, the Rephotographic Survey Project rejected the abstract, shifty definition of the West as frontier, and saw the West as a set of solid and continuos places. The project by its very nature assumed a connection between the western present and the western past. Placed next to each other, the paired photographs recorded the century that the old western history had banished to insignificance," *Ibid.*, 13.

[13] Seen together , the two photographs [of the former site of the Virginia City quarz mill] inoculate the mind against fatalism. They make such a strong statement on the unpredictability and improbability of historical outcomes that any student who sees these pictures should instantly grasp the uselessness of the word *inevitable. Ibid.*, 12.

[14] *Ibid.*

[15] *Ibid.*, 15.

[16] *Ibid.*

[17] "Mark Klett's convictions about the American West closely resembled my own," Limerick wrote. "Photographer and historian, visual person and verbal person—we had arrived at those convictions by very different routes. This was either an extraordinary and mysterious coincidence, or it was a sign that something big—a fundamental re-envisioning of the West—is indeed under way, and photographers and historians, as well as novelists and journalists, legal scholars and painters, are all playing their part in this larger enterprise." 10. Again, "Mark Klett presents the rare case of person who is not a professional historian, but who is nonetheless deeply aware, in everyday life, of the historical process." 16.

[18] The experience of rephotographing on the ground "caused an enormous change in the way those of us involved in the project saw landscape photographs." That change led to the awareness of the option of reinscribing the rephotographed view: "No longer were nineteenth-century photographs removed in time and space, nor were they impersonal documents of a now lost landscape. They became uniquely individual records of distant but related times. They became true access points into the past, which we engaged through the very active process of rephotography. The act of repeating photographs became an extension, amplification contradiction, and/or modification of the original photographer's perceptions, yet the rephotographs still retained their value as contemporary documents." Klett, et al., 37.

[19] That would be the case, for example, of the type of reinscription advocated by Richard Rorty. See: Richard Rorty, Consequences of Pragmatism (Minneapolis, MN: University of Minnesota Press, 1982).

[20] Klett, et al., 37.

[21] Ibid.

[22] The incline would be even more evident had the editors of Second View decided to reproduce the paired views in scale and in color. The original views would then appear covered with various types of photographic patina; the paired Polaroid contact prints would appear in the diminutive 4 x 5 format and their glossy/grayish hue.

[23] The connection between the European and the American context of that phenomenon is not only graspable at the symbolic level, but can also be found at work behind the financing of the New West economy. The building of both the Central and the Union Pacific Railroads were backed up in part by the American branch of one of Napoleon III's state-owned investment banks, the Crédit Mobilier. Unlike the British, the French had initially had difficulties in mobilizing private capital to finance of modern economic and transport infrastructures. One of Louis Bonaparte's prime objectives after the coup d'état that made him Emperor in 1851 was to develop a network of state-owned banking institutions capable of financing his ambition to overhaul the French national system. Once in place, those powerful institutions made France one of the most active exporters of venture capital of the nineteenth century. The French national banking system helped other European nations build their much needed railway infrastructures, while also aiding the construction of the Suez Canal via a public subscription. In the United States the operations financed by the American branch of the Crédit Mobilier came under intense scrutiny in 1872 when the *Sun* accused prominent politicians of having accepted its rising stocks in return for favors. As it turned out, the opening of the New West promoted by the Federal government had absorbed immoderate amounts of public capital that did not pour directly into the building of its infrastructures.

[24] Drew McCoy, The Elusive Republic: Political Economy in Jeffersonian America (Chapel Hill, NC: University of North Carolina Press, 1980).

[25] Linda Simon, Genuine Reality: A Life of William James (New York, NY: Harcourt Brace, 1998), 258.

[26] With the term 'cultural capital' Pierre Bourdieu intended to interrogate the connection between monetary and aesthetic values characteristic of capitalist societies. In that context, cultural expression is but the manifestation of the monetary hierarchy embedded in the systems of social distinction. See: Pierre Bourdieu, Distinction: A Social Critique of the Judgment of Taste (trans. Richard Nice; Cambridge, MA: Harvard University Press, 1984).

[27] William Henry Jackson, Time Exposure (Albuquerque, NM: University of New Mexico Press, 1986), 205.

[28] A canonic text in that regard is: Perry Miller, Nature's Nation (Cambridge, MA: Harvard University Press, 1967). In many respects, 'American exceptionalism' may seem a quaint 'Cold War' topic today. It is not a dead one, however. In a syndicated Op.Ed. piece published in the International Herald Tribune of March 28, 2000, Richard Reeves reinforced a pro-exceptionalist view of a recent survey by proposing his own list of what make Americans different. One of them read: "They [Americans] are anti-history. The past is just that, past. And that is not always a bad thing by any means. Americans don't kill each other over something that happened hundred of years ago. They don't even know what happened hundred of years ago. They try things that have failed before—and sometimes they work now," 9. On a more elevated plane, a new approach to the thematization of what *ought* to make America different as a democratic civil society can be found in: Richard Rorty, Achieving Our Country: Leftist Thought in Twentieth-Century America (Cambridge, MA: Harvard University Press, 1997).

[29] Henry Adams, The Education of Henry Adams, eds. Ernest Samuels and Jane N. Samuels (New York, NY: The Library of America, 1983), 804.

[30] Adams, 1002. The fictional character of The Education described the West as 'the land of the future' in reference to a visit to one of the Survey parties in 1871.

[31] The project behind Henry Adams's History of the United States of America duing the First Administration of Thomas Jefferson (1889) can be clearly read in a passage in John Quincy Adams and Charles Francis Adams's *Life of John Adams* (1856): "The character of Thomas jefferson presents one of the most difficult studies to be met with by the historian of these times. At once an object of the most exalted eulogy among those who made him their political chief, and of the bitterest execrations of his opponents, it is not very easy, between the two, to trace the lines which truth and justice alike demand," (Peter Shaw, ed.; New York, NY: Chelsea House, 1980) II,

376. The imperative to come to a historiographical resolution of the Adams-Jefferson dispute had already been proclaimed at the source by John Adams in a letter to Jefferson. "Whether you or I were right" Adams wrote on May 1, 1812, "Posterity must judge." The Adams-Jefferson Letters (Lester J. Cappon, ed.; Chapel Hill, NC: 1959), II, 301.

[32] No two sites are more different. Santa Maria Ara Coeli opened onto history; Monticello onto nature. The Church was erected in the sixth century on the ruins of the temple of Juno built by Augustus on the spot where the sibyl had told him that a Savior would come to redeem all humanity. On the monumental stairway leading to the hilltop Cola di Rienzo first spoke of an imminent 'renascence' of the glories of antiquity. On the top of that stairway Gibbon pondered over the mystery of the rise and fall of the Roman Empire. From there, one could physically sense the weight of the problem. What had caused the ruin of the Imperial Forum at the back of the hill? What had caused the rise of the Rome of the Popes in front of it? In-between the Empire and the Church, the Virgin and the 'renaissance,' the 122 steps leading to the Ara Coeli offered Adams the perfect vantage point from which to ponder over the failure of Jefferson's Republic on the eve of secession—and well after that. Monticello, on the contrary, was the very hilltop site where Jefferson had dreamt of deferring the corruption of time by opening his abode onto nature, and nature alone. Describing his situation there, Jefferson wrote: "And our own dear Monticello, where has nature spread so rich a mantle under the eye? . . . With what majesty do we there ride above the storms! How sublime to look down into the workhouse of nature, to see her clouds, hail, snow, rain, thunder, all fabricated under our feet! and the glorious sun when rising as if out of a distant water, just gliding the top of the mountains, & giving life to all nature!" Thomas Jefferson, Writings, Merrill D. Peterson, ed. (New York: Literary Classics of the United States, 1984), 879.

[33] Adams, 803.

[34] In the following reconstruction of what went into the making of a particular set of photographs, my use of the term 'pragmatics' (later in contrast to the term 'semantics') loosely follows at the cultural level the distinction formalized at the linguistic level by Jürgen Habermas in his theory of communicative action. What I intend to recover with the term 'pragmatics' is the network of situational placements that went into the making of particular images. The images in themselves may enjoy some independent semantic meaning, but to understand them in context one has also to recover the pragmatic situation that went into their making.

[35] In particular, Hayden dispelled the myth of the Great American Desert, the belief that a great desert had hiterto stopped the westward advance of civilization in North America. According to Henry Nash Smith, the other great accomplishment of Hayden was to substitute that myth with the myth of the garden. Smith, Virgin Land: The American West as Symbol and Myth (Cambridge, MA: Harvard University Press, 1950), 180–181.

[36] A 'Medical Doctor' by degree, Hayden was the last of the amateur geologists who had picked up the trade in the field. When the four Surveys were finally unified by Congress in 1879, the position in chief was given to the university-trained Clarence King—another sign of the raise of research universities in America.

[37] Ferdinand Vandeveer Hayden, Sun Pictures of the Rocky Mountain Scenery, with a description of the geographical and geological features, and some account of the resources of the Great West; containing thirty photographic views along the line of the pacific rail road, from Omaha to Sacramento, (New York, NY: Julius Bien, 1870), vii.

[38] Ferdinand Vandeveer Hayden, "Letter to the Secretary," in F. V. Hayden, Preliminary Report of the United States Geological Survey of Wyoming, and Portions of Contiguous Territories, (Being a Second Annual Report of Progress) (Washington, D.C.: Government Printing Office, 1871), 7.

[39] Ferdinand Vandeveer Hayden, "Letter to the Secretary," in F. V. Hayden, Preliminary Report of the United States Geological Survey of Montana, and Portions of Adjacent Territories, (Washington, D.C.: Government Printing Office, 1874), 9.

[40] Leroy R. Hafen and Ann W. Hafen, eds., The Diaries of William Henry Jackson, Frontier Photographer, to California & Return, 1966–67, and with the Hayden Surveys to the Central Rockies, 1872, and to the Utes and Cliff Dwellings, 1874 (Glendale, Cal.: A.H. Clark, 1959), 241.

[41] Ibid., 236.

[42] Ibid., p. 220-221.

[43] Ibid., 243.

[44] Clarence King, Mountaineering in the Sierra Nevada, (New York, NY: Penguin Books, [1872] 1989), 130.

[45] See on this particular aspect of Survey photography the magisterial treatment of King's survey photography in: Alan Trachtenberg, Reading American Photographs: Images as History, Mathew Brady to Walker Evans (New York: Hill and Wang, 1989)

[46] Ferdinand Vandeveer Hayden, Preliminary Report of the United States Geological Survey of Montana, and Portions of Adjacent Territories, Being a Fifth Annual Report of Progress (Washington, D.C.: Government Printing Office, 1872), 80.

[47] The Compact Edition of the Oxford English Dictionary, (New York, NY: Oxford University Press, 1971) II, 3177.

[48] As Martin Jay remarked, cultural pragmatics and cultural semantics should always accompany one another learning new ways of integrating each other. "Context determines not only meaning, but performative force. What might be called a 'cultural pragmatics' thus must always accompany a 'cultural semantics.' Such an approach must not, however, fail to acknowledge the inevitable locutory openness, perhaps even characteristic indeterminacy, of the terms whose illocutory function it hopes to reveal. One of the abiding lessons of deconstruction, whatever one may think of all of its other claims, is that rigorous definition, attempting to still the play in words, is bound to fail." Martin Jay, <u>Cultural Semantics: Keywords of Our Time</u> (Amherst, MA: University of Massachusetts Press, 1998), 2–3.

[*] A final note on the Rephotographic Survey Project should include the later trajectories of two of the group's photographers, Rick Dingus and Mark Klett. Both came to grips with the contradictions of the Project in their later work. Dingus questioned the machinic 'transparency' of the medium by finely penciling the surface of his photographic landscapes. The strokes reveal and obscure the photographic image calling attention to the paradoxes of eye contact. Klett's later work made contingency and historicity the very focus of his work. Each step in the landscape of the American West became an act of exploration in time as well as in space.

The Spirit of Chicago: Abundance and Sacrifice in Nature's Metropolis

William Boelhower
University of Padua

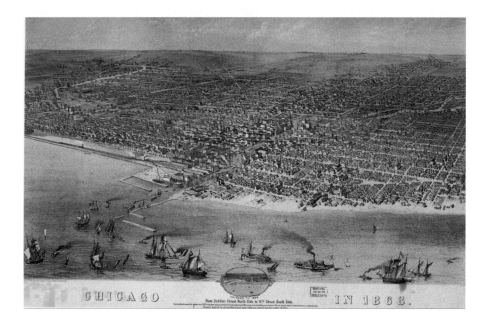

In the closing decades of the nineteenth century, popular novelists who set out to map the still largely unexplored topology of the modern metropolis often labeled their works mysteries. According to formula, they would routinely pierce through the city's brightly lit surfaces to discover in its shadowed depths the exotic worlds of false identity, vice, crime, poverty, debauchery, cruelty, and estrangement. But things were not really so gloomy, since such narrative tours were also accompanied by a positive hero (and heroine) who invariably skipped through the pitfalls of the city's underworld without a scratch. In effect, these mysteries are governed by a redeeming narrative law, namely that of adventure. And the hero-adventurer inevitably gets to the bottom of things and after being temporarily shipwrecked in the urban sea, is able, with a little luck and pluck, to refound the city. In late nineteenth-century Chicago, when this city was in its heyday, the words 'mystery' and 'adventure' functioned as masterwords for any number of people living in the city and eager to fathom the exceptional realities of the nation's fastest growing metropolis.

If concepts invariably failed to grasp what was boiling in the city's cauldron, then metaphors would have to do; not metaphors that would eventually be turned back into concepts once they served their purpose, but absolute metaphors, ones that would remain both literally and figuratively true (Blumenberg). Certainly a masterword for Louis H. Sullivan, *adventure* fully characterized the "great drama" of "the Modern" (1956:278) that he faced head on in Chicago. In The Autobiography of An Idea he calls this drama "the greatest of man's adventures upon his Earth" (277). And if Chicago had become the American Modern's central stage, then he would strut it as an adventurer. As he instructs us in his autobiography, great artists, scientists, and engineers were all Adventurers, the capital letter being his. After stalking the city's mysteries by walking twenty miles or more a day, until he had explored its every nook and cranny, "he came to know the why and wherefore of the City; and...said: *'This is the Place for me!'*" (244).

So he thought, but further on in his autobiography he confesses, "He was too young to grasp the truth that the fair-appearing civilization within which he lived was but a huge invisible man-trap, man-made" (289). In Chicago, he discovered, there was veil upon veil to be peeled away. As for finance—and how could one make it in this rough and tumble midwestern metropolis without knowing something about finance— "what a mystery it was" (289). Without telling us what Chicago's own Conradian horror might be, Sullivan heightens his semantic investigation of mystery and adventure with these stunning words: "Later he sent forth his soul into the world and by and by his soul returned to him with an appalling message" (289). Soon to become the city's foremost architect, he would eventually stake not only his career but his very life on seeing that his vision of the tall office building and the department store would come true.

By alluding to two different economies, one restricted (dealing as it does only with money) and the other general (dealing with whatever it means to invest oneís entire self in something), the word adventure helps us to remix the categories traditionally used to read the smokefilled but festive script of Chicago's coming of age. The nature of the two meanings, of the two ways of investing in the city, are radically different, and, as we shall see, they ultimately involve us in two distinct kinds of nature and two radically different economies. In historical perspective, both capital and population made Chicago the magnetic center linking the American East and West in one continental system. Both contribute to an understanding of Chicago as the site of *"un tout parle"*—a place where everything speaks (Ranciere 121)— and endow it with the ineluctible magic which, according to a character in Henry Blacke Fuller's novel The Cliff-Dwellers, is couched in the place name itself:

> the name of the town, in its formal, ceremonial use, has a power that no other word in the language quite possesses. It is a shibboleth, as regards its pronunciation; it is a trumpet-call, as regards its effect. It has all the electrifying and unifying power of a college yell.
>
> "Chicago is Chicago," he said. "It is the belief of all of us. It is inevitable; nothing can stop us now." (191)

In the second half of the nineteenth century, the most seductive, if not immediately convincing, way to present the mysteries of Chicago was through bird's-eye views of it. Such maps were always talismanic and implicitly suggested an almost exhaustless topography of adventure. In this lithograph of "Chicago in 1868" by A. Ruger, we have an aerial celebration of the city as a "sociospatial power" (Meinig, III, 319), and it is "this little glimpse"—as Truesdale Marshall, the flaneur in Fuller's novel With the Procession, would say (223)—that allows us to plunge into the rich scenario of Chicago sketched at the beginning. In Truesdale's opinion, the very least one could say of this synoptic view is: "It's full of interest" (223). For a young farmer from the hinterland, to descend into this gateway site from the Icarian perspective of the map was to immerse oneself in the life of the metropolis, its new freedoms and opportunities, the ethnic variousness of its population, the spectacle of its shopping corridors, the misery of its poor, the extravagance of the rich, the ruthlessness of its cartels, and the daunting indifference of urban society towards greenhorns from the surrounding country. In other words, what Ruger's map ultimately evokes is a method, a way of proceeding, in that its invitation to visit the city is extended to all of its myriad facets; the city, therefore, as "a total social fact" (Mauss).

A cursory glance at the map reveals that we are invited to enter Chicago by way of its cool blue harbor on Lake Michigan and then proceed west, up the river and along its business district. And if we keep going, no matter in what direction, we will eventually enter the lush green world of the prairie and the surrounding agricultural frontier. In the foreground of the map we have a prolific variety of ships and boats, some steam-powered and the others sailing vessels, but all involved in transporting various kinds of cargo. If we follow the two branches of the river, we will notice that they are filled with long lines of boats. The alignment of the traffic around the harbor suggests a thriving trade along the river and up into the heart of the city, where all the tall warehouses and grain elevators are. The city's heart is clearly a productive center, and the smoke from the steamships suggests a booming, modern scenario. Such smoke was a still positive sign in the 1870s. In the foreground to the left, there are trains entering and leaving the harbor's warehouse area, where such goods as lumber, ore, grain, corn, meat, and other products are unloaded and reloaded. Over most of the map's space there is a grid form that suggests a system of urban expansion and a standard way of turning land into real estate. It extends infinitely into the horizon where it finally disappears into untrammeled nature, and its lines represent so many incursions into the continent's future. There is no end to the possibilities of expansion, the grid seems to say.

Although it was common practice to think of Chicago as an autonomous, self-generated world, we should not forget that the energy it expended came largely from the prairie. As Louis Sullivan noted in his autobiography, Chicago had become "the center of a vast contiguous territory" (305). Always concerned about using the right word, Chicago's most creative regional architect referred to the city's exuberant spirit as a power that sprung from the place itself, a power expressed above all from below, by its people, but also by its powerful financiers and engineers, men possessed by a single grand idea. This power, whatever it was, was not something one could actually put one's hands on. It was more like an event or a kinetic reality than a substance. In effect, the way Sullivan and so many others of his day registered this power was by noting its flow. The word *flow* became another crucial word in the vocabulary Chicagoans needed to grasp their cityís energies. As his Autobiography clearly shows, Sullivan would have willingly agreed with this crucial qualification of Sherwood Anderson's:

> A city to be a real one has to have something back of it. Land, a lot of it. Rich land—corn, wheat, iron, rivers, mountains, hogs, cattle. Chicago back of it has the Middle West—the empire called Mid-America...in the center of which Chicago stands. (Memoirs 108)

When trying to understand Chicago energies, one also had to trace their flow across the entire spatial continuum represented by Ruger's bird's-eye view lithograph. Failing to do so meant putting oneself in the position of not being able to appreciate the reciprocities that kept the two topologies of city and hinterland within one energy economy.

Ruger's map is very much an image of Chicago as a flow chart. There are all kinds of factors that contributed to this flow: above all, transportation systems like the railroad, the cable cars, the ships coming in and out of the harbor; the extended use of elevators that allowed the wholesale and retail houses along State Street and the skyscrapers in the financial and industrial zones to expand upward; the use of conveyor belts and elevators in the vertical storage of grain and corn; the influx of masses of immigrants from Europe and of people from the surrounding towns and countryside of the Midwest; the establishment of the Board of Trade—better known as the Change—to regulate the movement of wheat and other products and to host the futures market that freed agricultural staples from their bondage to the cycle of the seasons; and even such cultural systems as the mimetic display of free-flowing foliate designs around the windows of the famous Schlesinger and Mayer Store (now known as the Carson Pirie Scott) by Louis Sullivan. As many of these different systems of flowing suggest, even if Ruger's map very obviously focuses on the city's industrial center, it cannot escape celebrating what is an essentially reversible topology. This interchange between city and country, which is the whole point of William Cronon's masterly study of Chicago, Nature's Metropolis: Chicago and the Great West, fixes the fulcrum of energy flow in the various kinds of negotiations that bound the two topologies together. In the preface to his book Cronon, too, commits himself to the study of "commodity flows" (xvi).

Given his central thesis, according to which Chicago is nature's metropolis, he equips himself with the disciplines of economic and environmental history in order to reconstruct and explain the city's unprecedented growth. And just as he surrenders himself to an absolute metaphor, namely that of "flows," so too does he take care to loosen up one—if not the major—of his principal categories. In what may at first seem an astonishing admission at the outset of such an ambitious work, Cronon has this to say about his problematic use of the concept of nature:

> It is one of the richest, most complicated and contradictory words in the entire English language. Those who like their vocabulary precise and unambiguous will surely be frustrated by the different ways I use "nature" in this text. To them, I can only apologize: I do not believe the ambiguities can be suppressed, and I regard the word as indispensable to my purposes. (xix)

In order to understand the nature of Chicago energy and its excessive expenditure particularly in the last thirty years of the nineteenth century, Cronon sets out to study the energy of nature, beginning with the "rich loess soil" that he describes as one of the "Ice Age gifts from the north" (23). Further on in his study, he pursues this point in greater detail: "The black soil they (the prairie grasses) had produced measured in feet rather than inches and contained well over 150 tons of organic matter per acre in what seemed an almost inexhaustible fund of fertile earth" (98). When we are talking about the awesome flow of wheat into Chicago in those early heydays, Cronon suggests, we must make sure not to forget its source in the incredible richness of the prairie earth. So much for the flow of Chicago energy and the reversible continuum of Ruger's cartographic vistas.

But Cronon's real interest is plotting out the process by which first nature (the raw products of the farm and the forest) become second nature (those products transformed into marketable and consumable commodities). Thus he titles one section of his book "A Sack's Journey," alluding above all to a sack of grain, and the section immediately after it "The Golden Stream." The golden stream was made possible by the building of grain elevators and the use of steam-powered conveyor belts. As Cronon notes, "Grain entering Chicago might arrive in wagons or canalboats or railroad cars, but to move up an elevator's conveyor belts, it had to be sackless. Only then could corn or wheat cease to act like solid objects and begin to behave more like liquids: golden streams that flowed like water" (113). Before the railroads, grain arrived in Chicago in sacks and until the farmer sold them, the very sacks that he brought to the city remained his. After the railroads and the setting up of a system of conventional grades and qualities of wheat, he no longer owned the actual physical grain he had harvested from his fields but an elevator receipt entitling him to so much equivalent weight of a certain grade. This is what Cronon means when he talks about the process of abstraction by which first nature becomes second nature. But after a few rather brief glances at the former, Cronon abandons his project of studying the two-way exchange of energy between country and city. The flow quickly becomes a one-way affair. Although in the early going he often quotes from novels dealing with Chicago, ultimately he does not invest in the symbolic order of cultural capital, where he would have found that the flow regulating the release of energy between his two topologies is indeed a reciprocal process. But the artistic order is beyond his scope.

In keeping with his courageous metaphorization of the term nature, what Cronon does say about the possible reciprocities between the nature of Chicago energy (second nature?) and the energy of nature (first nature) is highly suggestive: "In Chicago and its hinterland, first and second nature mingled to form a single world" (93). In Chicago novels of the period, it is amazing how many characters, usually but not always including the main protagonists, come from the farm or the countryside and often return there at the story's end: see, for example, Frank Norris' The Pit, Sherwood Anderson's Windy McPherson's Son, Hamlin Garland's Rose of Dutcher's Cooly, Henry Black Fuller's The Cliff-Dwellers, Robert Herrick's The Memoirs of an American Citizen, and Theodore Dreiser's Sister Carrie, to mention the most familiar. As George Ogden, the protagonist of Fuller's The Cliff-Dwellers, says, "Is there anybody in this town who hasn't come from somewhere else, or who has been here more than a year or two?" (12). It is not surprising, then, that such narratives often treat the reader to a very close and self-conscious descriptive celebration of the excesses and peculiarities of Chicago life. It is as if they wanted to say, I was there. In coming into the city, usually by train, the invariably young protagonist of most Chicago novels makes it a point to entertain us with the novelties of their experiences. Just about anyone coming into the city for the first time is bound to experience a rite of passage, especially if that person is from the country.

Here is the scene of Frank Lloyd Wright's entrance into Chicago as he describes it in his Autobiography:

> Chicago. Wells Street: six o'clock, late Spring, 1887. Drizzling. Sputtering white arc-light in the station, the streets, dazzling and ugly.... Crowds. Impersonal. Intent on seeing nothing. Somehow I didn't like to ask anyone anything. Followed the crowd. Drifted south to the Wells Street Bridge over the Chicago River. The mysterious dark of the river with dim masts, hulks and funnels hung with lights half-smothered in gloom—reflected in the black beneath. I stopped to see, holding myself close against the iron rail to avoid the blind, hurrying by.
>
> I wondered where Chicago was—if it was near. Suddenly the clanging of a bell. The crowd began to run. I wondered why: found myself alone and realized why in time to get off, but stayed on as the bridge swung out with me into the channel and a tug, puffing clouds of steam, came pushing along below pulling an enormous iron grain-boat, towing it slowly through the gap.... Later, I never crossed the river without being charmed by somber beauty. (85)

It is worth recalling that young Frank escapes to Chicago without his mother or anybody else knowing it. He leaves the beautiful little town of Spring Green, Wisconsin, in the late afternoon and reaches the big city in the early evening. The above passage is written in a kind of mimetic shorthand, presumably to dramatize his impressions as he makes his way into the city, looking for its heart. Alone now, he leaves behind the "dazzling" but "ugly" lights of the station (he's no longer in Spring Green!) and joins the crowd as it moves across the Wells Street Bridge over the Chicago River. This is his first time in Chicago and perhaps the first time he has ever been part of an urban crowd, so he appropriately "drifts" and "follows" instead of asking someone for directions. It is not surprising that he ends up nowhere in particular, namely in the middle of a bridge extending over the city's river. There, out of the blue, he wonders where Chicago is.

But before he raises this metaphysical question about the centerless nature of the modern city imprisoned in the Euclidean web of an orthogonal grid, he pauses to look into the "mysterious dark of the river" which, like a mirror, reflects back an essentially deeper truth: the city's vocation of mingling first and second nature. The "hulks and funnels" surely allude to cargo and tug boats instrumental in keeping Cronon's "golden stream" flowing. By 1870 Chicago already had seventeen elevators with a total capacity of 11.6 million bushels of grain (Cronon 135). Unwittingly, Frank has indeed happened upon the heart of the city, the Chicago River. Note, not a public square or plaza with cathedral and city hall on it, but a river filled with cargo boats. It is here, in fact, that he will shortly witness a primal Chicago scene when the bridge swings open and a tug pulls through "an enormous iron grain-boat." A more spectacular introduction to commodity flow he could not have hoped for. Let us for a moment reconstruct the scene as he tells it. He is just in time to get off the bridge before it begins to swing open, but caught up in this new adventure as he is, he decides to ride it. Maybe even risking his life. Then comes the tug belching its clouds of steam and very likely blocking out the world.

If this tug is anything like those on Ruger's map, then it is quite capable of emitting a colossal smudge. Perhaps, at this point, young Frank closes his eyes a few seconds or is temporarily blinded by the steam, and then, when he opens them again, there it is: "an enormous iron grain-boat." The scene was undoubtedly impressive since he is able to recall it in detail many years later. In addition, is there not a hidden link between young Frank, fresh from Spring Green, and the sudden epiphany of the grain-boat right in the heart of downtown Chicago? This coming together of the three—Frank, grain-boat, and the Chicago River—is too propitious for us not to suspect that Wright has assigned his entrance topos a precise symbolic errand: that of mingling first and second nature. The flow of Chicago energy is easily as complex as Cronon's nature, and we need not apologize for it. Like Icarus, Frank has fallen into the central conduit of Ruger's bird's-eye view of Chicago. And as he himself points out, he was forever "charmed by (its) somber beauty."

Another sequence of his entrance into Chicago begs our attention, since the experience of flowing and the merging of first and second nature is now attributed specifically to the cultural order and its primary agent, the democratic masses. Later that night, still "drifting with the crowd" (1977:86), young Frank gets his first sight of a cable car and, rightly curious, he decides to ride one:

> Got on one coming out headed north now.... Half-resentful because *compelled* to read the signs *pressing on the eyes* everywhere. They claimed your eyes for this, that and everything besides. They lined the car above the windows. They lined the way, *pushing, crowding* and *playing* all manner of tricks on the *victim's eye*. Tried to stop looking at them. Unfairly compelled to look again. (86, italics mine)

What overwhelms him are the signs, signs everywhere, until it dawns on him that he can not escape them. He is sitting in a world of signs, and he feels a victim of their play. What has happened is awesome, for without knowing it, Frank has crossed over into a semiocentric world and he will never be the same again. There are no longer *realia* and their signs. There are only signs. But there is more to the scene. Up to this point he was observing the inside of the car. Now he directs his gaze outside it, only to find more of the same:

> There were glaring signs on the glass shop-fronts against the lights inside, sharp signs in the glare of the sputtering arc-lamps outside. Hurrah signs. Stop signs. Come-on-in signs. Hello signs set out before the blazing windows on the sidewalks.... Coming from extravaganza, here was the beginning of phantasmagoria. (86)

The temptation is to read this passage outloud and allow ourselves to be carried away by the rhythm. In doing so, we can sense how young Wright must have been hypnotized by the thousand glaring eyes of the signs. Also striking is the way in which inside and outside become the same thing. Ultimately, there is no difference between the interior of the car and the world of signs on the streets. Nor is there any difference between the street and the interior of the shops, at least as far as the world of signs goes. Everything seems to flow together, in an extravagant and even phantasmagorical way. Such excess, such exuberance, is Wright's version of Chicago energy.

If we cross-check Wright's autobiographical experience of entrance with Louis Sullivan's, we get pretty much the same thing. Here is Sullivan talking about post-fire Chicago: "Louis thought it all magnificent and wild: A crude extravaganza: An intoxicating rawness: A sense of big things to be done" (Autobiography 200). Were it not for the shared comminglings of Chicago, one might suspect Wright of having plagiarized the master, for even Sullivan could not help observing of this aggressively self-promoting city, "It shouted itself hoarse in *reclame*" (201). There was, however, no doubt in Sullivan's mind as to where such extravagant intoxication came from. Few in his day were as attuned to the spirit of place as Sullivan: "Louis rather liked all this, for his eye was ever on the boundless prairie and the mighty lake. All this frothing at the mouth amused him at first, but soon he saw the primal power assuming self-expression amid nature's impelling urge" (201). Once again, we are being offered an absolute metaphor; it is useless to try to separate "primal power" from "nature's...urge" as if they were distinct concepts. What, after all, does nature mean here? Is it first nature or second nature Sullivan is talking about? In the end, we are no better off than Marcel Mauss when he engaged the Maori word *hau* to explain the spirit of the gift and its milieu. And yet, in reading Sullivan's Autobiography, which came out the same year as Mauss's famous essay, it is evident that he understood very well what turn-of-the-century Chicago was doing in "killing wealth" (Hyde 8) like no other city in the United States, and perhaps the world. Like Mauss, Sullivan reads the mingling of first and second nature not as a one-way movement from country to city, but as a circle—the kind of symbolic going back and forth that the very word 'reciprocity' implies (Hyde 11).

The city was not only manufacturing a new McCormick reaper so that farmers could work larger fields and produce more wheat, it also had invented a "disassembly line" by which throbbing pig flesh was efficiently converted into dead commodity in record time (Cronon 211). Laying himself down to sleep that first night in Chicago, one last thought flickered through the now posthumous Wright's consciousness: "Chicago murderously actual." When Sullivan told his own story of the hog in his autobiography, only this time (the first being Upton Sinclair's in The Jungle) taking the hog's point of view, he made a parable out of it: "And yet, upon reflection, what about other pink and whites at the breast today? Are they to grow up within a culture which shall demand of them their immolation?" (307). Sullivan, of course, is talking about himself as creative artist in the same oblique way that Kafka did when he told stories about bugs and other animals. Without an understanding of the relevance of sacrifice here, it is impossible not only to come to terms with commodity flow but also to talk intelligently about cultural capital. Take, for example, Sullivan's observation about the skyscraper from his autobiography: "The appeal and the inspiration lie...in the element of loftiness, in the suggestion of slenderness and aspiration, the soaring quality as of a thing rising from the earth as a unitary utterance, Dionysian in beauty" (313-14). Presumably, by "Dionysian" he is referring to the religious or sacred element the tall office building expresses in its vertical striving. Moreover, if we accept Sullivan's cue and reinstate the notion of sacrifice when discussing the flow of Chicago energy at the beginning of the last century, we will also have to become fluent in the circular economy of the gift. The two go together. Without this larger framework, the idea of Chicago as 'nature's metropolis' will remain forever obscure.

Having read of life on Halstead Street in the the Sunday paper, Theodore Dreiser decided on the spur of the moment to pack his bag and leave for the big city: "That ride to Chicago was one of the most intense and wonderful of my life. For to me it was of the very substance of adventure" (304). As open to experience as Sullivan and Wright, young Theodore stepped from the train "ready to conquer the world." As he tells us in his autobiography, Dawn, he was neither scared nor lonely; "if anything, there was something determined and even aggressive in my attitude.... I knew then and there that I loved Chicago. It was so strong, so rough, so shabby, and yet so vital and determined" (305). In describing the city, Dreiser is describing himself. He gives us an ecstatic picture of the city as "a living, breathing thing" (307). "Hail, Chicago!" he cries out to himself in greeting (163), and then joins the "moving tide of people" with their same "enthusiasm for living" (166): "Here came the children of the new world and the old, avid for life and love, seeking a patrimony" 163). And then, in order to capture the spirit of the place itself, he makes Chicago speak:

> I am the soul of a million people! I am their joys, their prides, their loves, their appetites, their hungers, their sorrows!.... In me are all the pulses and wonders and tastes and loves of life itself! I am life! This is paradise! This is that mirage of the heart and brain and blood of which people dream. I am the pulsing urge of the universe! You are a part of me, I of you!.... Take of it! Live, live, satisfy your heart! (307)

The Dionysian, exclamatory prose speaks for itself. Once again, a procession of nouns becomes the most fitting way to handle plenitude. Dreiser pictures the city calling to him, seducing him, until it becomes life itself that is speaking. And in the last brief phrases, the transaction is surely sacramental, evocative of the moment of transubstantiation at the heart of the Catholic Mass—*Take and eat, this is my body; now I live in you.* The passage deftly mixes sacred and profane, ritual and auto-biography. Even more importantly, Dreiser introduces the notion of sacrifice. The city's elaborate exhortation is manifestly a summons to feed from its life so that "life-hungry natives" (166) like Theodore may fill their hearts. As Lewis Hyde writes of the milieu of gift economy, "We long to have the world flow through us like air or food" (10). On the strength of such longing, Dreiser's longing, we have passed over into the realm of mystery, where the city's exuberance circles as a gift. Here is another sequence from Dreiser's scene of entrance: "The spirit of Chicago flowed into me and made me ecstatic. Its personality was different from anything I had ever known; it was a compound of hope and joy in existence, intense hope and intense joy. Cities, like individuals, can flare up with a great flare of hope" (166-67). When Dreiser talks of hope, we can sense that he has read the psalms. His phrasing echoes theirs. And nobody who has ever read him would want to drive a wedge between his account of life and trade, hope and market. For Dreiser, they are part of a general economy, it is surplus in a nonrestrictive sense that built Chicago's skyscrapers.

The task of tracking the absolute metaphor of flowing through a series of entrance topoi has consistently involved us in the symbolic order of creative energy. As the spirit of Chicago possesses the Sullivans and Dreisers of the city's heyday, they are transfigured by the gift they have received. Now a part of the city's vernacular economy, they invariably feel pressured into keeping the spirit, the gift, in motion. Not to do so would be a sign that one is, in Sullivan's words, "incapable of adjusting to the flow of living things" (Autobiography 325). So the city's life and the hope that it offers ultimately present itself as a challenge. As a youthful Dreiser takes stock of his situation in the city and sets about "to reinvestigate this vast plasm of hope" (308) that has transfused him since the first day he arrived, he finds himself burdened with an obligation. "Had I one gift to offer the world, it would be the delight of sensing the world as I then sensed it. This city was to me a land of promise, a fabled realm of milk and honey..." (308). Here Dreiser supplies us with the germ of his vocation as a writer, in particular, a novelist of the metropolis, and he is careful to sheathe it in biblical allusion. The gift he has to offer will be a version of the gift he has received; the difference between the two will be the result of a schooling process of self-sacrifice. His vocation will involve him in a form of sacrificial expenditure. "[D]esiring so much, I wanted to work and be a part of things and to share, if possible, the sweets of this loving cup" (339), Dreiser writes, again choosing to introduce a eucharistic atmosphere.

Let's watch him as he develops the idea further. "The whole cruel as well as kind, rough as well as smooth, working schemes of life set over against my enforced spectatorship and idleness stood fairly close, and in what sharp lines!... Yet daily, and for how long, as it seemed to me, I was pushed aside while and where so many were at table!" (339). And yet Dreiser speaks of this period of forced spectatorship as the inception of his vocation: "Rather, my one gift, and one only, appeared to be to stare about and admire this world so wide..." (338). Already in his idleness he was drinking of the cup that would lead to his inspired love for writing. His involvement in a street car strike taught him many things about sensuous surface scenes but nothing about social or economic theory. As he admits, "I had no gift for organic sociology." Trade for him was "a strange, at times even lovely, spectacle" (338). Still, in reading a novel like Sister Carrie or An American Tragedy, we cannot help admiring his acute understanding of money and of the magical thrill of spending it. Evidently, the description of such systems had become second nature to him. In some way—through his early years of apprenticeship in nature's metropolis and, of course, the alchemy of his literary vocation—the spirit of Chicago had become transformed into his own gift.

In the light of the heuristic clues that have emerged from our discussion of the entrance topos in the autobiographical narratives of Sullivan, Wright, Anderson, and Dreiser, we now have a rather clear-cut appreciation of a general economy which includes gift circulation. In this sense the above autobiographical scenes help us to discover facts that have been obscured by the glitter and dominance of the money economy. After all, in the passage from first to second nature that Cronon describes so thoroughly in his study of Chicago, it seems almost natural that something would get lost in the process by which trees become lumber, animals so many different cuts of meat, and corn a liquid stream reduced to the value of an elevator receipt. But what is that something that gets lost? The breath of life? The spirit that made a tree, a pig, a stalk of corn a living, even sacred, thing? Apparently, the production process converts living things into dead commodities, and these commodities have no more value than the price one must pay for them. In short, the process of obscuration would lead us to believe that we are dealing with dead matter, as if commodities no longer expressed a symbolic principle or an energy of their own. Remember, when Cronon decided to call Chicago "nature's metropolis," he did so because of the mingling of country and city, arguing that Chicago was ecologically rooted in its hinterland. As the entrance topoi examined earlier indicate, this rootedness takes the form of a circle. To investigate its motion further, let's take a single product that has gone through the semiotic transformation of the market—for example, corn.

In his Memoirs Sherwood Anderson gives us a map of the circle of reciprocity which links Chicago and "the Middle West, the real body of America" (154): "To the east, reaching up, Michigan. To the west, Wisconsin, Minnesota, the Northwest.... And to the south, smooth as a billiard table—fat land. No such corn land anywhere in the world. Innumerable droves of great sleepy hogs, eating the corn. Cattle off the dry western lands, coming in lean and bony, getting fat and sleek, eating corn" (107). As the gateway to the Great West, Chicago was the point of intersection for agricultural goods such as corn. Corn helped to make the city what it was. Further on in his Memoirs, Anderson tells the story of a young German immigrant who was trying to make it as a painter and who used to go with Anderson and others on weekends into the country to paint. The story can be read as a parable linking Chicago, its hinterland, and cultural creation within a single economy. Here is Anderson:

The big German Jerry came down to where I lay on my back on the dry grass by the sluggish stream. He had with him the canvas on which he had been working all day.... Across the stream from us we could see stretched away the vast corn fields....

He had been trying to paint the corn field. For the time he had forgotten to be profane. We others had all come from farms or from country towns of the Middle West. He had said that he wanted to paint a corn field in such a way that everyone looking at his painting would begin to think of the fatness and richness of all Middle-Western America.

It would be something to give men new confidence in life.... Jerry wanted by his painting to make people believe in the land....

"You fellows, your fathers and grandfathers were born on the land. You can't see how rich it all is, how gloriously men might live here." .... We didn't know our own richness, what a foundation the land, on which to build.

But he would show them through the richness of the fields. The skyscrapers in the cities, money piled in the banks, men owning great factories, they were not the significant things.

The real significance was in the tall corn growing. There was the real American poetry. (230-31)

We have corn in the corn field and corn represented in the painting. Why in the painting? To show where the real wealth lay, to point to the value of the land and its glory. The corn field in the painting converts the corn into a general or total fact, a *pars pro toto*. In other words, it represents much more than itself, especially when "itself" refers exclusively to elevator corn. The artist wants to recover this lost background and present the corn in its just milieu. In the painting the corn captures the spirit of the place, and the place is not just the corn field but Chicago as well. In this sense the painting alludes to the city's foundation. The spirit of the corn is the city's spirit. Chicago energy feeds off the poetry of "the tall growing corn." Presumably, it is on the basis of some such premise that Ruger chose to undergird his bird's-eye view of 1868 Chicago with a vignette map—at the bottom center— portraying the site as it was in 1820. Like Jerry's painting, Ruger's insert map opens up a different and forgotten conceptual space. While the bird's-eye view represents a city-country continuum as a reversible horizontal space, the insert map introduces a vertical axiology implying a change of scale. As the eye passes from the Chicago of 1868 to that of 1820, it also changes object. The two Chicagos are by no means the same. Most importantly, the two scales represent two radically different economies. 1820 Chicago, with its economy still regulated by Indian diplomacy (see the canoes coming into the Chicago River), displaces the money economy as the single metanarrative of late nineteenth-century United States history (Gregory 185).

In 1820 Chicago was a mere trading post frequented by various Indian tribes and French, English, and American traders. The Pottawatomi owned the land and were not expelled until 1833, after the Black Hawk War. On the site the American army had already built Fort Dearborn to control the area and protect the activities of the Americn Fur Company, but it still had to accommodate local trading conditions. It was still on middle ground. In the immediately surrounding area grew Indian corn and wild garlic or onion, which gave the river its name. If we want to understand the origin and significance of corn in 1820 Chicago, we must read the autobiography of Black Hawk, the great Sac warrior. It was his defeat that turned the site over to the American settlement. Here is his version of corn's original prestige:

> According to tradition, handed down to our people, a beautiful woman was seen to descend from the clouds, and alight upon the earth, by two of our ancestors, who had killed a deer, and were sitting by a fire, roasting a part of it to eat. They were astonished at seeing her, and concluded she must be hungry.... They presented it to her, and she eat— and told them to return to the spot where she was sitting, at the end of one year, and they would find a reward for their kindness and generosity.... When the period arrived, for them to visit this consecrated ground, where they were to find a reward for their attention to the beautiful woman..., they went with a large party, and found, where her right hand had rested on the ground, corn growing. (93-94)

This origin story, imbued with the gift economy, suggests an older order of sociality and exchange than that of the money economy. I have introduced it here because 1820 Chicago was just a step away in years from its boomtown version of the late nineteenth century. The temporal span between the two Chicagos on Ruger's map is unbelievably short; which makes what happened between 1820 and 1868 something of a miracle, at least as far as city growth is concerned.

The point is, the metaphor of *flowing*—whether applied to money, crowds, corn, railroads, or information—can not be reduced either to capitalist economics, aesthetics, or religion. The use of the same image to describe both city and country suggests that traditional oppositions between sacred and profane, useful and useless, necessary and superfluous, primary need and secondary satisfaction (Goux 208) are too simplistic. In effect, the various entrance topoi we have surveyed invite us to think of the two topologies in terms of a general economy of energy and power, if not of life tout court. This reinstatement of mystery, if you will, also implies a new epistemological context in which actors like Sullivan, Wright, Anderson, and Dreiser are less interested in explaining the mingling of first and second nature than in making us *see* the connections between them, as Wittgenstein advocated elsewhere (Karsenti 78). In readjusting our aims along these lines, we have actually come full circle, that is, back to the scenario "*d'un tout parle*"—a scenario in which everything speaks.

When Hilda Polachek would show guests around Hull House, the settlement house in Chicago run by Jane Addams, she would bring them upstairs and show them the murals on the walls of the Hull-House Theatre. There they saw a representation of Lincoln pulling a flatboat down Sangamon River and another of Tolstoy plowing a field. The two figures depicted the dignity of labor, she would tell them: "Then I would turn to the rear wall, where a beautiful landscape of golden waving corn had been painted, and I would say, 'And here is the dignity of rest'" (101). What the cycle of murals evidently sought to represent was not a partial image of man the worker so much as an image of the total human being—men and women as they work, enjoy themselves, and rest. If we apply this idea of wholeness to the kind of sumptuous mingling that Chicago specialized in, then we are in a perfect position to appreciate Louis Sullivan's exemplary struggle to aestheticize political economy through his theory and practice of architectural ornament.

Nobody was more sensitive than Sullivan to the votive power of the tall office building, soon to be known as the skyscraper. As Daniel Bluestone points out, these new buildings "achieved monumental status, calling for special homage and awed respect transcending their workplace character" (143). Sullivan understood Chicago and its architectural monuments strictly in terms of power, and he saw his theory of ornament as a means to connect this power to its source in the hinterland. His ecstatic decoration of the Schlesinger and Mayer Store brought the agricultural heartland to downtown State Street, to the teeming center of the city's shopping corridor. For him ornament became an active principle whose task it was to express the spirit of place. His work is a unique exhibition of the gift economy and its role in the creation of Chicago's most stunningly original civic-minded architecture, namely his own. He not only put himself into his work, he also paid for it with his life. He died a poor and broken man, spending his last years in a hotel room for which he could not even pay the rent.

Sullivan, like Cronon, set out to combine Chicago economics and Midwestern environmental history. When he left Philadelphia to go jobhunting in Chicago, the train-ride became for him a lesson in American geography:

> Next morning he was utterly amazed and bewildered at the sight of the prairies of northern Indiana. They were startling in novelty.... Here was power—power greater than the mountains. Soon Louis caught glimpses of a great lake.... Here again was power, naked power, naked as the prairies, greater than the mountains. (Autobiography 196)

Under this regional spell he arrived in Chicago transformed, and as he began to travel around the Midwest, he came to understand the message contained on Ruger's map: "Thus in time, and on his own account, he had acquired a bird's-eye view of the broad aspects of his native land.... And he came to wonder how many people could visualize their country as a whole, in all its superb length and breadth, in its varied topography, its changing flora... its immense prairies and plains, vast rivers and lakes, deserts and rich soils, immense wealth within the soil and above and below it" (Autobiography 299-300).

When he came to write his last work, A System of Architectural Ornament, published in 1924, its mantra became, "Remember the Seed-Germ." On the book's opening page, under the image of a seed split open, he writes:

> Above is drawn a diagram of a typical seed with two cotyledons. The cotyledons are specialized rudimentary leaves containing a supply of nourishment sufficient for the initial stage of the development of the germ.

> The Germ is the real thing; the seat of identity. Within its delicate
> mechanism lies the will to power: the function which is to seek and
> eventually to find its full expression in form.
>   The seat of power and the will to live constitute the simple working
> idea upon which all that follows is based—as to efflorescence.

With buildings like the Schlesinger and Mayer and his small midwestern banks in mind, it is fair to say that his theory and practice of ornament is summed up in the above image and gloss. His ornamental schemes are so many variations on the above theory of efflorescence. Once he had etched an equivalent of Ruger's bird's-eye view into his mind, his grasp of the circular flow of energy was thorough. As "Chicago rolled on and roared by day and night" (316), he writes in his Autobiography, "there was the thought, the seeming presence of the prairies and the far-flung hinterland. In such momentary trance his childhood would return to him with its vivid dream of power, a dream which had now grown to encompass the world" (317). In his trance Sullivan not only reverses the continuous topology of city—country, he also introduces the vertical axiology of turning back in time to his own commencement.

It is in his Ocean Springs retreat, where he would go to escape the stress of Chicago, that he gained visionary knowledge of the meaning of power. "'Twas here he saw the flow of life, that all life became a flowing for him, and so the thoughts the works of man. 'Twas here he saw the witchery of nature's fleeting moods.... 'Twas here he gazed into the depths of that flowing, as the mystery of countless living functions moved silently into the mystery of palpable or imponderable form" (Autobiography 297-98). During his days as Chicago's premier architect, Sullivan constantly studied the growth cyle of a variety of American plants; in A System of Architectural Ornament he encouraged his readers to consult Gray's School and Field Book of Botany. His ornamental motifs are mimetic, spellbinding attempts to trace plant growth of various kinds "from the seed to its full exfoliation" (Siry 154). While his contemporaries resorted to historical typologies of ornament, especially from the Greek and Neoclassical traditions, Sullivan sought to render the spirit of local place in his buildings. While his more successful colleagues went for the money and promoted readily recognizable, European building styles, he made it a point to say that "architecture is an expression rather than a style and is the outcome of certain conditions in a certain civilization" (Papers 153). This in 1901, when circumstances forced him to do more writing and lecturing than building.

As he says of his work on the Auditorium Building, "Louis's heart went into this structure" (Autobiography 303). In effect, sympathy was for him a crucial factor in the creative evocation of a building's urban context. The vitality of his ornamental designs—"impulses," he once called them (System, see his comment on Plate 4)—came directly from the energy-buzz that defined Chicago for Chicagoans. In his final years he saw himself as "a witness, a participant" (System: "Interlude") of the life of his city. In his address to the Chicago Architectural Club in 1899, he told those present to "take pains truly to understand your country, your people, your day, your generation, the time, the place in which you live;...seek to understand, absorb, and sympathize with the life around you" (Papers 124-25). And since his audience was made up mostly of young architects, he drew from his own experience to warn them of "the sorrow and bitterness of the struggle" (123) they would have to face if they dared to take the city seriously. Sullivan paid a high price for his originality; the creative energy he invested in his ornamental details paid off in prestige but not in commissions. While other architects in Chicago did no more than quote the forgotten tropes of violence and the sacrificial trophies intrinsic to classical ornament (Hersey 1988: 11-67), thus relegating their statements to the superficial status of literary redundancy, Sullivan passionately invested his system of architectural ornament with a sacrificial structure. This he did by attempting to embody the motion of Chicago energy in the very practice of ornament. At the same time, he tried to raise the anthropological order of the city's spirit of place to that of an aesthetic principle, by having his ornamental designs re-enact the circle of energy commuting back and forth between first and second nature.

The idea was to bring Dionysius back into the city, to give Chicago's two new building types, the tall office building and the department store, a Dionysian beauty. Sullivan's project was ambitious and grandiose. His fellow architects did not understand him. Through the investigative efforts of ornament alone—although Sullivan did not differentiate between mass and detail—the "single vast veil of mystery...might perhaps lift of a sudden...in a grand transformation scene" (Autobiography 207). In order to make ornament the scene of such a metamorphosis, he would have to capture the flow of Chicago energy, bring it momentarily to a standstill or a state of temporary arrest. To be sure, both in his writings and in his theory and practice of ornament, Sullivan was always peering beneath the surface of things, as was just about everybody writing on Chicago in its heyday. If one did succeed in fathoming the depths, Sullivan observes in his famous essay "The Tall Office Building Artistically Considered," he or she would see "how amazing the flow of life, how absorbing the mystery" (Papers 111). Sullivan is talking here about looking into "*the unfathomable depth of nature*," a category, we have already seen, that is useful not only in discussing the flow of grain in Chicago but also in admiring a field of corn in Iowa. As long as nature is seen in terms of the flow of power and energy, it is equally applicable to both life in the city and life on the farm. Sullivan is as metaphorical as Cronon in defending the ambiguities of "nature." For under its umbrella we now have, indifferently, not only first and second nature—laid out on Ruger's map as a topological continuum—but also two different economies, a restricted and a general one. And at the heart of the general economy, we also have the nature of the gift economy, with its structure of giving, receiving, and giving back again.

This, then, is the context within which Sullivan positions his theory of ornament. What ornament does, above all, is to recollect what has been transformed into second nature, but without sacrificing second nature's transformative power. At its most eloquent, Sullivan's ornament embodies a tremendous state of tension, which we can appreciate aesthetically as its inner vitality or mimetic voltage. Visually, his ornament turns back both spatially and temporally in order to embrace the circle that invests "nature" with its full array of complexities. In doing so, it winks at the origin of second nature's power and simultaneously reveals what has entered and disappeared in it. So we can say that Sullivan not only crafts his ornament to float in a sea of signs, but he also assigns it to the gift economy. This latter for the simple reason that while ornament registers what has disappeared in it, the energy of first nature is in reality inalienable. Chicago may be the site in which the energy of first nature is set free, but the spirit of this energy remains with the giver. As gift, it retains its original atmosphere. This is the paideia informing Sullivan's theory and practice of ornament. As he writes in his Autobiography, although in reference to architecture in general, ornament is "a token of a covenant..., a symbol of the city's basic significance as offspring of the prairie" (318). In short, ornament is for Sullivan essentially an ecological gesture.

As a turning back, as the scene of a potential transformation, Sullivan's ornament explicitly pertains to the sacrificial order. In his long essay "What is Architecture?: A Study in the American People of Today" (1906), his last major theoretical work, he clarifies what he meant when he said that he gave his heart to the Auditorium Building. In the last pages of the essay he has Nature speak as follows: "I center at each man, woman and child. I knock at the door of each heart, and I wait. I wait in patience—ready to enter with my gifts" (Papers 194). In his covenant with Chicago, Sullivan treated the city like virgin soil, and the ornament-seeds he "planted" there were tokens of the city's mingling of first and second nature. The opening gift was 1820 Chicago's, and his practice of ornament as a fine art was an attempt to reciprocate. The Carson Pirie Scott Building, now recognized as the most poetically glorious of Chicago's department stores of the early twentieth century, was an especially prestigious return gift, immediately recognizable as a work by Sullivan.

When the Schlesinger and Mayer Store was completed in 1903, much of its immediate prestige was due to the fact that it bore Sullivan's signature. At the base of the wreaths just over the doors of the rounded corner entrance are embedded the initials of the architect. As Siry points out in his definitive study of the building, "The exfoliations appear to have sprung from the letters LHS" (167). The wreaths themselves, "the most literally naturalistic motifs in the building's ornamental scheme" (Siry 158), sum up the festive imagery of Sullivan's decorative statement. It is as if the master wanted to locate the anthropological structure of his ornament in a new architectural drama of sacrifice. After all, the word ornament "has implications of honor, achievement, religious duty," George Hersey reminds us (149). As Sullivan spent his life repeating, architecture as a fine art must be "of the people, for the people, and by the people" (Papers 113). The Schlesinger and Mayer Store captured the flow of civic vitality like no other department store in Chicago. Looking at the buildings of the city's other architects, you would be hard put to find any conscious celebration of Chicago's complex mingling of first and second nature. Their use of traditional typologies of ornament effectively closed off research into the city's originary dispensation. Only Sullivan was willing to investigate the terrain of Ruger's vignette of 1820 Chicago.

A year before his death, Sullivan set down a final account of how the flow of energy works in his practice of ornament. Naturally, he did not talk about it in terms of the gift economy as such; nor could he have known Marcel Mauss's famous essay on the gift. But his absorption in tracing Chicago energy back to its "out-working" (*System*: "Interlude") in first nature distinctly marked Sullivan as Mauss's fellow traveler and gave his ecologically sensitive designs their unmistakably sacrificial aura. By conceptualizing ornament as an atmospheric emblem of the mingling of different economies of energy, Sullivan was expressing the equivalent of Mauss's *hau*. Both sought to circumscribe the spirit of place intrinsic to the gift economy. Sullivan wanted ornament to witness to this mingling by freezing this latter momentarily in a visual gesture. Thus contemporary Chicago would recall the Chicago of 1820, and in celebrating itself the city would also celebrate its surrounding hinterland. In this way, Chicago would also hold the original spirit of place—and the gift economy it represents—in mind. When we recall the trajectory of Sullivan's life and the fate of his buildings, the sacrificial nature of his project shines even more brightly.

The first task Sullivan set himself was to free the monumental from the restrictions of rigid geometry. His intentions were anti-architectural. In his gloss on Plate 4 in A System of Architectural Ornament, we can see how he reconceptualized architectural volume by enfolding it in a theory of efflorescence. In his system of ornament, geometrical forms became "containers of energy, extensive and intensive" (His gloss on Plate 3). The radials that crisscross circle and pentagon in his designs represent energy flow, and this flow in plants is what gives them form and identity. Far from being static, these vectors are actually radiations. As he points out in his gloss for Plate 3, "All lines are energy lines." In short, the purpose of Sullivan's philosophy of ornament is to make all things flow. Plate 4 he titles "The Awakening of the Pentagon" and in this crucial exercise he seeks to trace its "fluescent phases of expression tending toward culmination in foliate and efflorescent forms." The miracle here lies in converting rigid geometry into the lifelike forms of plant-life. The large ornament in Plate 4, which represents the end-process of the pentagon's awakening, is titled "Pentagon in Action." What makes the conversion of rigid geometry possible is the seed-germ as primal type (see Plate 5). The seed-germ is a reservoir of energy.

If we were to step back now and observe the overall effect of ornament on the Schlesinger and Mayer Store, we would see how its spiralling tendrils and curling leaves craze over the building's surface in repeated shocks of floral explosion, reminding us that Sullivan intended his monument as an act of bioarchitectural memory. The Schlesinger and Mayer is a good example of what George Hersey would call genetic architecture, that is, a building which recapitulates the growth of a plant species (1999: 30). Like Leonardo da Vinci, Sullivan saw "strong common currents in all flowing, curving, twisting, and turbulent things" (Hersey 1999: 32). Identifying the prototype of these currents in the seeds of plants, he based his system of ornament on the precept "Remember the Seed-Germ." This act of remembering meant using ornament to capture Benjamin's "primal history of the present" (462:N2a,2), in which ornament "is that wherein what has been comes together in a flash with the now to form a constellation" (463:N3,1). For Sullivan, Benjamin's "what has been" is first nature, and by mingling first and second nature into a common current, his ornament becomes "dialectics at a standstill" (463:N3,1). It is no wonder that his architectural ornament sought to repeat the inaugural effect of his and Ruger's bird's-eye view of nature's metropolis, and in doing so, it gave his buildings their characteristic "fluency" (*System*, gloss on Plate 7). In his day, no one more than Sullivan knew what the price was for killing wealth in Chicago.

I wish to thank Liam Kennedy and Maria Balshaw for publishing a non-linear multimedia version of this essay in their Three Cities CD-ROM and Udo Hebel who published a shorter and thematically different version of this essay in his recent volume Sites of Memory in American Literatures and Cultures. The copyright of this essay belongs to the author.

WORKS CITED

Anderson, Sherwood. Sherwood Anderson's Memoirs. New York: Harcourt, Brace and Company, 1942.

Anderson, Sherwood. Windy McPherson's Son. Urbana: University of Illinois Press, 1993.

Benjamin, Walter. The Arcades Project. translated by Howard Eiland and Kevin McLaughlin, Cambridge, MA, and London: Belknap/Harvard University Press, 1999.

Black Hawk, An Autobiography. ed. Donald Jackson, Urbana: University of Illinois Press, 1990.

Bluestone, Daniel. Constructing Chicago. New York and London: Yale University Press, 1991.

Blumenberg, Hans. *Paradigmi per una metaforologia*, translated by Maria Vittoria Serra Hansberg, Bologna: Mulino, 1969.

Cronon, William. Nature's Nation. New York: W.W. Norton & Company, 1992.

Dreiser, Theordore. Dawn. London: Constable & Co Ltd., 1931.

Fuller, Henry B. The Cliff-Dwellers. New York: Holt, Rinehart and Winston, Inc., 1973.

Fuller, Henry B. With the Procession. Chicago and London: The University of Chicago Press, 1965.

Goux, Jean-Joseph. "General Economics and Postmodern Capitalism", Bataille: A Critical Reader. eds. Fred Botting and Scott Wilson. Oxford: Blackwell, 1998.

Gregory, Derek. Geographical Imaginations. Oxford: Blackwell, 1994.

Herrick, Robert. The Memoirs of an American Citizen. Cambridge, MA: Belknap/Harvard University Press, 1963.

Hersey, George. The Lost Meaning of Classical Architecture. Cambridge, MA: The MIT Press, 1988.

Hersey, George. The Monumental Impulse. Cambridge, MA:
    The MIT Press, 1999.

Hyde, Lewis. The Gift, Imagination and the Erotic Life of Property. New
    York: Vintage Books, 1983.

Karsenti, Bruno. "The Maussian Shift: A Second Foundation for Sociology in
    France?" Marcel Mauss, A Centenary Tribute. eds. Wendy James and N.J.
    Allen, New York and Oxford: Berghahn Books, 1998.

Mauss, Marcel. The Gift: the Form and Reason for Exchange in Archaic
    Societies. translated by W.D. Halls, New York: W.W. Norton & Co., 1990.

Meinig, D.W. The Shaping of America, vol. 3, Transcontinental America
    1850-1915. New Haven and London: Yale University Press, 1993.

Polacheck, Hilda Scott. I Came a Stranger. Ed. Dena J. Polacheck Epstein,
    Urbana: University of Illinois Press, 1991.

Ranciere, Jacques. Les mots de l'histoire. Paris: Seuil, 1992.

Siry, Joseph. Carson Pirie Scott, Louis Sullivan and the Chicago Department
    Store. Chicago and London: The University of Chicago Press, 1988.

Sullivan, Louis H. The Autobiography of an Idea. New York: Dover
    Publications, Inc., 1956.

_____. The Public Papers, ed. Robert Twombly. Chicago and
    London: The University of Chicago Press, 1988.

_____. A System of Architectural Ornament. New York: The Eakins Press, 1967.

Wright, Frank Lloyd. An Autobiography. New York: Horizon Press, 1977.

The Three Muncies:
Buckongahelastown, Munseytown, Middletown

Martha Banta
University of California, Los Angeles

Robert and Helen Lynds' Middletown (1929) and Middletown in Transition (1937), classics in the field of social anthropology, are considered "pioneering" studies of "a typical American town." Continuing attempts to pry meaning from a site selected for its averageness have turned Muncie, Indiana, (the actual location of "Middletown") into the site for on-going academic enterprises conducted by The Center for Middletown Studies and the Middletown III Project. Muncie's cultural capitalists have been successful in tapping funds from the Lily Foundation, the Ball Brothers Foundation, the National Endowment for the Humanities (which funded the six-part PBS television series), and other grant agencies. Indeed, access to late twentieth-century forms of cash flow is as important to the scholarly entrepreneurs lured from the East to capitalize the resources of a small city located along White River in Center Township, Delaware County, Indiana.

Current "Middletown" projects that produce an ever-growing list of publications continue to focus on the town's sociological and demographic significance as that statistical "mean" by which Americanist scholars hope to gauge what "Americanness" is. However, before I trace the evolving modes of attention paid to post-Lynd Muncie, I want to go back to the origins of its site, geological, archaeological, and historical.[1] The "natural history" of Muncie reaches back, back beyond the colonial era into the prehistorical time-zones marked out by geologists and archaeologists.

In 1816 the State of Indiana (talk about an overdetermined name, ironically given to lands almost denuded of indigenous tribes) was carved out of the densely forested land of the Old Northwest Territory. (This was well before the Lewis and Clark mapping expedition pushed the meaning of "northwest" thousands of miles toward the Pacific Coast).[2] In 1791, a chief of the Delaware Indians (allied with the Munsee or Wolf clan) settled Buckongahelastown at the bend of the Wapahani, sometimes known as the Opecomeecah (later dubbed "White River" by white settlers suffering from the lack of imagination Thoreau so often deplored). The second Indian settlement was Tetapachit Town located on a hill overlooking the river, closely followed by Smithfield and Munseytown, settled by whites once the westward removal of the Indians began with the signing in 1818 of the Treaty of St. Mary's.

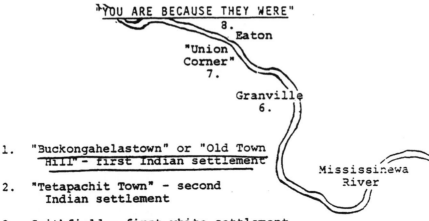

"YOU ARE BECAUSE THEY WERE"

1. "Buckongahelastown" or "Old Town Hill" - first Indian settlement

2. "Tetapachit Town" - second Indian settlement

3. Smithfield - first white settlement

4. Munseytown - second white settlement

5. Yorktown - early white settlement

6. Granville - early white settlement

7. "Union Corner" or "Henpeck", as it was first called

8. Eaton - early gas discovery

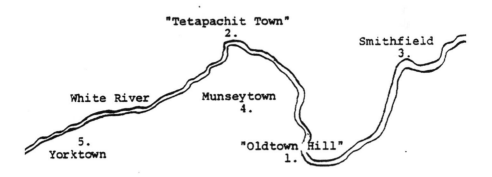

LOCATIONS OF THE EARLY VILLAGES

FIGURE 1

In 1821–22, Federal surveyors measured the land and set up the township system. Goldsmith Coffeen Gilbert used government money to purchase "the Hackley Reserve," six-hundred and twenty-seven acres owned by the granddaughter of Little Turtle, chief of the Miamis. By 1827 four families had settled around Gilbert's trading post at Munseytown, known variously as Munseetown and Muncey Town until 1845 when "Muncie" became the official name.

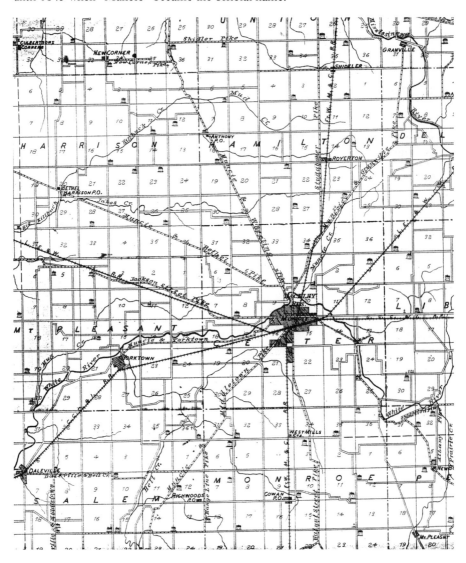

FIGURE 2

Though designated the county seat, for decades Muncie remained a raw backwoods village. In the 1830s and 1840s it missed out on crucial canal connections. Although Muncie managed to wrangle a stop on the railroad by 1852, when the village received the rights of incorporation in 1854, the population was no more than eight hundred. Muncie's identity was that of a village that serviced the farmers of the surrounding township. Muncie was "ordinary" beyond the standards of the ordinary that warrant draw attention a sociologist's attention and time. Everything changed, almost over night, with discovery in 1886 that natural gas lay underfoot. Five Ball brothers expatriated themselves from Buffalo, New York, wooed westward by the Muncie Citizens Committee and a promise of $5,000, a seven-acre tract of land, and a nearby gas-well if they would relocate their glass factory to Delaware County where, eventually, the famous Mason Glass fruit jars went into production. The initial stages of the process had begun that would lead, within the next generation, to the mixed blessing of Muncie's entry into American cultural lore as "Middletown."[3]

People of the Stony Country

Muncie is the site (layered by history, both natural and nationalistic, both prehistoric and history-driven) chosen in 1924 by the Lynds almost out of a hat.[4] Their intention was to annotate what was "typical" and "average" about a small mid-western city in the late 1920s. That they got a number of things wrong is only part of the interesting saga of how a town becomes famous for being ordinary; how it continues to be a remunerative cottage-industry for scholars long after its original character changed into something quite different; how the questions asked by sociological anthropology leaves unresolved questions that practitioners of geology and archeology might put to the site.

Is it not appropriate that the particular clan of the Delaware Indians which first settled Buckongahelastown were the Munsees, meaning "people of the stony country[5]?" What was hidden within the "stony" land would, in later generations, become the basis of the material economy and the cultural community of Middletown's people. The story of "The Three Muncies" begins thousands of years before peoples inhabited the North American land mass, with the advent of geological formations that gave physical shape and substance to the area now known as western Ohio and eastern Indiana.

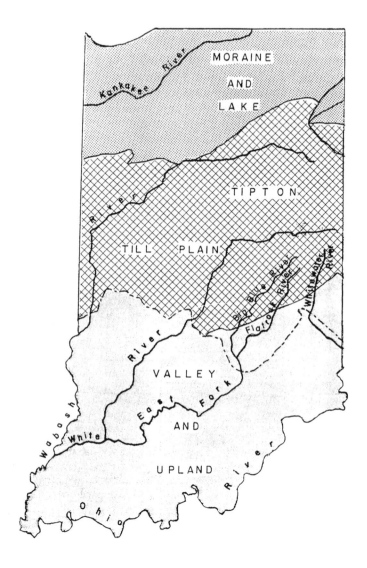

FIGURE 3

Major physiographic zones and rivers of Indiana. Dashed line represents the
furthermost advance of the Illinois glaciation. Modified from Indiana Geological
Survey.

Once we arrive at the crucial moments in modern history when the discovery
was made of the vast fields of natural gas lying with the layered area of Trenton
limestone, I shall include data tabulated by geological experts on the environment

that laid the (literal) foundation for Muncie's fortunes. I start, however, with reference to attempts by the material archaeologists to mark out the stages of human habitation in the Middle Mississippi region; their diligent work has implications for the sociological anthropology practiced by the Lynds and their successors.[6]

Archaeologists struggle to devise histories that pre-date the history recorded by the white settlers who move into an area centuries after other kinds of narrative evidence is left by the primal land and its indigenous people. Some stake out highly localized digs that extract from the pliant earth the artifacts that yield evidence about a particular culture; others work with "interpretative frameworks" covering wide expanses of territory and broad spans of time. Keep in mind that "from the perspective of natural areas," Indiana itself is "an artificially defined part" of "the whole of eastern North America" and that its so-called Historic Period is only a blink of the eye in regards to the ten thousand years these "frameworks" attempt to cover.[7]

Muncie, Indiana, registers little, if at all, in either of these archaeological enterprises. Burial mounds feature prominently in the Woodland Tradition (1000 B.C. to A.D. 900), the third of the four "traditions" itemized by archaeological theorists studying the vast area between the rivers of the Ohio and the Mississippi, preceded by The Big Game Hunting Tradition and The Archaic Tradition, and followed by The Mississippian Tradition that extends from A.D. 800 to The Historical Period (Ibid, 15). Alas, Muncie has no Indian mounds on hand to draw curious visitors, like those at the Mounds State Park near Anderson or on the New Castle State Hospital grounds (Ibid, 40).

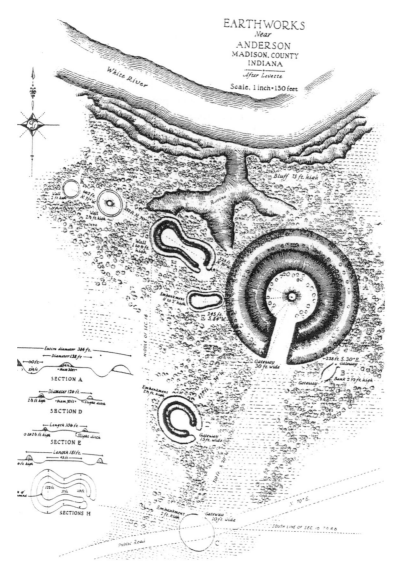

EARTHWORKS
Near
ANDERSON
MADISON, COUNTY
INDIANA
After Levette
Scale, 1 inch = 150 feet

FIGURE 4–5 The southern group at Anderson Mounds and the New Castle Site.

Even when one moves along into the Mississippian period, Muncie has nothing special to offer from the archeologist's point of view (unique examples of projectile points made from chalcedony or chert, mussel shell middens, Glacial Kame-cemeteries, or Marion Thick pottery), and nothing to excite interest from the state's tourist-industry. However, certain observations made by the archaeologists studying the evidence of the Indian cultures that developed during "the Mississippian period" might well have seized the attention of sociological anthropologists of "the Middletown period." Settled "town life" is in place, as is "marked social stratification," together with "elements of social control . . . vested in institutions having a religious-political function." Even the complex earth-works of the preceding Woodland tradition are "symptomatic of co-operative endeavor"; they suggest that "the motivations for their long-term accretion and use must certainly rest in some form of institutionalized social control beyond that customarily present in the small kin group" (Ibid, 45–46). One might meditate on the applicability of the following description of its material culture to latter-day Middletown, as viewed by commentators on the Middletown community as interpreted by the Lynds: "remarkably uniform and lacking in stylistic variation and evidence of experimentation," with "overall a sense of monotony, of sameness, and of local isolation" (Ibid, 43).

Indian legends left behind by the Choctaws told that the prehistoric mound-builders of Indiana, ancestors of the Choctaw nation, came out of a hole in the ground; further legends had it that they disappeared into the caves of the Ohio River area upon the arrival of white men. A wonderful tale, but the fate of the Choctaws is negligible in establishing Indiana's white-settlement-history. More to the point is the appearance of the Delaware Indians in the mid-seventeenth century in an area which had, at that late period, very few Indians at all, and those being "refugees" in flight from the East depredations of the warring Iroquois tribes (27).

The Indiana territory was filling up with increasing numbers of white settlers, followed later by the Delawares, together with random bands of the Miamis and Potawatomis, the Shawnees, the Piankashaws, Kickapoos, and Weas (Ibid, 26; Barnhart/Riker, 52). It is the Munsee (Wolf) clan of the Delawares who figure in the settlement of Muncie, and it is their brief, sad saga that receives note here, as it seldom did in any detail in the town that later appropriated their name.

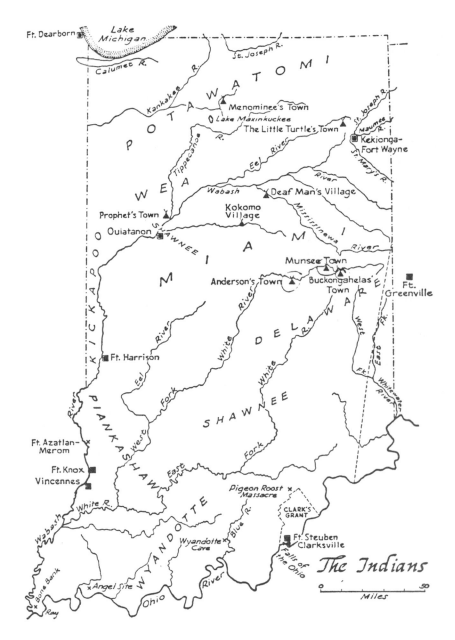

FIGURE 6

A brief personal point of reference: as a fourth-grader in the Muncie elementary schools (that school-year when little Americans once learned everything there was to know about the world's geography), I was aware that Delaware was one of the states along the Eastern seaboard (capital: Dover), and that its name referred to an Indian tribe from that region. I also knew that I lived in Delaware County and that Muncie got its name from the chief of the Delawares who had made camp nearby on White River. Why had I not then asked an obvious question: How and why did the Delawares get from Point A (the Eastern state) to Point B (my home county)?

Granted that the Muncie school system in the 1930s had pressing socioeconomic matters on their Middletown collective minds that might preclude its giving classroom time to the trials undergone in the 1700s by the Delawares and the Munsees. Whatever passing reference was given to Muncie's Indian past was highly romanticized. "The Appeal to the Great Spirit," cast in 1903 by Cyrus E. Dallin from the original in Boston's Museum of Fine Arts was situated at the bend of White River near the home of Edmund Burke Ball, in whose honor it was erected and in memory of "all the Indians who inhabited our nation before the coming of the white man" (Abel, 46–47). But then, the history of the white settlement of Indiana tended to romanticize itself, not just the annals of the Indians it replaced. Had not the revised Centennial Edition of Historic Indiana announced itself in 1916 as "Chapters in the Story of the Hoosier State from the Romantic Period of Foreign Exploration and Domination through Pioneer Days, Stirring War Times, and Periods of Peaceful Progress, to the Present Time[8]?"

Whether contained in the Walam Olum, the body of history passed down by the Lenni Lenape that includes the Delaware and Munsee tribes, or in set down in records of the white settlers, tales of the Delaware Diaspora are those of a series of removals, ever westward.[9] Walam Olum speaks of migrant members of Delawares wandering in Indiana territory hundreds of years before white history took note of them, but originally the Delaware confederacy was located in Delaware, eastern Pennsylvania, New Jersey, and southern New York. In 1682 their leaders signed a treaty with William Penn and established their council fire near present-day Germantown. By 1720, however, the whites, in league with the Iroquois who now dominated the entire area, began to push the Delawares westward: toward the Susquehanna in 1742, across the Allegheny mountains in 1724, and into eastern Ohio in 1751, where the tribe tried to dig in and face off both the Iroquois and the whites.[10] By 1770, the Delawares gained permission from the Miamis and Piankishaws to settle between the Ohio and White Rivers in Indiana. The 1795 treaty of Greenville was the end of the end for the Delawares.[11] Some were removed to Missouri and Arkansas, others to Texas. By 1838 those who survived the infamous "Trail of Death" were gathered into a reservation in Kansas.[12] In 1867, the depleted number of Delawares were pushed still farther westward into Indian Territory, where they were incorporated into the Cherokee Nation. In 1930, Delawares, including members of the Munsee tribe, numbered 971; only 20.2 percent were of "full blood."[13]

Era of Flaming Plumes of Gas

Muncie was denied direct participation in the historical dramas leading to the establishment of the Indiana Territory in 1813 and of the State of Indiana in 1816. Just as the mound-builders of prehistoric times left no mark near the Buck-ongahelastown settlement but allowed Anderson and New Castle (each twenty miles distant from Muncie) top priority on the favored list of field trips for school children, Muncie is absent from seventeenth-century annuals as the site of the major events that shaped enduring, often traumatic, relations between the Indians and Europeans, and the colonists from the colonizers. Historians have much to tell about Fort Wayne (sixty miles to the northeast), Vincennes (clear across the state, down in the lower southwest corner, Tippecanoe (over to the west near Lafayette), as well as Greenville and Corydon (almost to the Ohio River, on the way to Louisville, Kentucky). These are the sites where Indiana was created out of the Old Northwest and fame came to Mad Anthony Wayne, William Henry Harrison, Little Turtle, Tecumseh, and the Prophet.[14] True, Muncie had a connection (albeit fragile) with these exciting events by way of its reference to Buckongahelas, the Delaware chief whose name was attached to the first Indian settlement in the Muncie area, and to Little Turtle, whose granddaughter (named Setting Sun by the Indians and Rebecca Hackley by the whites) sold the land allotted to her for the tribe's service to Goldsmith Gilbert, original founder of Munseytown.[15] So weak a link, it seems, that when the 1916 Centennial was celebrated in grand style across the state, it was largely ignored by the people of Delaware County. Only a single day was given to its observance; no contribution to the state celebration was made; no money was forthcoming for the erection of permanent memorials.[16] Post-bellum Muncie seemed well on its way to being no more than ordinarily ordinary. It was hardly an obvious candidate for selection as America's Typical American City, site of extraordinary averages. Muncie's moment would come in 1886 with the discovery that deep wells of natural gas lay just underfoot.

The conditions that brought public attention to Muncie as one of the centers of the gas boom of the 1880s had been there all along. As the waters of the great sea that once covered the entire area of Indiana receded, fragments of igneous rocks that had been carried down from the north during earlier geological ages began to emerge. Geologists identify the strata from bottom to top as Potsdam sandstone, Lower Magnesian limestone, St. Peter's sandstone, and Trenton limestone. It is the latter layer, "covered by a mantle of glacial drift," that would furnish the largest source of the state's oil and gas wells, and in so doing, altered Muncie's future by creating the conditions that made it known as the site of extraordinary averages.[17]

Geology with its probing of the natural resources hidden away under layers of rocky strata brought attention to Delaware County that archeology with its study of artifacts crafted elsewhere by "the people of the stony country" could not. Although the first wells in the county were drilled in Eaton (about twelve miles to the north), it was Muncie's luck to rest on the Tipton Till Plains region with Trenton limestone below the surface. This allowed it to become the site of the glass companies and other factories, whose presence would offer the sociological anthropological data the Lynds sought for their study well after the gas wells had given out. Natural gas brought sudden wealth, energetic boosterism, and rapid industrial growth to a formerly prosperous but quiescent agricultural area.

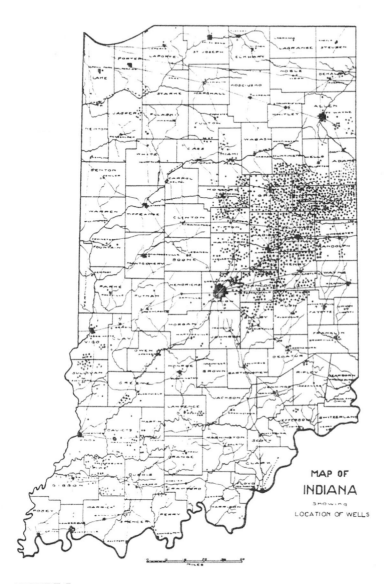

FIGURE 7

Map showing distribution of <u>oil, gas, and dry wells drilled in Indiana</u>. Space does not permit the location of all wells drilled in the oil and gas producing areas.

Historians of the Indiana natural gas boom delight in recording both the statistics and the romance of "its fantastic but short life," lasting but twenty years until its peak in 1906.[18] It can be argued that they glory even more in relating the tragic extravagance that led to the rapid depletion of this exceptional natural resource. True Americanists, they take a certain perverse pleasure in detailing the follies of ignorance that accompanied "the gaudiest, most glamorous boom [Indiana] has ever known," at a time when "there was virtually no understanding that a gas accumulation was a finite thing, and the voices of those who did understand were not heard" (Heiney, 11). The waste was tremendous. In some places night was virtually indistinguishable from day. Flambeau torches of natural gas burned wastefully along city and country roads. It became the fashion to erect arches of perforated iron pipe over roads leading into the town, fire gas into them, and let them burn night and day. For weeks after wells were tapped and ignited, they were allowed to blast showy flames into the sky for up to 100 feet (Ibid). [19]

Today the mid-west is dependent upon its supply for natural gas brought in by pipelines from the fields of the Texas panhandle, Kansas, and West Virginia, but at the close of the nineteenth century, there was no tomorrow in sight: only flames reaching to the heavens. The aftermath of the bonanza would introduce the Lynds to Muncie, followed by the publication of Middletown in 1929. Nonetheless, the times of the gas boom brought the town its one flush of literary fame.

The discipline of archaeology had not made a name for Muncie and its immediate environs, although geology's analysis of its natural resources would. Unfortunately, the literary world of Indiana found nothing of worth to say about Delaware County or Muncie, its county-seat.

There is a commendable tradition of Indiana fictive literature, but it dotes on the southern part of the state, venturing no further up-state than Indianapolis, placed dead-center. It is as though the "flat monotonous landscape" characteristic of the Tipton Till Plains surrounding Muncie—lying as it did to the north and east, directly in the path of "the Valders Stadial," the last stage of "Wisconsin glaciation"—was thought as well to characterize the imaginative locale of the Three Muncies. The southern-most regions of the Old Northwest inspired Maurice Thompson's Alice of Old Vincennes and Kenneth Roberts' Northwest Passage. The backwoods years of early statehood are made memorable by Edward Eggleston in The Hoosier Schoolmaster and The Hoosier Schoolboy, while Robert Owen's New Harmony community located in the lower left-hand corner of the state inspired numerous memoirs recalling this important reform movement. The Magnificent Ambersons, Booth Tarkington's novel of refined society in Indianapolis, the state's capitol, received the Pulitzer Prize, while his Penrod narratives image Indiana adolescence as a time of bliss. Hoosier vernacular gained recognition through Frank 'Kin' Hubbard's "Brown County" humor, George Ade's Fables on Slang, and the verse-narratives collected in James Whitcomb Riley's The Old Swimmin' Hole. Even the authors given most notice today by literary critics (Theodore Dreiser and David Graham Phillips) chose to situate their hard-eyed view of society outside the state, perhaps to the advantage of the pride Indiana takes in itself as the pleasant, all-American heartland of hope and prosperity.[20]

Eyed from the position taken by the Indiana literary establishment, as well as by the general run of archaeologists and geologists, the Muncie area stands in uncomfortable relation to "the absent things in American life" drawn up by Henry James as he set the seeming blankness of his native culture over against what one "might enumerate [as] the items of high civilization" existing abroad. That is, the take by the Hoosier state on Delaware County might approximate the "English" assessment of "America" where "everything is left out."[21]

FIGURE 8

It was the gas boom that made Muncie an important literary resource for William Dean Howells. New York City is the main focus of Howells' 1890 novel, The Hazard of New Fortunes, but a lengthy description of the excitements taking place during the late 1880s in and around the town of Moffitt (which I insist is as good a portrait of the Muncie locale as needs be) claims major attention. The following account comes from Fulkerson, the narrative's founder of a new magazine "angeled" by Old Dryfoos, newly rich and recently arrived from Moffitt. Fulkerson "saw the place just when the boom was in its prime" (Hazard, 84–86).

[T]hey took me round everywhere in Moffitt, and showed me their big wells—lit 'em up for a private view, and let me hear them purr with the soft accents of a mass-meeting of locomotives.... They say when they let one of their big wells burn away all winter before they learned how to control it, that well kept up a little summer all around it; the grass staid green, and the flowers bloomed all through the winter. I don't know whether it's so or not. But I can believe anything of natural gas. My! but it was beautiful when they turned on the full force of that well and shot a Roman candle into the gas—that's the way they light it—and a plume of fire about twenty feet wide and seventy-five feet high, all red and yellow and violet, jumped into the sky, and that big roar shook the ground under your feet!

Flowers blooming in winter; rainbow flames across the sky; and "the first thing that strikes you when you come to Moffitt is the notion that there's been a good warm, growing rain, and the town's come up overnight." That's in the suburbs, the annexes, and additions. But it ain't shabby—not shanty-town business; nice brick and frame houses, some of 'em Queen Anne style, and all of 'em looking as if they had come to stay and they've got a lot of new buildings that needn't be ashamed of themselves anywhere; the new court-house is as big as St. Peter's, and the Grand Opera-House is in the highest style of the art.[22]

New industries flooded into the Trenton limestone area to take advantage of the cheap fuel from the gas fields. By 1893 some three-hundred million had been invested in the region (Heiney, 11). Glass factories headed the list, leaping from four in 1880 to twenty-one in 1890 (Beck, 14). [23] Of these, Ball Brothers, once it began to produce Mason Glass Fruit Jars, would become the most important by far. All accounts of the Indiana gas boom highlight the coming of the five Ball brothers from Buffalo (Martin, 7–10; Beck, 22–23; Birmingham). Interesting, that the accuracy of the Lynds's project would be placed in question by later sociologists for their not having taken into account the strong presence of the Ball Company (designated as the unnamed "X" factor) and for slighting the far-reaching influence the family had upon the city's financial, labor, and social history. But whatever the Lynds may have missed about the Balls in their 1929 study, and whatever their lacks in the use of sophisticated sociological methods, they get the highest marks for their Howellsian narrative skills and the sharpness of their perception that in Muncie they had the makings of a good story.

The gas boom and the big dramas that flamed across the region had long since ended by the time the Lynds came to town in 1924. But history kept happening to Muncie.[24] The bits and pieces ("projectile points" made not of chert or mussel shells but of everyday events) were "on site," there for the Lynds to find and fit into an "interpretive framework" as cogent as those traced by material archaeologists or geologists.

Making Cultural Capital of Middletown

This paper does not intend to review the nature of the Lynds' report on Muncie in 1929 or its sequel of 1937. The focus is placed on what it meant over the years to Muncie's citizens to be singled out for attention by a book later listed in Books That Changed America: what it meant, that is, to undergo Wharholian spurts of fame that extended well past a single set of fifteen minutes of national attention. Whether the town liked it or not, Muncie had been chosen as a sociological test case; and almost by accident, since it had originally been placed low on the original list of possible survey sites by a man who was neither an accredited sociologist nor the first choice of his employers. It was all somewhat of a fluke that Muncie became Middletown, but once it was so designated, its citizens had to bear this peculiar fate, both resenting and enjoying it. At first, Munsonians had little or no say on the narratives the outside world imposed upon them, although eventually the city did its best to take some control. Overall, however, Muncie provided material, which certain several individuals and enterprises viewed as a sow's ear, which needed to be converted into prime cultural capital.[25]

On October 29, 1924, the Muncie Evening Press ran a little notice on the second page titled "Nearly Everybody Now Has Car Here: Robert Lynde [sic] Gives Interesting Figures about Muncie in Talk to Kiwanians."[26] Whichever metaphor one chooses (the cat was out of the bag; the lid of Pandora's box opened), this innocuous mention was evidence that Lynd (and his wife, however invisible) were in town to do a "social survey" of Muncie's work and leisure habits.

In 1928 the word got out that a book about "Middletown" was soon to be published. Responses of every kind and from many different quarters began to appear. Robert Benchley's wrote a humorous piece for the Yale Review insisting that "the typical New Yorker" is more of a "real American" than any resident of Muncie. Gilbert Seldes in the Bookman compared the forthcoming Middletown to Sinclair Lewis's Main Street, and found the former more realistic. On its publication in 1929, Middletown elicited further references to Lewis's novels. This time it was Stuart Chase in the New York Herald Tribune who alluded to Babbitt to back up his argument that Muncie residents were part of "The Bewildered Western World," experiencing less control over their individual destinies.

By 1929 the existence of Muncie was recognized by major national publications, both in the United States and abroad in the London Times Literary Supplement; and by well-known commentators like Allan Nevins and H. L. Mencken. This new notoriety was not entirely pleasing: not when Mencken's piece, "A City in Moronia," printed in the American Mercury set up Muncie's citizens as excellent evidence of the typical American's "unbelievable stupidities"; not when John Dewey in the New Republic objected to the deterministic flavor of the "money culture" interpretation laid upon Middletown; not when Raymond Fosdick urged the graduating class of Smith College to avoid lives lived according to the dull uniformity of the Middletown community.[27]

Things calmed down as time passed. On June 13, 1935 the Morning Star mentioned that Robert Lynd had returned to Muncie to do a new survey that would check whether changes had taken place since his original visit. The Post-Democrat testily noted that Lynd had "carved our vitals ten years ago" and that his few days in town were insufficient to make sound judgments, while the Star expressed relief on June 26 that the Lynds had left town undecided whether or not to publish a sequel. Any sense of relief ended, however, in early 1937 with the announcement of the coming publication of Middletown in Transition. Ever hopeful about the positive results of being singled out for cultural fame, the local papers announced the arrival of Margaret Bourke-White, "the Country's Ace Photographer," on assignment by Henry Luce's Life to get images of the town that was once again on the verge of national exposure. When the City Council went "on parade" before this "famous" and "famed" woman, the Morning Star declared that "Muncie is Honored" by Bourke-White's presence in town. It concluded that the residents appreciate the national recognition given to Muncie as "the typical American city," but within the week the Evening Press made the prediction that "Muncie Unlikely to Agree With the Findings of Dr. Lynd," who had been "made the victim of certain community gossips."

The early reviews were mildly negative (Commonweal's piece, "If Rip Van Winkle Awoke," did little to enhance the city's image as a lively center of economic and social growth), but they had nothing like the impact upon Muncie's sense of self-worth effected by Bourke-White photo-essay, "Muncie, Ind. Is the Great 'U.S. Middletown'," appearing in the May 10 issue of Life. The photos were cleverly selected from the hundreds of negatives made by Bourke-White, and cleverly laid-out for maximum effectiveness as an entertaining expose of Haves and Have Nots (one of the Ball couples seated in style in the drawing room of their Tudor-style home placed in contrast to a work-worn pair "at home" in their chicken-coop dwelling). The visualizations were a mix of Grant Wood with a touch of Thomas Hart Benton and the Farm Security Administration photographs of Walker Evans and Dorothea Lange, but the resulting tone was more farcical than sympathetic; more eager to "get a good story" than to provide a balanced overview.

Munsonians were not pleased with how the world was asked to view their town. But should they not have known by then what it means to live under another's eye: the journalist's camera or the cultural anthropologist's notes? On the first pages of Middletown Lynd stated his credo:

> A clew to the securing both of the maximum objectivity and of some kind of orderly procedure in such a maze [that confronts all attempts at "a total-situation study of a contemporary civilization"] may be found in the approach of the cultural anthropologist.

Lynd allowed that:

> To many of us who might be quite willing to discuss dispassionately the quaintly patterned ways of behaving that make up the customs of uncivilized peoples, it is distinctly distasteful to turn with equal candor to the life of which we are a local ornament. Yet nothing can be more en-lightening than to gain precisely that degree of objectivity and perspective with which we view "savage" peoples.[28]

Muncie's savage breasts continued to be soothed and ruffled throughout 1937 by the various "interpretive frameworks" laid upon it by such contemporary notables as Malcolm Cowley, Alvin Johnson, and Howard Mumford Jones, as well as a man from Vienna who was excited by the fame accruing to the town where his relatives, the Scherbaums, lived. The peace of public indifference by the outside world gave relief during the 1940s, 1950s, and 1960s (though there were occasional inquiries about how Munsonians reacted to World War II and its immediate aftermath). A new wrinkle was added once students at Ball State University (and later those from other academic institutions) began to write dissertations on the community. Muncie also became a check-point for television newscasters, desirously to read its cultural pulse re the Vietnam War and other agitations.[29] Only at this point did members of the local population start to take aspects of the Muncie story into their own hands. Yet three of these accounts came from members of the Ball family: one, the history of the Ball Company by a son of the original dynasty; another, the dissertation written by one of the sons-in-law; the third, a privately printed memoir by one of the granddaughters.[30] Not the sort of tales to which the scholarly mind can give much credence; more in the line of the Walam Odum, perhaps. These were voices on the wind, in any case, since the Ball Corporation's highly diversified activities were relocated in Colorado in the 1950s, with all local plants closed down in 1963.

A major turn-around came when The Center for Middletown Studies initiated in 1980, its activities soon institutionalized by Ball State University, helping to counterbalance the "Middletown III" project begun in 1975 by outsiders financed through the National Science Foundation, and the Black Middletown Survey of 1981. If publications like Time, Money, and Now (a British magazine) took interest, and Middletown studies were absorbed by scholarly periodicals in Paris and Brussels, the "natives" sought to be seen if not heard.

Nonetheless, no one in Muncie was prepared for the fire-storm that resulted in 1982 when PBS ran the six-part "Middletown" series (originally intended as a seven-episode offering until "Seventeen" was blocked from airing by a group of Muncie citizens because of its too-close-to-the-bone depiction of high-school sexuality, race tensions, and improper language). The rocky development of this series under the hands of its director, Peter Davis, and the members of the local Middletown Film Series, constitutes a fascinating tale in itself, in which several interpretations contend as the final reason for "Middletown, The Movie," and the failures and successes of the enterprise.[31] Consider, however, the match between the difficulties faced by material archaeologists who attempt "to obtain knowledge about human life and culture," as described by a study of prehistoric Indiana, and the challenges met only in part by the PBS television series in the 1980s.

The details of social organization, political organization, and religious ritual, among other social attributes, may be only dimly perceived, if at all, because the materials that survive are often insufficient to document such practices (Kellar 10)

Since the late 1980s, the Middletown scene has been relatively quiet. An exhibit of "The Middletown Photographs" was held at the Ball State Art Gallery, followed by their publication in Magic Middletown. The Center of Middletown Studies keeps finding worthy projects to sponsor. Dissertations are written on such topics as "Testing Coalition Theory in The Great Gatsby and the Babbitt Trilogy" using methods for analysis followed by the Middletown III scholars. Bibliographical listings record the frequent references made to the Lynds and the subsequent visitations made to psychologize the city. But frankly, Muncie has nothing that lures tourists to other cultural sites, such as Williamsburg in Virginia, Niagara Falls in New York or Greenfield Village in Michigan. It is a very nice town in a pretty region of the state, but as an Indiana locale it offers none of the attractions of, say, Columbus, Indiana, that phenomenal cultural site brought into being by the Cummins Engine Foundation.[32] Flamboyant, flaming gas fields no longer exist. Turkey Run, Spring Mill, McCormick's Creek, the Dunes, Tippecanoe Battlefield, the Lincoln Boyhood Monument, New Harmony, Brown County—Indiana's many state parks and pleasure-grounds—are far from the vicinity of Middletown. Yet people come to Muncie, although not as family groups on vacation checking into the local Holiday Inn intent on seeing local sights. They have come ever since the Lynds stumbled upon the town, making it "a field of dreams" (sometimes nightmares) for scholars, reporters, and documentary film-makers who arrive to reap the special cultural capital it has to offer.

Whatever narrative forms are seized upon to tell tales about the Three Muncies, none command the expressive style of the sentence with its prideful cadences taken from a history of Delaware County set down in 1881. Listen to the words by which this narrator announces his happy task:

> To recall in brief review in successive steps in the march of civilization as developed in the local changes wrought by the progress of the star of empire westward bound, is the province of the historian in this most inviting field.[33]

Twentieth-century accounts (whether their medium is prose, photography, film-images) are driven to the nervous use (verbal or visual) commas, colons, parentheses, and scare-quotes—any device that imposes qualifications, doubts, hesitations, indeterminacies upon their material. Long gone is faith in Muncie's place in "the progress of the star of empire," the faith that enabled the prose of 1881 to roll, unimpeded, "in the march of civilization . . . westward bound." The language that defines the Three Muncies does not strive for sublimnity. Rather, the many rhetorics imposed upon this particular social phenomenon insist on averageness; but an averageness that is extraordinary, nonetheless. After all, as even Henry James was willing to concede after lining out "the absent things in American life," "The American [add, Munsonian] know that a good deal remains—that is his secret, his joke, as one may say"(James, Hawthorne,[38]).

NOTES

[1] Let me inform readers that I was born and raised in Muncie, one very small resident of the city at the time the Lynds first arrived. Almost all the data used in this paper comes from sources available to anyone from anywhere. Certain facts, however, derived from personal knowledge or are gleaned from special contacts I have in Muncie. Whether any biases have seeped into this project, it is impossible to say for certain. Nonetheless, warmth of interest is no doubt apparent.

[2] The first surveyor of the Old Northwest Territory, and one of its original land speculators, was George Rogers Clark, who worked for the Ohio Company. He was the elder brother of William Clark who later joined Meriwether Lewis in the surveying expedition of 1803-06 that opened up the "new" Northwest Territory. A convenient survey of the stages of the settlement of this region (by both Indians and whites) is in Haimbaugh, History of Delaware County, vol. 1, 46-48.

[3] This paragraph draws from basic information that traces the succession of settlements by both Indians and whites leading up to Muncie's founding included in You Are Because They Are, a little pamphlet compiled by Mary Frances Abel from material massed by Muncie's Paul Revere Chapter of the Daughters of the American Revolution. A more complete account (albeit clearly biased against the "savage" Delawares) is contained in Haimbaugh, Vol. 1, 55-56, 60, 88.

[4] The account of the haphazard manner in which the Lynds chose Muncie as the site of their study, and how the Lynds were chosen to serve as its analysts, has been carefully told on several occasions by Dwight W. Hoover, founding director of the Center for Middletown Studies. Hoover's "Middletown: The Studies," is his detailed introduction to Middletown. The Making of a Documentary Film Series.

[5] See Ronald L. Baker and Marvin Carmony, Indiana Place Names, 111 (also Baker's From Needmore to Prosperity, Hoosier Place Names); Jacob Piatt Dunn, True Indian Stories with Glossary of Indiana Indian Names: 260, 285, Haimbaugh, History of Delaware County, I: 45, 50, 67-69; A Book of Indiana, 408.

[6] Key information is available in James A. Kellar, An Introduction to the Prehistory of Indiana, B. K. Swartz, Jr., Indiana's Prehistoric Past, John. D. Barnhart and Dorothy Riker, Indiana to 1816, William A. Wilson, Indiana. A History, and Native American Cultures in Indiana, ed. Ronald Hicks.

[7] Barnhart and Riker, 16; subsequent pagination within parentheses. Kellar defines archaeology as "a scientific activity designed to obtain knowledge about human life and culture during the long time interval" designated as prehistory – "that period in human experience before the invention of writing systems" (10).

[8] Julia Henderson Levering, Historic Indiana, 1916.

[9] See Haimbaugh, I: 45-55. Further information supplied by David Agee Hoar's preface to "The Greenville Treaty 1795" discussed by Helen Hornbeck Tanner, and by "Ethnohistory of Indian Use and Occupancy in Ohio and Indiana Prior to 1795" by Erminie Wheeler-Voeglin, authors of Indians of Ohio and Indiana Prior to 1795. In Kellar's words (18), the Walam Olum is "a series of mnemonic signs which reportedly were in the possession of the Delaware Indians and chronicled the movement of the Algonquian-speaking Indians from Asia into the New World." (Also see Dunn's chapter on the Walam Olum.) Kellar underscores the consequences of the disjunction between the evidence for which archaeologists search and its general absence in the Indiana landscape. Connecting "prehistory to history requires that American Indian ethnic groups be identifiable through unique house styles, pottery, tools, or other material objects accessible to archaeologists. However, in Indiana, no such body of data exists, or is it likely to be recovered, since the historically documented groups were late migrants into the region. And by the time they had entered the state the native material culture had been all but replaced by items of European manufacture. The archaeologist/historian is faced with an impossible task in the quest for ethnic identification in Indiana" (61-62).

[10] Tanner (4-6) reviews the consequences of the Iroquois Wars that lasted fifty years from their start in 1648. The turmoil of these years, primarily struggles for domination over the Great lakes fur trade carried on between rival Indian tribes, and by the Indians against the French, British, and Dutch, had severe and lasting consequences for the Indians of the Old Northwest. Tribal populations were drastically altered, refugee bands fled from their camp sites, and separate tribal identitites were destroyed, as French and British forces entered into the void caused by these upheavals.

[11] In 1779 the Delawares presented a formal protest to Congress, asking for return of territory they had "long inhabited and Hunted on," including lands that extended up "the River Wabachee [Wabash] to that Branch call'd Opecomeecah [White River]," lands where they had "seated our Grand Children the Shawnees upon in our laps." In return, the Delawares agreed to give "to the United States of America, such a part of the above described country, as will be convenient to them and Us, that they may have room for their Children's Children to sit down upon." From Wheeler-Voeglin (II: 502), which cites the Wisconsin Historical Collections (XXIII: 320-21). As it turned out, the future residents of Muncie on the bend of the White River would have "room for their Children's Children," with none left for the Delawares. No more would the Delawares enjoy "settled town life" or experience continuities of "institutions having a religious-political function." As Haimbaugh states baldly in his 1924 History of Delaware County, "But the white man came, with desire in his heart to possess these lands. And the white man won and the red man departed, and of the latter we have only the name to remind us of his former occupancy of these lands. The savage had to go. There was no place for him here" (I: 46).

[12] See Wilson (38-39) and Dunn (214-252) for descriptions of the Trail of Death in 1838. Menominee, chief of the Potawatomis (the tribe, that together with the Delawares and Miamis, originally occupied the Indiana territory) and eight-hundred and fifty-nine of his people were rounded up by troops under General John Tipton. By the time this "caravan of exiles" reached the Illinois border, scores had already died; survivors were herded into Kansas. One hundred and fifty perished during the two month trek. A monument to Menominee now stands near Plymouth, Indiana, at the site where he was lassoed and sent with his people into permanent exile.

[13] Tanner (28) cites these figures, taken from The Indian Population of the United States and Alaska, 1930.

[14] In 1791 Little Turtle led the Miamis, Shawnees, and Delawares in victory against American forces in the southeastern region. So severe was the defeat that some in Congress were ready to give up all claims to land north of the Ohio River. President Washington refused to comply and gave General Anthony Wayne command of five thousand troops. After Wayne's victory at the Battle of Fallen Timbers, Little Turtle, together with the Delaware chief, Buckongahelas, were forced to attend a council in Greenville; there, the Treaty of 1795 signed over half of Ohio and a long strip of eastern Indiana to the Americans. Tecumseh, the Shawnee chief, did not agree with the capitulations he felt had been made by Little Turtle. He marshalled forces to resist white settlement, but in 1811 at the Battle of Tippecanoe, the Indians led by The Prophet, twin brother of Tecumseh, were routed by the troops of William Henry Harrison, governor of the Indiana Territory. Harrison's political fortunes were made, and Tecumseh's pan-Indian movement was lost. Corydon was named the new capital of the territory in 1813 and later as capital of the newly formed state in 1816 (named by the choice of its inhabitants). Indian resistance continued into the 1830s, but to no avail. (See Wilson, 30-38)

[15] In relating his version of the Muncie Creation Myth, Thomas B. Helm's history of Delaware County singles out the trading-post started by Gilbert in the Mississinewa River area in the northern part of the country. Gilbert "was fortunate enough to be robbed by the Indians, in a drunken row, and his wife, during the melee, was struck with a hatchet and slightly wounded." Fortunate, because Gilbert was awarded two thousand dollars by the local government agency, which deducted this amount from the annuity assigned by the United States to the Delawares. Using these unexpected funds, Gilbert bought the Hackley Reserve, which had, as stated earlier, been given as a reward to the grandaughter of Little Turtle by the white authorities. What goes around, comes around!

[16] Frederick F. McClellan, Muncie attorney, managed to put together a parade, aided by the local D. A. R. Chapter and some of the original pioneers. It was claimed that "civic and political turmoil" distracted Muncie's attention from the significance of the Centennial, and that local "business interests behind a dollars-and-cents

enterprise" that touted the industrial growth of "Magic City" took priority over Indiana history. See Harlow Lindley, The Indiana Centennial, 1916 (106-107).

[17] These notations appear in Petroleum and Natural Gas in Indiana, the "preliminary report" of 1920 supplied by W. N. Logan, State Geologist, to the Department of Conservation, Division of Geology (50). The strata overlying Trenton limestone (whose thickness varies from 470-586 feet) are the Cincinnatian, the Silurian, the Devonian, the New Albany, and the Missisippian (53). The number of wells drilled at and near Muncie by 1920, as well as figures on wells abandoned by this date, are given on pages 85-86. Logan's report also treats the reasons for assuming a common origin for petroleum and natural gas, and gives the rates of production for each, which peaked in 1904 and 1902 respectively (18, 20, 85). Logan's Introduction is a stern warning against "quacks" who live by the "diving rod" and the "witching" method, practices that led to the "unscrupulous" bilking of ignorant investors in fraudulent oil fields. "No industry is more dependent upon science than is the petroleum industry upon the science of geology. The petroleum and natural gas industry of Indiana is of so much importance to the industrial development of the State that it should be given every aid which this science can supply for the solution of its problems" (10). The prehistory of natural history is outlined in J. W. Heiney, The Story of the Indiana Gas Company, Inc., and Bill Beck, Natural Gas for the Hoosier State. Gas street lighting in the early nineteenth-century relied on manufactured gas (commonly created by roasting coal); by the 1860s, gas was introduced into the home for the purposes of lighting. Indiana had several coal-gas companies in place before 1886, but the natural gas discovered in the Indiana field was enormous. By 1889 and expanse of 5,000 square miles (with Muncie and Anderson at the center) was yelding vast quantities of the colorless, usually odorless gas. It is estimated that between 1886 and 1915, nearly one trillion cubic feet came from the Trenton field in Indiana. Consider that the total amount of natural gas consumed in the United States in 1970 came to 22 trillion cubic feet (Heiney 10-11). Note that archaeologists will (albeit quietly) rhapsodize over the Red Ocher used in burial artifacts found in the Tipton Till Plains region (Swarz 14), while geologists care most about the gas deposits that lie beneath the ocher in the Trenton limestone layer.

[18] See Heiney, 10-12, Beck, 10-16, Book of Indiana, 407-410; and Haimbaugh, I: 386.

[19] Logan, as State Geologist, lacked flamboyance in his written report on Indiana's natural gas fields, but his analaysis and charts vividly convey a harsh tale of the end of this great natural resource (21-24). Also see John Bartlow Martin, "The Gas Boom" (4-11) and J. C. Leach, "Decline of the Field" (11-18), from The Hoosier State, ed. Ralph D. Gray. Other consequences of the boom were less festive than those celebrated by Heiney and Beck. Below the surface, natural gas is at high pressure. "At one drilling site in the late 1880s rocks as big as hen's eggs gushed out of a hole at Hartford City [twenty miles from Muncie], and the drilling crew watched helpless as 50 million cubic feet of gas a day escaped as they attempted to pack the

runaway well," while "residents of Anderson, Muncie and other towns in the gas belt became depressingly familiar with gas explosions from leaking pipes that could level whole city blocks" (Beck 12-13). Then there was the warning uttered from the Indianapolis pulpit of Reverend David Swing that natural gas would lead to the end of the moral and natural order; and the prediction made by an Indianapolis doctor that eye disease would greatly increase as a result of the drying qualities of natural gas heat (Beck 13).

[20] See Meredith Nicholson, The Hoosiers; Hoosier Caravan and Indiana Authors and Their Books, 1815-1916, both compiled by R. E. Banta; Donald E. Thompson, Indiana Authors and Their Books, 1967-1980. Indiana realists include Charles Austin Beard and Mary Ritter Beard, noted home-bred historians, who turned their attention to the charting of patterns of economic and political motivation that cut across larger swathes of American history than Indiana could encompass. But A Hoosier Holiday (1916) reveals that even Theodore Dreiser could express those pangs of nostalgia that tended to keep Indiana authors from taking a harder look at the actual conditions of the lives led by its citizens. In light of the Muncie experience, consider the nostalgic title of Mary Frances Abel's little chronicle, You Are Because They Were and the words placed on Haimbaugh's dedication page, "This Work is Respectfully Dedicated to THE PIONEERS Long Since Departed" and "'Remember the days of old./Consider the years of many generations.'" In contrast, Wilbur Sutton's "Muncie, City of Progress," states, "The early history of Muncie is not important, perhaps, except as supplying a background for the present .... 'Those who deal in reminiscenses,' says an ancient Greek motto, 'are fearful of present facts" (Book of Indiana 407). Whatever Sutton's admonitions, nostalgia and fantasy were the most profitable literary commodities coming out of the Hoosier state prior to the Lynds' recapitulation of the "Middletown" ethos. Indiana's authors published an inordinate amount of children's books and escape literature: Nathaniel Moore Banta, compiler of the Brownie books, Martha Finley, perpetrator of the Elsie Dinsmore series, Annie Fellows Johnston, writer of The Little Colonel Books, Booth Tarkington's Penrod sagas, Clara Ingram Judson, author of the many Mary Jane titles, and Gene Stratton Porter's A Girl of the Limberlost and Freckles. The highly popular escape-artists were George Barr McCutcheon (Graustark), Charles Major (When Knighthood Was In Flower). William Vaughn Moody (all those ethereal verse-dramas), Lew Wallace (Quo Vadis and The Fair God), and Tarkington (Monsieur Beaucaire). (See R. E. Banta, Indiana Authors and Their Books.) Since Hoosiers preferred to fableize the southern regions of the state, Ross Lockridge, Jr.'s best-selling Raintree County rightly takes its place in this romance traditon. The desire to flee the land of the average would later send masters of dream-desire such as Cole Porter, Halston, Bill Blass, and James Dean into early exile from their home state. But in any case, Munsonians eventually nurtured their own memories; usually romantic, yet on at least one occasion, notably harsh. The first was Emily Kimbrough, daughter of one of the town's oldest, most elite families, educated at Bryn Mawr and the Sorbonne, with editorial experience at the Ladies Home Journal, and co-author with Cornelia Otis Skinner of Our Hearts Were Young and Gay. The

titles of Kimbrough's memoirs, How Dear To My Heart (1944) and The Innocents from Indiana (1950), suggest the light-hearted approach she took to social frolics that could have taken place in almost any mid-western town of the period between the two world wars. It is painful to set Kimbrough's charming accounts of growing up as a privileged white girl over against Gregory Williams' 1998 autobiography, Life on the Color Line, The True Story of a White Boy Who Discovered He Was Black. Brought at age ten to Muncie in 1954, Williams is informed by his father that he is black and that it is as black that he must live. Muncie has also had its flush of privately-published poets: Thomas Thornburg, Saturday, Town and Other Poems (1976), a series of publications by Charles F. Coldwater, M.D. (pseud. Philip Ball, son of our family doctor, in 1978, 1979, and 1980), titled Coldwater Runs Deep, Middletown and Normal City, and The Ghost of Gas Boom Past; and Growing Up in Middletown by Bob Cunningham (1982). But let me observe that "the fantasy of the ordinary" is also at work in most accounts that try to counter "fantasies of the extraordinary."

[21] James, Hawthorne, 37-38.

[22] Featured in Leslie's Illustrated Newspaper of May 4, 1889, Muncie's courthouse was erected in 1887, later demolished in 1966 and replaced in 1969 by a "modern" shoe-box building. [Figure 8] If Gilbert's wilderness trading-post of 1827 can be likened to The Jail eulogized by William Faulkner in his telling of the Yoknapatawpha County Creation Myth (see Requiem for a Nun), Muncie's courthouse of 1887 was the town's icon for established respectability. The Wysor Grand Opera House opened in 1892 (its photograph is included in Hoover's Magic Middletown). See Abel (28-31) for a house tour of Muncie's most distinctive domestic architecture dating from the late 1890s into the early 1900s. Note that this tour includes both an Underground Railroad Station (circa 1855) and the future headquarters of a branch of the Ku Klux Klan in the 1920s. Notation of other changes that came to Muncie in the aftermath of the gas boom are given in Martin's piece (7); by the end of 1886 a syndicate bought real estate worth $150,000, Muncie was being called the "Birmingham of the North," rents rose, houses were in short supply, James Boyce erected a brick building with a ninety-six foot front equipped with plate glass windows, and Indianapolis newspapers took note of a "thriving city of eight thousand." On May 11, 1887, Muncie's newspaper reported "1,136 Strangers in the City. Men of Wealth and Influence Seeking Locations. Real Estate Men Busy and All is Serene" (Birmingham 68). In the same year the paper boasted that speculators found "not a Hoosier village but an Indiana city" (Martin 7).. "Once the hoopla died down, real progress began" (Birmingham 71) Reality necessarily replaced the excitements of fantasy once the gas wells gave out. But as Wilbur Sutton has it, Muncie possessed the right "spirit" and "unbounded faith in herself," and so won through. Compare the anxious views held by Henry James in The American Scene as he wandered the streets of New York City, the place that did not believe in itself. Whatever the faith, the facts are thus: between 1886 and 1900, Muncie's population increased four-fold, up to 20,942; between 1900 and 1910, a period of staganation set in as the smaller industries folded. Between 1910-1920

there was a surge in population and the establishment of new industries, with a 50% rise in population. Only because of this spurt was it possible for Muncie to be considered for the Small-City Survey the Lynds were asked to record since a 35% increase was mandated by the sponsoring Committee on Social and Religious Surveys.

[23] The importance of the infant automotive industry on the local economy must not be overlooked. Although Michigan became the center once the Ford Company, together with General Motors and the other auto manufacturers, won out over Indiana in wars of competition, the state had been at the heart of the earliest innovations. See Beck (31) on Elwood Hayes, and the building of Indiana's first car in 1894; and Hayes on his own ventures in Gray's Hoosier State (69). Muncie drew a number of auto-parts manufacturers which strenghtened the town's industrial base.

[24] For the story of how Muncie dealth with a smallpox epidemic in 1893 that placed the town under quarantine, and with the imposition of martial law in 1908 during a local strike, see M. Banta, "Medical Therapies and the Body Politic," Prospects 8 1983: 105-106 – further examples of how history continues to stir up lives lived by the averages. From the view of Muncie's self-designated historians down to the time the Lynds arrived in 1929, "history" was defined as "biography" –specifically, the success-stories of "representative men" written in the Chamber of Commerce prose-style satirized by Sinclair Lewis. Archaeologists, geologists, and sociologists like the Lynds coming after 1929 had to present Indiana and Middletown stories by means of narratives quite different in kind from the biographies that make up a large part of the bulk of the earlier histories compiled by Helm (1881). A Portrait and Biographical Record of Delaware and Randolph Counties (1894), A Twentieth Century History of Delaware County (1908), Haimbaugh (1924), and A Book of Indiana (1929).

[25] Dwight W. Hoover relates the quirky story of how the Lynds were brought to Muncie in the first place. The Cripple Creek Massacre brought shame and embarrassment to John D. Rockefeller, Jr.; he sought to assuage his guilt by founding and funding the Committee on Social and Religious Surveys in 1923. The committee first named the sociologist William Louis Bailey of Northwestern University to inaugurate the Small City Survey, then decided against him and picked Robert S. Lynd. Lynd was no sociologist but rather a recipient of a degree from the Union Theological Seminary and the author in 1922 of a sharp attack against Rockefeller's treatment of the miners in his company's employ. Lynd first considered making a survey of South Bend, Indiana, then added Decatur, Illinois, and Kokomo, Indiana to his list, before deciding to try Muncie. See Hoover, "Middletown Again," Prospects 15 (1990): 445-486; reprised in his 1992 introduction to Middletown. The Making of a Documentary Film Series.

[26] This and the following items are drawn from Middletown. An Annotated Bibliography, eds. David C. Tambo, Dwight W. Hoover, and John D. Hewitt.

[27] Fosdick's denunciation adds another irony to the Middletown saga. It was Fosdick (brother of the well-known minister, Harry Emerson Fosdick) who, as John D. Rockefeller, Jr.'s lawyer, had urged Rockefeller to name Lynd as the head of the Small-City Survey. When Middletown was published, however, Fosdick became one of its strongest critics (Hoover Film, 4-6).

[28] Middletown, 3-5.

[29] NBC kept its eye on Muncie throughout the decade. The crew for the "Huntley-Brinkley Report" came in 1970; in 1978 and 1980 the "Today" crew stopped by. In 1979 a Finnish film crew made a documentary on the Middletown phenomenon.

[30] Edmund B. Ball, a history of the Ball Corporation; Alexander E. Bracken, Jr. (husband of one of the Ball daughters), an early history of Muncie in the period prior to the gas boom; Lucina Ball Moxley, a memoir that comments on the negative impact caused by the Lynds' studies on the family's privacy and reputation.

[31] Hoover relates his side of the story in Middletown, The Making of a Documentary Film Series in a manner that persuades this reader that his account is as accurate as is possible for such a tangled situation. I must admit my own, quite accidental, involvement in the project. I had not lived in Muncie for several years when I was asked to serve on an NEH Media Committee. It happened that the Davis documentary was among the proposals I was asked to evaluate. (At that time no one at the NEH knew that Muncie was my home town.) I find in reading Hoover's account that his own views coincide with the reservations I voiced at the time of the Media Committee's meeting. We both wished to use the occasion of a documentary to mount a reasonably accurate "historical" and/or "sociological" appraisal of the various foci planned for the series, which included politics, religion, employment, education, marriage, sports. David opted to stress dramatic story over historic accuracy or analysis. Local particulars were sacrificed for a more impressionistic and universalized view. Indeed, David had originally selected Hamilton, Ohio, as the site for his next film project. Even when the scene was switched to Muncie, Davis saw no problem in his conflation of the properties of two quite different communities. The film series that resulted was very good for its kind. The question remains open whether that "kind" continued to distort the (admittedly impossible) task of "knowing Muncie."

[32] See Robert Campbell's "Modernism on Main Street," Preservation (September-October 1998): 38-45, for a recent assessment of what it means for a small, out-of-the-way Indiana community to become the site of some of the most exciting twentieth-century architectural structures in the nation.

[33] Helm, from his introduction to "Township History," in History of Delaware County. The oratorical grandeur of Helm's sentences are replaced in 1924 by Haimbaugh's blunt statement, "And this, all too briefly, is the story of the coming of

the Delawares to this region and of their going. The white man needed their lands"
(I: 67).

Post Script: "The Three Muncies" was delivered on April 15, 2000, at the conference
of the European Association for American Studies in Graz, Austria. I returned to Los
Angeles late on April 18. On the morning of April 19, the front page of the Los
Angeles Times featured an article titled "'New Economy' Deepens the Wealth
Divide," by-lined by Mary William Walsh reporting from Muncie, Indiana, on how
that economy is "affecting different groups in wildly different ways." The extensive
article goes on to state: "Muncie is a natural place to watch these forces at work.
More than 75 years ago–during another economic boom—a husband and wife
research team picked Muncie as the quintessential American town for their study of
go-go growth's impact on middle America. Robert and Helen Lynd produced an
exhaustive account, called 'Middletown,' of how the Roaring '20s had enriched the
few at the expense of the many." It never lets up, this compulsion to return again and
again to Muncie, whose cultural capital has yet to run dry, as had the natural gas
wells all those years ago.

WORKS CITED

Abel, Mary Frances. You Are Because They Were. Muncie, Ind.: Royal Printing Co., 1976.

Baker, Ronald L. From Needmore to Prosperity. Hoosier Place Names in Folklore and History. Bloomington, Ind.: Indiana UP, 1995.

Baker, Ronald L. and Marvin Carmony. Indiana Place Names. Bloomington, Ind.: Indiana UP, 1975.

Banta, Martha. 'Medical Therapies and the Body Politic.' Prospects. The Annual of American Culture Studies, vol. 8, 59–128. New York: Cambridge UP, 1983.

Banta, Richard E. Hoosier Caravan A Treasury of Indiana Life and Lore, selected with comment. Bloomington, Ind.: Indiana UP, 1975.

Barnhart, John D. and Dorothy L. Riker. Indiana to 1816. The Colonial Period. Indianapolis: Indiana Historical Society, 1971.

Beck, Bill. Natural Gas for the Hoosier State. An Illustrated History of Indiana Gas Company Inc., 1945–1995. Indianapolis: Indiana Gas Company, 1995.

Birmingham, Frederick A. Ball Corporation. The First Century. Indianapolis: Curtis, 1980.

Campbell, Robert. 'Modernism on Main Street.' Preservation (September–October 1998), 38–45.

Downs, Robert B. Books That Changed America. New York: Macmillan, 1970.

Dunn, Jacob Piatt. True Indian Stories with Glossary of Indiana Indian Names. Indianapolis: Sentinel, 1909.

Gray, Ralph D., ed. The Hoosier State. Readings in Indiana History. The Modern Era. Grand Rapids: Eerdmans, 1980.

Haimbaugh, Frank D. History of Delaware County. Indiana. 2 vols. Indianapolis: Historical Publishing Company, 1924.

Helm, Thomas B. History of Delaware County, Indiana, with Illustrations and Biographical Sketches. Chicago: Kingman, 1881.

Hick, Ronald, ed. Native American Cultures in Indiana: Proceedings of the First Minnetrista Council for Great Lakes Native American Studies. Muncie, Ind.: Ball State University, 1992.

Hoover, Dwight W. Magic Middletown. Bloomington, Ind., Indiana UP, 1986.

Hoover, Dwight W. .'Middletown Again,' Prospects. The Annual of American
    Cultural Studies, ed. Jack Salzman, vol. 15, 445–486. New York: Cambridge
    UP, 1990.

Hoover, Dwight W. Middletown. The Making of a Documentary Film Series. Chur,
    Switzerland: Harwood, 1992.

Howells, William Dean. A Hazard of New Fortunes. Bloomington, Ind.: Indiana UP,
    1976.

Hubbard, Kin, ed. A Book of Indiana. The Story of What Has Been Described as the
    Most American State in the American Democracy. Told In Terms of
    Biography. Indianapolis: Indiana Biographical Association, 1929.

Indiana Authors and Their Books, 1816–1916, compiled by R. E. Banta.
    Crawfordsville, Ind.: Wabash College, 1949.

Kellar, James H. An Introduction to the Prehistory of Indiana. Indianapolis: Indiana
    Historical Society, 1983.

Kemper, G. W. H., ed. A Twentieth Century History of Delaware County. 2 vols.
    Chicago: Lewis, 1908.

Levering, Julia Henderson. Historic Indiana. New York: Putnam's, 1916.

Lindley, Harlow, ed. The Indiana Centennial. 1916. A Record of the Celebration of
    the One Hundredth Anniversary of Indiana's Admission to Statehood.
    Indianapolis: Indiana Historical Commission, 1919.

Logan, W. N. 'Petroleum and Natural Gas in Indiana.' The Department of
    Conservation. State of Indiana. No. 8. Fort Wayne, Ind.: Fort Wayne Printing
    Company, 1920.

Lynd, Robert S. and Helen M. Lynd. Middletown: A Study in Contemporary
    American Culture. New York: Harcourt Brace Jovanovich, 1929, 1957.

Michael, Ronald L. Bibliography of Literature on Indiana Archaeology. ed. B. K.
    Swartz, Jr. Muncie, Ind.: Ball State University, 1969.

A Portrait and Biographical Record of Delaware and Randolph Counties. Chicago:
    Bowen, 1894.

Swartz, B. K. Jr. Indiana's Prehistoric Past. Muncie, Ind.: Ball State University, 1973.

Tambo, David C., Dwight W. Hoover, and John D. Hewitt. Middletown. An Annotated Bibliography. New York: Garland, 1988.

Tanner, Helen Hornbeck and Erminie Wheeler-Voeglin. Indians of Ohio and Indiana Prior to 1795. 2 vols. New York: Garland, 1974.

Thompson, Donald E. Indiana Authors and Their Books, 1967–1980. Crawfordsville, Ind.: Wabash College, 1981.

Wilson, William E. Indiana. A History. Bloomington, Ind.: Indiana UP, 1966.

"Mathematic of Creation": Lane, Olson, and the Problem of Loss

Tadeusz Sławek
University of Silesia

Mourning consists always in attempting to ontologize remains.

Jacques Derrida.

1.

We are concerned with a certain topography: one cannot attentively read a sign or carefully look at an image without the operation of grounding which destroys their transparency and silkiness. What is interpreted cracks the surface of transluscence and disturbs the thinness, or fleshlessness, of the everyday. Clarity becomes blurred, perceptive glance is born out of obstructed vision, and reality loses its vitreous smoothness. In the everyday there is no topo-graphy of signs because (a) they are not supposed to leave traces on the glassy structure of the world which they constitute, there is no *graphie* of signs, and (b) therefore they cannot occupy any specific *topos* on a smooth and transparent surface of the everyday.

In the most general sense, we could say that what distinguishes a poetic or painterly image from our observations of the quotidian reality is the absence of a geo- or rather GRAMMOgraphy. No placing of signs is possible in the everyday where signs function due to their "facades" of generally recognized, remembered rather than carefully inspected, meanings; and where they do not display to the viewer an intricate system of relationships holding among them and between them and the world. Thus, both literature and painting must, on a certain level of analysis, become a metaphysics of vision, leading us from a permanent and "flat" to an impermanent and "all round" perception. Using Merleau-Ponty's terminology, we could claim that the movement of vision takes place in the field of polarities between the frontal view (in the everyday) and the in-depth perception (in poetry or painting): "There is that which reaches the eye head on, the frontal properties of the visible; but there is also that which reaches it from below—the profound postural latency whereby the body raises itself to see—and that which reaches vision from above like the phenomena of flight, of swimming, of movement, where it participates no longer in the heaviness of origins but in free accomplishments" (Johnson and Smith 147).

We can see that the idea of placing inherent in GRAMMOgraphy lets the invisible ("postural latency") into the structure of the visible, thereby puncturing the present with the absent. It thus allows for such a placing of signs which, on the one hand, takes into account all dimensions and directions ("frontal", "below", "above") but, on the other hand, does not lock it up in the irreversibility of one specific place or *topos*. On the contrary, it liberates it both from a strict unidirectionality of reasoning (which always wants to get back to a clearly determined "origin") and from the permanence of one location in which the accepted meaning seals off the sign (Merleau-Ponty's Nietzschean critique of "heaviness"). Grammmography discovers the importance of place in the general placelessness of the everyday (Olson: "a place as a term in the order of creation.... is worth more than a metropolis"; Olson 1970).

2.

The visible is constituted by the work of the invisible within its territory; the articulate is founded upon the labour of the inarticulate. In this way our vision discovers two sides of an image: First, that which is "ready" and "finished" (and as such becomes subject to economic transactions of exchange, semiotic parity of the signifier and the signified, as well as aesthetic operations of collecting, etc.). Second, that which is present, which is "there" but only through absence marked by what has been omitted, left out. The work, the deed, the event of the image are due to what does not happen there. This is what Charles Olson, a formative intellectual authority behind new American poetries of the 1950s and 1960s, recognizes as a cornerstone of his approach towards the painterly images of his Gloucester compatriot Fitz Hugh Lane (see Wilmerding 1971 and 1988; Novak on Luminism). In a poem celebrating the hundredth anniversary of Lane's death, Olson offers us the following interpretative work:

> When I think of what Fitz Lane didn't do
> painting all this light which almost
> each day is enough, at least at twilight,
> to rouse one as a change of air does
> to the direct connection our lives bear
> to the mathematic of Creation surrounding us,
> I love him the more for his attempts pre-
> Hawthorne to draw in silk the pinks and
> umbrous hills and rocks surround
> on this reflexive and reflexing
> Harbor-light sits under one's eye
> & being as the saucer to the in
> the instance of this evening high al-
> most exactly perfect half moon al-
> ready going westward too. (<u>Archaeologist of Morning</u>)

We shall not be able to do justice to the intricacy of either the poem or the painting. What we can do is only set out a few methodological lines which will help to delineate a theory of vision as GRAMMOgraphy (a science which reads not only signs as traces but is concerned with traces left by signs) and man as the geo-graphic subject.

(a) One should not let the opening verb go unnoticed: the work of seeing is a labour of thought. There can be no true practice of vision which can divorce itself from thought. This is the first operation of grammography—to anchor thought in a series of points of view, to make thought aware of the flesh in which it functions; in a word, seeing is an operation which places thinking. This gambit, with its close relation to seeing and thought, seems to have a Cartesian flavour, but it is, in fact, a critique of Cartesianism. As Merleau-Ponty claims for Descartes, "everything we say and think of vision has to make a thought of it" (Johnson and Smith 137) i.e. the work of the eye is secondary to the reflection which, first, recognizes each abstract element, and, second, combines all of them in identifiable units (so that we eventually see, for instance, a port rather than a collection of colourful spots). Olson goes even further in proposing that what is visible does not find its ultimate explanation in the rational strategies of identifiability ("hills", "rocks", "Harbor-light"), but that it sinks into a *loss*, into what can be thought only as absent but upon which the visible is founded. Thought remains essential in the operations of vision, but it is a thought which is closer to Whitehead's than Descartes's concept of thinking. It is surprising how Whitehead's thought resembles Merleau-Ponty's visualizations of thinking: "His [Whitehead's] thinking is a prism. It must be seen not from one side alone but from all sides, then from underneath and overhead...as one moves around it, the prism is full of changing lights and colours" (Price 19).

In short, to see a painting is to think about what the painter did not do ("When I think about what Fitz Lane didn't do") because the articulation of the painter's hand is based on the constant intervention of the invisible. Merleau-Ponty quotes Balzac's story *"Le chef-d'oeuvre inconnu"* whose protagonist, a painter Frenhofer, says, "A hand is not simply part of the body, but the expression and continuation of thought which must be captured and conveyed..." (Johnson and Smith 68). In the equivalent phrase Olson links the painter's hand with his eyes which are, as we have already observed, the domain of thinking acquiring visual forms. In "Letter 7" which is dedicated to the painter Marsden Hartley, Olson begins by evoking the artist's eyes— *Marsden Hartley's/ eyes - as Stein's/ eyes (M)*, (1: 30)—and later moves to a statement that *hands are put to the eyes' command* (1: 32). The event of the painting emerges from a larger scene which, due to the absence of any specific visible data, can be described only as a non-event. This non-event could also most likely be referred to what Merleau-Ponty calls depth and what is represented in a painting as the sky permeated and saturated by a particular kind of light.

(b) We stand within a paradox: a painting is characterized by a certain blindness (the painter "didn't do" because either he did not see or was dazzled by what he saw), but it is this obstruction of perception which allows both the objects represented and the spectator to enter the orbit of thinking. What is produced is, in effect, a questioning of the reality of the image. If what we see is constantly emerging from the realm to which we have no access, and if the deed of the painter is punctured by its contrary (let us remember that, in the footsteps of Blake, a "contrary" is not a "negation"), by what has not been done, then the object represented must undergo a process of irrealization in which it does not simply become less "real" but, which is significantly different, less completely real.

The scene of painting does not and cannot exhaust itself in what is visible and what has been clearly and cleanly (in a technical sense) painted. Painting becomes doubly ob-scene—it tells us something which cannot be publicly and visibly manifested (by hinting at what was not done) and remains at fault, somewhat soiled and dirty (another etymology of *obscene* derives it from *caenum*, dirt). This is so because there exists in a painting something distant from the clean clarity of what has been immaculately presented to our eyes. Although we will not be able to follow this path to its end, let us remember that sexuality is not distant from the context of blindness. The following remark by Derrida allows us to construct a link between this "ob-scene" quality of painting and the blindness (loss) that is at its center. Talking about Samson, Derrida claims that he "is not only a figure of castration ... but, a bit like all the blind, ... a sort of phalloid image, an unveiled sex from head to toe, vaguely obscene and disturbing" (106).

c) There are two stages in our approach to the image. First, the invisible (what the painter "didn't do") must be told over and over again; the loss must be meticulously described. This phase which moves from representation to description is also based on the same mechanism which locates the loss and absence amidst profusion and presence. Therefore, while describing "what Fitz Lane didn't do", Olson simultaneously constitutes, through the description of what he sees, other losses and other absences. The second stage is of a more dramatic character. While the former, through description, still explores a link between a represented object and the scene of representation (we are able to diagnose the hills and rocks as belonging to a geographic location called "Gloucester"), the latter explores the realm of the ir-real by trying to make up for what the painter "didn't do" and by supplying the invisible, the loss and its description, with a whole network of relationships obtaining between various objects and the general scene of the non-event, or what Merleau-Ponty called the visible's "profound postural latency".

This effort is coded by Olson as a reference leading from each individual object to what he calls the "mathematic of Creation". The "mathematic" in question is by no means merely operational-calculative thought, but a science of relationships and connectedness. This understanding of mathematics links it with the Emersonian science of the ethical relationship between nature and man ["behold the sea...beautiful as the rose or the rainbow full of food, nourisher of men, purger of the world... in its mathematic ebb and flow... giving a hint of that which changes not and is perfect" (Smith 264)], the Bachelardean concept of mathematics as a discipline concerned rather with "absent" relations than "present" facts ["*un phénomene particulier est une veritable fonction de plusieurs variables et l'expression mathématique est encore celle qui l'analyse de plus pré*" (Bachelard 209)], and the Whiteheadean concern with mathematics as dealing with a certain absence of actual entities ["while mathematics is a convenience in relating certain types of order to our comprehension, it does not...give us any account of their actuality" (Price 175)].

What the irreal signifies is the crucial need for relatedness or connectedness with the Other (almost like a variation on the topic of the Romantic theory of correspondence) which is, however, centered around the sense of loss (what we "didn't do") and the impossibility of rendering the connectedness, the "mathematic of Creation", in the language of images or signs [Whitehead again: "the language of literature breaks down precisely at the task of expressing in explicit form the larger generalities—the very generalities which metaphysics seeks to express" (Whitehead 11)]. As in Cavell's analysis of Thoreau, Lane's contemporary, the image maker "comes to us from a sense of loss; the myth does not contain more than symbols because it is no set of desired things that he has lost, but a connection with things, the track of desire itself. Everything he can list he is putting in his book; it is a record of losses" (Cavell 50).

(d) We could say then that description is inevitably perforated by sub-scription. To see a painting or to read a poetic image is to simultaneously describe its contents, retell what is there, and to deal with what has not been done by the image-maker. Sub-scription refers to the power of the invisible, of the small print which, by providing the represented object with further perspectives and wildly distant points of view, relates it not only to the immediate scene of event (a port of Gloucester, for instance, depicted either at the time of Lane or Olson) but to the invisible scene of non-event, of what Olson called "the mathematic of Creation", from which the represented objects have emerged and which is representable as the almost monochromatic blue sky or grey earth.

In Olson's analyses of Lane's work and his own images of Gloucester (in other words, the space he shared with the painter), sub-scription can take the form of, for instance, geological reference to the rock formations upon which Gloucester was founded, archeological referral to Dogtown (a part of Gloucester famous as the "only ruined town of America"), and historical transference of Gloucester to the ancient Middle East, more particularly Phoenicia [Olson: "Lane's eye-view of Gloucester/ Phoenician eye-view" (Maximus 279)]. In sub-scription perception does not erase memory but is strengthened by its hidden operations. The act of perceiving a given space (for instance, Gloucester) as a lived location means living it—rather than merely living IN it. Through reaching out toward and undertaking a desperate effort against the spirit of the time, in order to maintain a link with its distant past, Olson describes himself in a characteristically unfinished phrase (we must soon return to this incompleteness): *I who hark back to an older polis/ who has this tie to a time when the port* (1: 20). In a much later poem we read: *17th Century within my eyes & on my skin as/ in my mind...*(3: 135).

In a fragment from his conversation with Herbert Kenny, Olson provides us with several important clues about the force of sub-scription underlying and forming his perception of Gloucester:

> Because Gloucester began this continent...the North Atlantic turbine...
> Vilhjalmur Stefansson: that the motion of man upon the earth has a line,
> an oblique, northwest-tending line, and Gloucester was the last shore in
> that sense. ... I use it as a bridge to Venice and back from Venice to Tyre,
> because of the departure from the old static land mass of man which was
> the ice, cave, Pleistocene man and early agricultural man, until he got
> moving, until he got towns. So that the last polis or city IS Gloucester.

> Therefore I think that in a sense we're—man now is either going to
> rediscover the earth or is going to leave it. ... The Gloucester becomes the
> flower in the pure Buddhist sense of being the place to be picked.
> (Muthologus 161-162)

Sub-scription is a force that is instrumental in shaping man's responsibility to and for
the landscape. It opens an important moment in the drama of human perception and
dwelling as it allows the person viewing a given scenery to hold a position of a being
between rather than that of a typical resident who tacitly assumes he is merely in the
landscape. The between in question is tropologically rendered as "a bridge"; the
metaphor which Olson uses not merely spatially (a bridge to Venice and to Tyre) but
also temporally (a bridge from Pleistocene to modernity) and culturally (a bridge
from agricultural to urban humanity).

In the 27th Letter of the Maximus sequence, Olson names this between in yet
another manner. It is the experience of landscape as the "beyond" which, however, is
fundamentally constitutive to man. Landscape is a lived experience when we emerge
from it, when we view landforms as a passage, which opens to let me *be*. Although,
at the same time, I know that I *am* only to the extent to which I am constituted by the
beyond, by the *other*, by the ultimately *other* Other: That which is so powerful and
extensive that it can be named only as the earth, as *geo*. Hence, I myself am nothing
more than the writing of this other, i.e. the script of the earth. *I am geo-graphy.*

Thoreau metaphorically applies geographic categories to man. In "Conclusions"
to Walden he claims that "there are continents and seas in the moral world, to which
every man is an isthmus or an inlet, yet unexplored by him, but it is easier to sail
many thousand miles through cold and storm and cannibals, in a government ship
(...), than it is to explore the private sea, the Atlantic and Pacific Ocean of one's
being alone" (212).

Olson undertakes an even more ambitious task and begins by outlining a
trajectory of the displaced return of the same, which is mandatory for the act of
understanding. To understand is to "come back" but the logic of displacement makes
this, paradoxically, a return to something else. One can say that understanding, to be
what it is, must necessarily miss its point. It must turn out to be a return to a different
thing, from which vantage point only are we able to truly understand what we have
just missed. To use an archer's terminology, you hit the target by missing it. The
opening line of the poem dedicated, at least in part, to the reconstruction of a
childhood memory reads: *I come back to the geography of it* (2: 14).

The "geography" in question refers to two scenes: that of the landscape and that
of the self. Both scenes are perilous. The former is determined by such a reading of
land which dramatizes and activates formations while the man occupies a middle
position, looks from a perilous passage upon the land breaking away or "falling."
Thus we have: *To the left the land fell to the city, / to the right it fell to the sea.* The
landscape of Gloucester is then read as a structure of "falling" where the verb not
only contributes its dynamic quality to the dramatic potential of the scene but also
alludes to the Biblical original transgression. Thus the land "falls", i.e. it inclines, but
it also opens for us a much wider perspective from which we can perceive such
phenomena as the "city" and the "sea" as the "fallen" land. For a discerning eye the

land is where there is no land, where the land ceases to be land. "To come back to the geography of it" means to be able to see the invisible in the visible, or—as Olson claims in the concluding section of the poem—to "compell Gloucester backwards", to see crushed particles of rocks in the sea, to look, as Blake wished, *through* the eye to open the geological framework of the visible. If we listen to Merleau-Ponty, we see that Olson repeats Cezanne's tactics: "he inquired about the geological structure of his landscapes, convinced that these abstract relationships, expressed, however, in terms of the visible world, should affect the act of painting" (Johnson and Smith 67).

But the "geography" of which Olson writes constitutes yet another between, which—this time—describes a situation of the geo-graphic subject. The subject scripted by the earth, written down and marked by the land, the subject which establishes a bond between himself/herself and the landscape, is not a completed construction. Since the writing of the land never stops, to truly respond to the landscape, to *see* it rather than merely glance at it, means to un-finish oneself, to leave a gap in one's self, to be—in Olson's formula— "a man plus":

> *I have this sense,*
> *that I am one*
> *with my skin*
>
> *Plus this - plus this:*
> *that forever the geography*
> *which leans in*
> *on me I compell*
> *backwards I compell Gloucester*
> *to yield, to*
> *change*
> *   Polis*
> *is this*

The geo-graphic subject is not quite "one with his/her skin". The self turns out to be non-self-identical as it is eaten out by geography, which overwhelms it and makes it regress (*compel backwards*), so that the landscape demonstrates that it is in truth metamorphic. Olson's geo-graphic subject could say what Cezanne maintained about himself: "The landscape thinks itself in me, and I am its consciousness" (67). First of all, when I perceive the landscape, I passively register it and commit an act of originary violence. But I also "compell" it "to yield", and this action of mine speaks not only of a force before which a given view has to "capitulate" but also of a semi-erotic movement which results in making the place productive, fertile. When Olson claims that the true seeing of Gloucester overcomes it and forces it to "yield" (i.e. bear and bring forth as a natural product, particularly as a result of cultivation), we read it as an enlargement on the previous thesis which held that we need to see the land as "fallen" in order to become the city, i.e. the land which has forgotten its fertile, originally and originarily rural past sub-scribed in it.

The geo-graphic subject is a man-plus. He/She is open to what is no longer him/her; he/she hospitably receives what-is-coming and therefore he/she needs to be constantly hollowed out by "the geography" which creates the empty place where what-is-coming can be received (Olson: *it is coming/ from all that i no longer am*). This emptiness which is necessary for the constitution of the geo-graphic subject as hospitable being allows for such a positioning of man which removes him/her from the central location and anchors even man's hospitality in the primordial hospitality of the world. Beyond the factual, scientific knowledge of the world there lies the domain of the "Mathematic of creation", i.e. man's profound acceptance (like Nietzsche's *Ja-sagen*) of the contingency of being. In a dense fragment of <u>Maximus</u> for the analysis of which we have no time here, Olson says:

> *I know the quarters*
> *of the weather, where it comes from,*
> *and where it goes. But the stem of me,*
> *this I took from their welcome,*
> *or their rejection, of me*
>   (1: 53)

The geo-graphic subject "stems from" the elemental hospitality, which transcends human language as well as categories of knowledge. It stems in the depth of what Merleau-Ponty speaks about in his analyses of painting and what painters like Lane and Mark Rothko represent as a space of almost monochromatic color, to which we give the name of "sky" or "earth."

As such a subject, the man who reads what is sub-scribed in land formations is able to distance himself from the economic order of contemporaneity. If to see Gloucester is to regress visually and mentally so that we are able to witness its metamorphosis into *polis,* which escapes the modern system of power, then it is synonymous with a rejection of the strictly individualistic system of culture and its economy of inheritance: *There is no strict personal order/ for my inheritance.* To see properly is to break away from the hegemony of the word and to let eyes and ears perform their pre-linguistic operations (*And words, words, words/ all over everything/ No eye or ears left/ to do their own doings),* (1: 13). It also means to escape the limitations of the modern power system which the poet, borrowing a term from Pound's *Pisan Cantos,* refers to as "pejorocracy". "Pejorocracy" is founded upon ethical reductionism (*love is not easy/.../ now/ that pejorocracy is here,* (1: 3); this deprivation must have been particularly acute since man, Olson claims, is not only *omnivore* but, first of all, *amorvore,* (1: 96). It is also founded on the corruption of cultural capital *[mu-sick (the trick/ of corporations, newspapers, slick magazines, movie houses]* (1: 10).

3.

It is only on such a complicated ground—only after we have been able to overcome the loss and absence and "see" these supposedly disconnected things—that man's responsibility to and for the landscape can develop. This responsibility is constituted by a twofold endeavor: first, by an attempt to understand and see what representations and images "cannot do"; and second, by an effort of interpretation that will never be completed, since the more we become immersed in the production of signs and images the more loss and absence we will have to diagnose. Thus we must understand Olson's remark "I realize how much stuff there is around, and what could be done on Gloucester" (Muthologos 174) along the lines of Merleau-Ponty's inexhaustible potentiality and latency rather than the Cartesian call for precise knowledge. The incompletenss of the process of interpretation is also a critique of contemporaneity for Olson as much as it was for Thoreau, who in the final pages of Walden deplored the situation "in this part of the world [in which] it is considered a ground for complaint if a man's writings admit of more than one interpretation" (Thoreau 215).

The knowledge in question has no claim to generality. In effect, unlike the Cartesian model, it is precisely a knowledge, i.e. knowledge *of a place*, an epistemological project which is profoundly anchored in the local. Thus to think means to perceive the present of the place in such a way that it bursts open to show the past. Thinking is a presencing of the past, not a re-calling or claiming of the past in the way we retrieve archival materials, but exactly a presencing the past—making the past present. Knowledge thus conceived is the result of a promise, a revelation of history, which a given place extends to us. Due to knowledge conceived of as a "promise," only that which has reached the status of the gift can truly be known. Asking himself about "the known", Olson replies: *This, I have had to be given ,/ a life, love, and from one man/ the world* (1: 52).

But such a lore which presents itself only as a promise and gift hardly answers to a description of "knowledge"; it certainly is a kind of knowing but of a different order and whose particular epistemological turn Olson signals by a characteristic letter change. When his interviewer suggests, "if knowledge is the material for your writing ... you must derive this knowledge ... in a given place at a given time, namely Gloucester, and its entire heritage?" (Muthologus 107), Olson launches into a diatribe in which he links the type of knowledge he develops "in" and "of" Gloucester with the gift of immediate cognition of spiritual truth (Muthologus 108):

> Neither the term "knowledge" nor the term "Gloucester" have any ... they might rhyme if I spelled it GN, as it should be spelled. Would you come to Gnowledge to get to Gnoucester? You'd have to do GNA GNA GNA, right?...Gnature ...Mr.GNoster who made Gloucester..."

The change from "K" to "G" is significant for a number of reasons. First, it shifts epistemological protocols towards gnosticism. Now knowledge is of a gnostic character, i.e. it links cognition with religion. The sacred ambition to know is now re-linked (*re-ligare*, to connect again) with the divine. It also marks a territory of the mature thought, of thinking which has reached its melancholic climax, which saves existence from the general ruin. In a late poem from the Maximus sequence Olson says: "I am/ not twenty any more, only/ the divine alone interests me at/ all and so much else is other-/ wise I hump out hard &/ crash in nerves and mashed/ existence only" (3: 198).

Second, "Gnowledge" turns out to be local and idiomatic. It does not refer to what is general but depends upon its immediate neighbourhood. It is constituted as a fragment of the rhyming pattern, Gloucester and "Gnowledge" which "might rhyme". This "rhyming" is nothing else than a careful listening to details, minimal signs which fill our everyday life and which should not go unnoticed. If "Gnowledge" is a case of what Derrida calls the "hermeneutic compulsion", then this epistemological practice operates on the border between superstition, paranoia, and science: "what is the difference—asks Derrida—between superstition and paranoia on the one hand, and science on the other, if they all mark a compulsive tendency to interpret random signs in order to reconstitute a meaning, a necessity, or a destination?" (Smith and Kerrigan 20).

Third, "Gnowledge" is formed as a rhythmic repetition, as a poetic revelation of the structure of Being. Hence Olson may be right when he claims in the same conversation, "I don't think it's knowledge at all." Rather, it is a mantric repetition ("GNA, GNA, GNA") which teaches us to discover this pre-history of meaning in all the standard, Cartesian articulations of thinking. Thus Knowledge turned Gnowledge unconceals the originary rhythms of the weather, whose "coming" and "going" Olson speaks about in one of his poems. In the signs of language we are instructed to disclose the rhythm of approaching the original creation—siGNAture becomes GNAture which in turn stems from the fundamental GNA, GNA, GNA.

4.

Since we have been preoccupied with landscapes, let us clarify the three levels of its appearance which we have been concerned with. First, there is a landscape of a certain real placing (for instance, Gloucester). Second, there is a painterly rendition of it (Lane's views of the port of Gloucester). Third, there is an interpretative reading and seeing (Olson's poetic analysis). So far we have been concerned with the last two levels, trying to detect in them mechanisms of irrealization, description, and sub-scription, which is centered around the concept of loss. The distinction between these two realms and the first is by no means unimportant, but here let us say only that what is most significant is that in a "real" landscape all its elements are by definition "well-placed" and firmly anchored in their locales. In Emerson we read, "The landscape. A place for every thing, & everything in its place. No waste, and no want" (Smith I: 263). Even if, like Gilpin, we would like to observe some "mistakes" which nature has made, nevertheless, the very fact that they have been committed by nature turns our critique into a mere figure of speech. We do not have a philosophical power that would allow us to question the originary placing of things in the scheme of nature. All we can suggest is "re-placing" some of the natural elements. But this only more overtly suggests that the force of the *place* has been there before us, and we can do no more than "re-place"—put in a different location. This different location, however, is not the originary "place". Even if we assume that loss is already inscribed within nature, it is only art that allows us to see it. Only through a necessary meditation on what absents itself from the work process—on what has not been done in it, has been dislodged from the "mathematic of Creation" and has to be reinstated there by the detours of sub-scription—can we realize that in the image things are always already dis-placed, re-placed, and dis-lodged. The effort of painting (Olson speaks merely of Lane's "attempt") aims precisely at this impossible reinstituting of the individual object into what Merleau-Ponty calls a "broader ontological power." (Johnson and Smith 133).

Gilpin's reaction to a landscape as flawed is generated precisely by his projection of the image upon natural scenery, and his criticism of the latter does not stem directly from objects but from a mental imagining of their representation as images. For example, in Humphrey Repton's books, a painting of the real landscape is accompanied by an artistic rendition of it, so that one can impose the latter upon the real scenery and see the "failures" of nature. If Gilpin claims that nature could be better placed, then it is the effect of the workings of dis-placement, always active within the image.

5.

Finally, let us note that the philosophy of loss located at the center of the image, as well as the impossible historiography of the non-event beyond the chronology of an occurrence, have their economic turn. The economy of painting is ruled by the principle of loss and waste. The more we try to fill in what the painter "didn't do", the wider we spread the circle of absence. The objects constituting an image are, as we have seen, dis-placed, deprived of their "proper" element and location, and therefore cannot be incorporated in the economic exchange based precisely on the idea that each thing has its own value and place in the scheme of goods.

In short, the philosophy of loss problematizes a question of ownership and property. One can own a piece of land as well as a canvas with its representation. One can even own the image as a product, but the protocols of appropriation are closed for the machinery of the image, or image as process, whose ever-active operations of loss and absence in principle deny the logic of appropriation. What has not been done, and what I think of when I look at a painting, does not succumb to the rule of the money economy, which circulates only completed objects. What has not been done or produced cannot be a subject of market economy. Neither can it be collected—which is not an incidental thing if we remember that collecting and mercantile capitalism are viewed as stemming from the same economic tradition: *"la généalogie du capitalist ... se trouve deduire aussi le collectioneur. Mieux même, le premier n'est pour ainsi dire qu'une variante du second"* (Pelckmans 11). To see or to carefully look at a painting or a poetic image is to think along the lines of another economy involving loss, sacrifice, or wasteful expenditure rather than miserly hoarding or straightforward profit—namely one of "wondership" rather than "ownership" (1: 9). This is an important point for Olson, a pronounced critic of the capitalist mentality of postwar US ruled by the "pejorocracy". In one of the <u>Maximus Poems</u> we read: "I met Death—he was a sportsman—on Cole's/ Island. He was a property-owner," (3: 69). To see in such a way which allows us to live the landscape, to think oneself the geo-graphic subject, is to maintain the vital connection between the eye and the hand, to be a painter, the man with *this living hand, now warm, now capable/ of earnest grasping* (3: 177). The artist, the geo-graphic man who responds to the sub-script of the world—the man of gentle and earnest grasping (a rare species).

WORKS CITED

Bachelard, G. *La valeur inductive de la relativité*. Paris: Vrin, 1929.

Cavell, S. The Senses of Walden. New York: Viking Press, 1972.

Derrida, Jacques. Memoirs of the Blind. The Self-Portrait and Other Ruins, translated by P. Brault, M. Naas. Chicago: University of Chicago Press, 1993.

Johnson, Galen and Michael B. Smith, eds. The Merleau-Ponty Aesthetics Reader: Philosophy and Painting. Evanston, Illinois: Northwestern University Press, 1993.

Novak, B. Nature and Culture. American Landscape and Painting 1825–1875, New York, 1980.

Olson, Charles. Archeologist of Morning. New York: Grossman Publishers, 1970.

---. The Maximus Poems. Berkeley: University of California Press, 1983.

---. *Muthologos*. Bolinas: Four Seasons Foundation 1979.

Pelckmans, P. *Concurrences au monde. Propositions pour une poétique du collectionneur moderne*. Amsterdam: Rodopi, 1990.

Price, Lucien. Dialogues with Alfred North Whitehead as Recorded by Lucien Price. New York: Mentor Books, 1954.

Smith, J. and W. Kerrigan. Taking Chances: Derrida, Psychoanalysis, and Literature. Baltimore and London: John Hopkins University Press, 1984.

Smith, S. S. ed. The Topical Notebooks of R.W.Emerson. Columbia, London: University of Missouri Press, 1990.

Thoreau, H. D., ed. O. Thomas. Walden. London and New York: Norton 1966.

Whitehead, A. N. Process and Reality. New York, London: Free Press, 1978.

Wilmerding, John. Fitz Hugh Lane. New York: Praeger, 1971.

---. *Paintings by Fitz Hugh Lane*. Washington DC: National Gallery of Art, 1988.

Freeways in the City of Angels

William R. Handley
University of Southern California

In Los Angeles, people think of space in terms of time, time in terms of routes ...and of automobiles as natural and essential extensions of themselves. [1]

Los Angeles seems endlessly held between these extremes: Of light and dark—of surface and depth. Of the promise, in brief, of a meaning always *hovering* on the edge of significance.[2]

This paper explores texts and images through which the territory and experience of the Los Angeles freeway circulate. Fiction, non-fiction, and film on Los Angeles are replete with representations of the freeway that register a wide range of themes and affects: it is a site that seems to offer freedom but demands subjection, a site where fear and desire arise, where revelations and communion are possible and forgetting and numbing are made easy; it is a liminal space between public and private, mobility and paralysis, past and future, point A and point B. It is a site of greater social convergence than shopping malls, but it can be one of the most private and isolating experiences in one's day. Its signs are more determinative than advertising and "must be obeyed because they are infallible."[3] (In Steve Martin's film L. A. Story, one even passes on life-changing romantic advice.) The most shared pragmatic structure in the city, certain freeway interchanges have also been called works of art (see figure 1)—and not just because of the considerable number of large murals painted in underpasses and along sidewalls. "Of all the changes man can visit upon his urban environment, few are as monumental as an eight-lane freeway," John Chapman claimed in a 1967 study of Los Angeles that dubbed the city "Roadsville, U.S.A."[4] The freeway is in place (except during some earthquakes), but no place in any social sense. Among its other paradoxes, according to Martin Wachs, it invites people "to experience ocean, mountain, and desert within minutes of one another [yet] it is a major source of the smog that makes them invisible. It is a lifeline by which millions are supplied with their daily sustenance, yet it can be a place of carnage and police chases."[5] Like the city described in the epigraph above, this mundane site seems to promise a meaning always hovering on the edge of significance, asking to be read both as surface and in greater depth.

Since its beginning, but especially recently, the freeway is where Los Angeles sees itself—and often, like Narcissus, misrecognizes what it sees there. The freeway is the intersection of Los Angeles's extremes, a specific yet amorphous site that both erases historical memory and produces a wide range of literary and visual representations, like the city it runs through. And like the city it often stands for, the freeway resists easy or stable socio-cultural mapping and lends itself to contradictory meanings. For that very reason, this site of transportation transports meaning, via its representations, between Los Angeles's divergent realities, images, imaginaries, and histories. As I will discuss in four quite different but related routes to this site, these include the freeway's totalizing form for the "postmetropolis" (in Edward Soja's term); the history of land speculation and transportation routes that shaped the city; the convoluted relation that the freeway and the city have to the natural environment; and the spectatorship of/via the media—a kind of virtual transportation made possible by helicopters—that objectify Los Angeles's racial and class divsions and render the social as hyperreal. As the sign of Los Angeles as "city of the future," the freeway has thereby served to erase a deeper past. But while the Los Angeles freeway has often been aestheticized to historically blinding abstraction, it is nevertheless a textual territory in which forgetting is located, in Norman Klein's phrase—and where forgetting is remembered.[6]

I. Covering Los Angeles: Freeway as Totalizing Form

> **FREEWAYS,** vast expressway networks that has unified and defined the physical structure of the Los Angeles area since the 1960s.
> —entry in Los Angeles A to Z [7]

In his 1971 groundbreaking study Los Angeles: The Architecture of Four Ecologies, Reyner Banham writes emphatically that the city's freeway system "in its totality is now a single comprehensible place, a coherent state of mind, a complete way of life, the fourth ecology of Angelenos" after the city's beaches, foothills, and sprawling plains. This "autopia"—which was a ride at Disneyland when Banham used the term—is where the Angeleno "is most himself, most integrally identified with his great city" and it marks a "special way of being alive." [8] While one might qualify Banham's exceptionalist and celebratory rhetoric and question what coherence or integrity the city possesses, especially as social space, Banham's characterizations of Los Angeles as a freeway city and of the freeway as a single (because continuous) place is arguably as true today as when he wrote his study. Though it is rarely on a tourist's wish-to-see list, it has become perhaps the most substitutable image for the city: "Just as the Eiffel Tower defines Paris and the Statue of Liberty symbolizes New York, the freeway is the universal icon by which Los Angeles is described."[9] But while the first two sites announce to the visitor "you are here," the freeway is always directing visitors and natives alike to somewhere else. Indeed, while there is a continuity to the interconnected freeways in Los Angeles, they are in no way bounded by the city: if one enters the Santa Monica freeway (Interstate Route 10) at the coast and drives away from Santa Monica, east toward downtown, one will see a sign that announces that this is also the Christopher Columbus Transcontinental Highway, which runs all the way to Florida (and nominally refers us back to seafaring and the "discovery of the New World.")

Easily mapped cartographically, the freeway is impossible to visualize in its totality either as a structure or as an experience; indeed, overhead images of the freeway give a false picture of both aspects: the frame violates its real structure and often makes the intersections stand in for the whole, while it represents "driving" as going in all directions at once, which no actual driver can experience (see figures 1 and 2). Any fixed point on the freeway photograph or map points in at least two opposite directions. The freeways are most characteristic of Los Angeles in part because, like the city itself, they have no center and form a circuitry that imitates the city's supposed postmodern geography: "the city has no end, no middle and no limits. Any attempt to find a fixed point from which to look at the urban region must fail in the final instance," Roger Keil writes of the city, in terms more accurate of the freeways that overlay it.[10] Can the freeway be experienced in its totality through any one of its parts, in the manner in which Jean Baudrillard claims any Burger King will tell one all there is to know about America? In theory, yes, especially if we think of the freeway as, in Edward Soja's words:

> a concentrated representation of the restructured spatiality of the late capitalist city [what he now prefers to call the postmetropolis]: fragmented and fragmenting, homogenous and homogenizing, divertingly packaged yet curiously incomprehensible, seemingly open in presenting itself to view but constantly pressing to enclose, to compartmentalize, to circumscribe, to incarcerate. Everything appears to be available ....but real places are difficult to find, its spaces confuse an effective cognitive mapping, its pastiche of superficial reflections bewilder coordination and encourage submission instead. . .[11]

Does it matter that Soja is here describing, as many others after Fredric Jameson have done, the Bonaventure Hotel in downtown Los Angeles? Is Los Angeles a hologram à la Baudrillard, in which information concerning the whole is contained in each of its elements, or are we always looking for elements of L. A. to describe the complicated space of the freeways that not only metaphorically stand in for the city but make its sprawl possible?[12] It does matter that Soja is describing a hotel, but what also matters is that that hotel is located within the intersections of the many freeways near downtown that form, one could say, the coiled heart of their vast body. While one cannot pretend to visit the freeway as a site in its totality, the hotel provides a simulacrum of freeway travel through the city as a "more concentrated representation" of such "restructured spatiality" under late capitalism.

The freeway system is the only site in Los Angeles that both is mappable and approximates the city's size. Since Los Angeles is geographically immense by any American urban standard, its size makes it difficult to represent in its entirety on a manageable yet detailed map. Overviews of the region on single maps therefore tend to trace the skeleton or veins of its major freeways as its distinguishing features, to the extent that the freeways not only provide cartographically the image of an internal structure to the city (rather than a superimposed surface on it), but they also often stand in for it metaphorically and visually. This double need is evident in many films that begin with images of the freeway such as The Loved One, City of Industry, Colors, and even Blade Runner, in which the freeway in 2019 is a free-form autoscape in the air. This imaging of Los Angeles as freeway is also evident in books about the city that appeared after the Santa Monica freeway—now the city's busiest—was completed in 1965. (Before the 1960s, there had been only a few works of real distinction, such as Carey McWilliams' masterful 1946 study Southern California: An Island on the Land and Anton Wagner's 1935 study, Los Angeles: Zweimillionenstadt in Südkalifornien). The freeways were becoming, as Banham would later remark, a single comprehensible place that seemed to embody the extremes of the city and these studies adopted the freeway system for the design of their dust jackets, cover boards, inleafs, and illustrations.

The dust jacket of Christopher Rand's 1967 Los Angeles: The Ultimate City (see figure 2) shows a picture that hardly lives up to the book's title, but that captures the "ultimate" character of this novel city-space at the time: a straight stretch of freeway in the foreground leads the viewer toward the looping intersection of the Santa Monica and Harbor freeways, drawing us toward and then swirling us outward and away from the city's downtown, which is nearby but not visible. The eye's movements imitate the historical move away from the downtown (that the freeways were meant to lead to) and toward its decline—both economically and symbolically—with the proliferation and increased visibility of the freeway as not only a site but also a "way of life." Take away the dust jacket, and the book's front cover board reveals an abstraction of arrowed lines pointing in all directions (see figure 3): the freeway is not only disconnected from the inner city but is abstracted from itself. Perhaps that is its meaning hovering on the edge of significance. What the freeway represents—mobility, dispersity, decenteredness, the postmodern city—"covers" Los Angeles. The dust jacket and inleaf of John Chapman's Incredible Los Angeles, which also appeared in 1967, are more comprehensive and no less abstract: on the entire dust jacket is the sprawling L.A. basin, its peninsula seeping into the ocean in the foreground. On the book's front and back inleaf is an even more incredible map of "Los Angeles and its Freeway System": the sparest topographic rendering of the region's natural features with the solid black lines of the freeway—none named or numbered, all thus becoming naturalized like rivers, or veins—coursing and circulating through the body of the land. The more the freeway stands in for Los Angeles, these images suggest, the more Los Angeles is thereby emptied of its social content—as the price of achieving an abstract or pure form.

The freeway as visual abstraction or spectral sign assumes its own recognizability but withholds any significance beneath its surface meaning. Its iconic abstraction lacks, like the driving experience itself, situatedness and context. We can see this on the cover board of Rand's book (figure 3). But when these lines approximating those of the freeway are given context, the abstracted freeway is made historical and given social shape, as in the lines of white flight from downtown since 1940. When these abstracted lines are inverted and made to circle in on themselves in Edward Soja's diagram of the "trialectics of being" and in the campaign for "Rebuild L.A." after the 1992 riots, the diagram suggests an even more curious layer to the abstracted freeway palimpsest. In the name of "radical" postmodernist theory and political progress, postmodern sprawl is reined in, the curving lines are given harmony. If, on the edge of these images' surface meaning, we see the freeways hovering, then the implication is that no one can leave downtown for the suburbs.

It would seem that when Rand's and Chapman's books appeared in 1967, the city had become its freeways almost as soon as they were completed, producing a need for new narratives of the city's distinctiveness. This need is curious if one considers that the freeway as a totalizing form or experience also resists narration by virtue of its abstraction from meaningful particulars. As Joan Didion argues in her essay "Pacific Distances,"

> a good part of any day in Los Angeles is spent driving, alone, through streets devoid of meaning to the driver, which is one reason the place exhilarates some people, and floods others with an amorphous unease. There is about these hours spent in transit a seductive unconnectedness. Conventional information is missing. Context clues are missing ... Such tranced hours are, for many people who live in Los Angeles, the dead center of being there, but there is nothing in them to encourage the normal impulse toward "recognition", or narrative connection. Those glosses on the human comedy ... that lend dramatic structure to more traditional forms of urban life are hard to come by here.[13]

The driving experience can be narrated almost as pure metonymy: "There are the same pastel bungalows... There are the same laundramats, body shops, strip shopping malls ..."[14] Yet Didion's description is of driving "surface streets": on the freeway itself there is even less to differentiate between or connect to. When space becomes less differentiable, so does time. Chapman's book argues, "drivers sometimes succumb to an illusion of speed on long stretches of elevated freeway. The up-in-the-air, airplane-like environment makes trees and rooftops seem as though they are going by slower than they really are."[15] But while things seem slower, the trip can speed by almost unnoticed. Christopher Isherwood's George in A Single Man (1964) becomes "less and less aware of externals" as he drives and goes "deep down inside himself." But soon, when the traffic thickens and slows: "God! Here we are, downtown already! George comes up dazed to the surface."[16]

This is a fairly common driving experience, but its distracted resistance to narrative is particularly consonant with the difficulty of reading the past in Los Angeles's built environment. We cannot recognize historical and narrative coherence in the freeway's form also because of the rapid transit between past and present built environments. In a rumination on the empirical and theoretical significance of place, J. Nicholas Entrikin argues that "the technical abilities involved in the manipulation of the environment seem to be poorly matched with the cultural narratives that connect an individual or group to an environment."[17] This is particularly the case, as I will explore in section three, for a city that owes its very existence to the technological manipulation of its environment.

Where Chapman and Rand sought to cover the city as "a single comprehensible place," no matter how reduced to ahistorical abstraction in their covers, an earlier study, Remi Nadeau's 1960 Los Angeles: From Mission to Modern City shows us, on the verge of the freeway's dominance, the city's Janus-face, below the title is a Spanish mission, while above is the freeway coursing toward downtown. From past to future, or 0 to 60, in just a few seconds. The title both presumes and elides a sequence of events that explain the city's total transformation and the relationship between its past and present. More self-consciously, Roger Keil's 1998 study <u>Los Angeles</u> gives another split screen. In this image, the commuter-laden freeway in the foreground, surrounded in an uncommon instance by luxurious homes, seems to lead us into the past of the electric railway above—and to direct our vision toward the present social realities of those whom the freeway is not primarily meant to serve, the young people of color playing between the graffiti-covered iron walls along the track. For Keil and other contemporary critics, neither the freeway nor the city of Los Angeles is a single comprehensible place, and images of freeways must be placed against other images to get a more complete picture of what they mean.[18] The pastiche of Los Angeles both resists coherent narration and demands a contextualizing of its otherwise disjointed histories and sites. It may be that the free-way, as a recent and still dominant stage of what Banham calls L.A.'s "transportation palimpsest," offers only the fastest and most convenient route through history. In this sense the freeway resembles Frederick Jackson Turner's notion of the "frontier." As palimpsest and as text-territory, the freeway/frontier recapitulates the stages of civilization; as a measure of "progress" it explains and justifies everything that came before and after it historically.

Angels Fall to Asphalt: The Wreckage of History
　　In downtown Los Angeles, near the Bonaventure Hotel, angels sit atop freeway signs above the Harbor Freeway in the film <u>City of Angels</u>. Inspired by Wim Wenders' <u>Wings of Desire</u>, a rumination on history, mortality, and love, <u>City of Angels</u> is devoid of explicit considerations about history even as it is visually preoccupied with downtown Los Angeles, that area of the city that has witnessed the greatest historical transformation. That the angels are perched above the freeway and haunt the downtown is at best subtly suggestive of what is made explicit in the original film: that these angels are witnesses to the wreckage of history. In one of Wenders' original scenes, an angel sits in the vacant no-man's land of Potsdamer Platz in divided Berlin, once the teeming heart of the city, and contemplates the ravages of history. <u>City of Angels</u> is mainly preoccupied with the romance between a woman and the angel who so desperately has fallen in love with her that he falls the height of a tall building to the asphalt in order to become mortal. The former angel then hitches a ride and leaves Los Angeles to find the woman, who has retreated to a Lake Tahoe cabin, and he experiences for the first time such things as the pleasures of sex and the sensuality of a piece of fruit. But their time together physically is brief, because the woman soon becomes roadkill: while riding a bicycle on a road through a forest, she smashes into a logging truck. Though steeped in romance, thereby ostensibly denuding Wenders' angels of their historical gravity, this film's visual preoccupations and narrative trajectory nevertheless take us back into history and into nature, from freeways to forests, from automobiles to bicycles. In a twist that would redeem Los Angeles from its *noir*-side if not from history itself, the film makes nature—and not the city of freeways—the site of mortal danger for the heroine.

In his "Theses on the Philosophy of History," Walter Benjamin reads a painting in order to reimagine historical process:

> A Klee painting named 'Angelus Novus' shows us an angel looking as though he is about to move away from something he is fixedly contemplating. His eyes are staring, his mouth is open, his wings are spread. This is how one pictures the angel of history. His face is turned toward the past. Where we perceive a chain of events, he sees one single catastrophe which keeps piling wreckage upon wreckage and hurls it in front of his feet. The angel would like to stay, awaken the dead, and make whole what has been smashed. But a storm is blowing from Paradise; it has got caught in his wings with such violence that the angel can no longer close them. This storm irresistibly propels him into the future to which his back is turned, while the pile of debris before him grows skyward. This storm is what we call progress.[19]

Inspired by a picture, Benjamin's angel of history also is one: an image, which spatializes historical time by transforming it into an accumulation of physical wreckage. What has been visibly erased by progress and lost to history piles up before the angel's feet as the storm blowing from paradise hurls the angel into the future. The image is also a text that tells us what the angel knows: that looking back makes one helpless to change what has accumulated like so much strata over time. The angel "would like to stay, awaken the dead, and make whole what has been smashed," but its wings are stuck open by the storm's traffic, propelling it both spatially and temporally into the future.

The image is a particularly potent one for my analysis of the Los Angeles freeway as a site that both makes visible and hides historical transformation in the name of progress and "the city of the future." What the freeway erases, whether the past "paradise" of a city of orchards or even the wreckage that has accumulated on its pavement, cannot be seen. But it can be read into literary and visual representations of Los Angeles's freeway culture just as Benjamin's angel allows us to read the history of progress: what is lost to the visual environment is represented by texts and images that seem to remember what the freeway forgets and to know the price of that forgetting. At the beginning of the wide-ranging, 1995 documentary on Los Angeles, Shotgun Freeway (the title of which metaphorically substitutes the freeway for the city), a black and white film from what seems to be the 1940's—given the style of automobile and dress—shows us what is blowing from paradise in the City of Angels.[20] A literalization of the city's name, an angel hovers in the air above orange groves as a man takes a photograph of his car in front of them. When the Polaroid develops, the angel has disappeared from the picture; in its place is a sign that says "Angel Body Shop" and in the place of the orange trees is a city street with the man's car parked along it. "Development" banishes the angel from the fruit trees of paradise and gives us the fallen body of an automotive culture. The visual palimpsest suggested by what is on the screen and in the photograph elides the question of historical causality: now you see it, now you don't. Watching this brief segment, and thinking about Benjamin's angel, I was troubled that the makers of the documentary elided the question of the film segment's historical place and meaning: who made it when, and why? Was this a "booster" film? If so, why did it offer a vision of the "future" (presumably the original audience's present) that showed Los Angeles as a fallen paradise? But that elision proved very much the point when I contacted one of the film's makers, who told me that they had in fact staged that sequence themselves, intending not to pass it off as historical but as a rumination on historical transformation. The filmmakers looked back to L.A.'s "pastoral paradise" and imagined an angel who foresaw the wreckage wrought by progress—hence the need for "angel" body shops to make whole what has been smashed, in an ever-receding progression from the smashed but putatively once-existing paradise. That which gives us the power to envision the invisibility of history, the angel, vanishes in this fabricated old footage within the built environment.

Historical elision—the nearly Polaroid-quick "development" from the pastoral to the urban-automotive—is everywhere visible in Los Angeles' built environment but no more so than on its freeways, if only because many of them carry old Spanish names, including the names of missions, and are banked with flowers and greenery. One authentically 1940's film, by the California Department of Transportation (Caltrans), imagines a mythologized Spanish past as sequentially connected to the modern freeway, though the sequence is elided. As we watch a film of an early Spaniard walking on a dusty trail, a voice says: "This was the trail of the Padres, marked out and smoothed by weary sandaled feet in the pastoral days of California— El Camino Real: the primitive beginning of one of the great road systems in world history." The phrase "beginning of" establishes an imaginary chain of causally linked, sequential events and thereby gives the illusion of a coherent history, of the present as a straightforward product of the past. Reyner Banham's "transportation palimpsest" situates the freeway more historically, given the space made available to it by a longer history of comparably spread-out development. Nevertheless, he also marks its discrete, sequentially linked stages, originating with the Spaniards:

> The uniquely even, thin and homogeneous spread of development that has been able to absorb the monuments of the freeway system without serious strain (so far, at least) owes its origins to earlier modes of transportation and the patterns of land development that went with them. The freeway system is the third or fourth transportation diagram drawn on a map that is a deep palimpsest of earlier methods of moving about the basin. In the beginning was the Camino Real, the Spaniards' military road . . .[21]

That road, of course, is no longer visible: "its exact route seems pretty difficult to establish nowadays," he adds (though it presumably passed just south of where I live, along the Miracle Mile Shopping District on Wilshire Boulevard). Banham's narrative, like the much less historically minded Caltrans film, puts the freeway "there," on the trail of the Padres. This palimpsest is not the "single catastrophe" that Benjamin's angel sees piling wreckage upon wreckage; it is a chain of events, or a partitioning, that both visualizes and conceals history.

The invisibility of historical transformation is largely due to the fact that Los Angeles developed after its Pueblo days as a monopoly capitalist city, which never experienced the typical dense growth of the industrial capitalist city of the nineteenth century. Suburban life in Fordist Los Angeles required, first of all, personal automobile transport. As a result, Roger Keil argues, "Freeways—the vital infrastructure of suburban-based automobile transport—disemboweled the inner city. The city was functionally divided into dichotomous cities."[22] And the dichotomy was enabled by freeway infrastructure. Keil's claim bespeaks a nostalgia for an inner city or city center that is not uncommon in writing on Los Angeles. But the nostalgia is arguably for something that, even before the automobile, was never quite true of Los Angeles after its pueblo days; the inner city underwent a loss of dominance even before the freeways. If Los Angeles never developed as a modern industrial city, its purported postmodernist sprawl may best be understood, rather, as the continuous circulation of capital—at first, monopoly capital—across a vast land area beginning in the 1870s.

Sandwiched between the Spaniards' trails and the freeways in Banham's transportation palimpsest are the railroads and the electric rail system, each of which also approximated the general lines of transportation routes radiating from the original pueblo near modern-day downtown. The deal that Los Angeles struck with the Southern Pacific railroad in the 1870s, in which the SP agreed to divert their line down through the San Fernando Valley to Los Angeles rather than go straight across the high desert to the northeast of the city, was and still is, according to Banham, the "most important single event" ever in the history of the area, after the foundation of the pueblo in 1781. Not only did it ensure the economic viability of the region, but also set in motion the historical relationship between land speculation and sprawling lines of transportation that shaped the present city. In narrative terms, it was the conversion moment from publicly to privately funded transportation, since the SP bought the only publicly funded railroad in the deal, the Wilmington. The five Southern Pacific lines that radiated from the Pueblo towards San Fernando, San Bernardino, Anaheim, Wilmington, and Santa Monica constitute, according to Banham, "the bones of the skeleton on which Greater Los Angeles was to be built, the fundamentals of the present city where each of these old lines is now duplicated by a freeway." And they also brought the flesh: "subdivision of adjoining land proceeded as fast as the laying of rails," drawing a population of "commuters" after 1880.[23] The downtown area was already becoming less dominant before the turn of the century. The development of the world's most extensive urban electric rail system began as early as 1887 but especially with Henry Huntington's Pacific Electric Railway (known as the "Big Red Cars"). In 1923, at its point of greatest extension, the PE operated 1,164 miles of track that sketched out contemporary Greater Los Angeles. Some of these rails are still visible today, but the system is gone. The demise of this system was due in part to a corporate conspiracy—but also to longstanding consumer dissatisfaction with trains that were dirty and late and with the monopolists who owned them.[24] The auto-freeway lobby had, since the 1920s, actively opposed public subsidies for transportation. Corporations that had a stake in cars and buses—General Motors, Standard Oil, Firestone Tires, Phillips Petroleum, and Mack Truck Manufacturing Company—organized a dummy operation to buy up and dismantle mass transit lines throughout the country, including the Red Cars.[25] (A comic version of this plot underlies the film Who Framed Roger Rabbit?) The last Red Car made its last journey in 1961.

Regardless of its historical accuracies, Banham's classic study of Los Angeles "ecologies" is "on the land"—topographically situated, one could say, in a manner that naturalizes, as in some evolutionary model, the development of transportation in Los Angeles leading to the freeway. The first sentence of his text takes us on a continuous and coherent route from electric railways to regional profitability and, by the end of the paragraph, "the transportation infrastructure for an area of land that was to contribute much to the present character of the city." The Pico electric line "was the true beginning of the process" because it was "directly linked" to a subdividing company and to land speculators. Just as it was early on "directly linked" to a subdividing company, the eventual electric railway that divides Banham's text links the Spanish and railroad pasts to the freeway future, by means of a palimpsestic text-image. That this palimpsest is as much if not more the product of Banham's text-images than of history is evident when one notices the only other signs on Banham's map of the 1923 Huntington lines: 18th-century Spanish missions and the Watts Towers, begun in 1921 and completed in 1954. If driving has taught Angelenos "to think of space in terms of time," which is what the urban historian does in a different sense, Banham's maps and text encourage the reader to think of historical time as space in this drive through three centuries—but not as any space that is lived or, despite its "flesh" and "bones," alive. Though Frederick Jackson Turner presumed an immanent force in history, his rhetorical diorama in the frontier thesis works to the same effect as Banham's palimpsest:

> Stand at the Cumberland Gap and watch the procession of civilization, marching single-file—the buffalo following the trail to the salt springs, the Indian, the fur-trader and hunter, the cattle-raiser, the pioneer farmer—and the frontier has passed by. Stand at the South Pass in the Rockies a century later and see the same procession with wider intervals between.[26]

Like Turner, Banham's text-image provides a stance from which to see, as Benjamin describes it, "a chain of events" in singular space. By itself, however, Banham's image represents spatially coterminous events, in the manner in which an organic body embodies its historical experience. Neither stance nor representation can be experienced while being in Los Angeles, let alone while transporting oneself through it.

This skeleton upon which the transportation palimpsest is read is evident if we superimpose on the five lines of the Southern Pacific railroad radiating from downtown Joan Didion's famous description of Maria Wyeth's driving route in her 1970 novel Play It As It Lays. Maria drives "the San Diego to the Harbor, the Harbor up to the Hollywood, the Hollywood to the Golden State, the Santa Monica, the Santa Ana, the Pasadena, the Ventura." I have traced this route. It is continuous until it reaches the disjunction between the Santa Monica and the Santa Ana, pulling it in a sequence of incompatible directions that imitate the impossible intersections of the places these freeways are named after. At the intersection of most of these freeways near downtown, her narrative names five lines of direction that are roughly the same as the "the five Southern Pacific lines that radiated from the Pueblo towards San Fernando, San Bernardino, Anaheim, Wilmington, and Santa Monica," as Banham describes them. Indeed, when Didion writes that "Sometimes the freeway ran out, in a scrap metal yard in San Pedro," her narrative returns the reader to the site of the first railroad line: Phineas Banning's Wilmington line in 1869, which was the first and last railroad financed by public money in the region, and a key bargaining chip in the deal with the Southern Pacific, which extended it to San Pedro, causing the decline of the community of Wilmington. As much as it might be read as a non-linear, postmodern labyrinth, Maria Wyeth's journey recapitulates rapidly and takes us back to an earlier layer of L.A.'s transportation palimpsest, when capital began to flow and the privatization of transportation began.

The Machine on the Freeway in the Garden on the Desert
    As convoluted as its freeway interchanges, is Southern California's relation to foundational American myths about nature. The unadorned form of a snake is on the dust jacket of Didion's Play It As It Lays, an image that most obviously suggests the fall from paradise but also obliquely suggests, given the way it mimics the forms of Maria Wyeth's circuitous route, the fallenness of a freeway culture. Los Angelean versions of the myth of the Fall are often convoluted ones, in part because Paradise was originally man-made. (The original sin of Faye Dunaway's character Evelyn in Chinatown is incest with her father Noah Cross, the powerful land speculator.) In the history of the dialectical relationship between human beings and the natural environment in the American West, beginning with western Massachusetts, Southern California's history is distinctive. No wilderness to be subdued by the "back-woodsman" or "pioneer," it took technology to populate this semi-arid region on a large scale and to turn it into a garden. What Carey McWilliams observed in 1946 is even more true today: "Southern California is man-made, a gigantic improvisation. Virtually everything in the region has been imported: plants, flowers, shrubs, trees, people, water, electrical energy, and, to some extent, even the soils. While potentially a rich and fertile region, the land required a highly developed technology to unlock its resources." And those resources are immense. Though the vast majority of its life forms have been brought from somewhere else, including such trees as the eucalyptus, acacia, pepper tree, and varieties of palm (even the weeds of the region are not native), with water and scientific cultivation, the land "will raise more things faster, and in greater quantities than any other section of America," which was true in 1946 when McWilliams made this claim. Nature on steroids: it is a "deceitful and illusory" and "artificial region."[27] It remains today both garden and desert, both city and suburb, surely one of the most unlikely places on earth, given its massive population—and certainly one of the most precarious cities, as Mike Davis has recently reminded us in The Ecology of Fear. The qualities worth boosting and boasting about are inseparable from its potential for natural and man-made disaster, even and especially the plentiful sunshine, the effects of which can produce drought, fires, and, when the plentiful rains come, floods, mudslides, and debris flows.

Just as this history between human and natural forces is distinctive, so is the literature that has been written about it, to the extent, I would argue, that none of Leo Marx's three founding American myths that describe approaches to nature—progressivism, primitivism, and pastoralism—have by themselves taken lasting root in southern California's literature (though the progressivist myth, for one, has rarely produced great literature anywhere, as Marx argues).[28] Politically and culturally, they have all sprouted here or there, then or now: William Mulholland's progressivist faith in technology's ability to subdue aridity via the L.A. aqueduct (while turning the fertile Owens Valley dry); New Age primitivist faith that, as Mary Austin put it in her 1909 Lost Borders, "Great souls that go into the desert come out mystics;"[29] and the "rurban" and super-suburban arrangements throughout the region that are bastard children of the pastoral myth. But what distinguishes the literature about Southern Californian human and natural environments and the relation between them is that all these myths have been grafted onto each other to produce anti-myths that reverse or invert the founding myths' lines of historical and metaphorizing influence between the human and the natural. Transplanted to this new human-natural arrangement, they have each come to look like what they were intended to efface: progressivism becomes more wild and threatening than the wilderness, as we see in the futuristic LA of the film Blade Runner; primitivism brings not wisdom but insanity, as when Didion describes in "On Morality" that instinct that tells people "that if they do not keep moving at night on the desert they will lose all reason;"[30] and the pastoral becomes the deceptive site of homicide and surveillance, amidst lovely gated gar-dens, in the literature and film of L.A. noir.

What these inversions of foundational myths produce quite often is paranoia—paranoia about nature, about human beings, and, for the writer especially, about metaphor's transference of meaning and agency among human, natural, and technological entities. Who's shaping whom—the environment or man? And which environment: the natural or the built, if these distinctions mean anything in L.A. especially? Do the people drive the freeway or does it drive them? Literature on Los Angeles affects not so much how we see nature and hence how we act on it, as in one tradition of nature writing, but becomes the self-conscious symptom of how our acting upon nature is so patently just "an act," a preposterous conceit, to the extent that nature has become imagined (because it often acts like) some evil avenging double, a destructive con-artist who is the agent not only of our own entrapment in artifice but of our loss of agency. When the Santa Ana winds blow in Los Angeles, Raymond Chandler writes in his story "Red Wind," "every booze party ends in a fight. Meek little wives feel the edge of the carving knife and study their husbands' necks. Anything can happen."[31] "To live with the Santa Ana," Didion writes in "Los Angeles Notebook," "is to accept, consciously or unconsciously, a deeply mech-anistic view of human behavior."[32] Nature in L.A. is, in other words, a mirror of the human nightmare—that continuous wreckage piling on itself before the angel of history—repressed by progressivist, primitivist, and pastoral myths.

The distinctions among the natural, the human, and that unhelpful catch-all "the artificial" are completely blurred in much of Southern California's literature and film. (In Nathanael West's 1939 Day of the Locust, for example, people are plant-like and transplants waiting to die, while nature seems artificial.) As one index to how the region's social and literary history has blurred the lines between the natural, the human, and the built environment, consider the Los Angeles River. L.A.'s "natural" river once narrowed near modern downtown and came to the surface there, drawing Indian and Spanish settlement. After particularly bad floods in 1938, the natural river became, in effect, man-made or manipulated with the construction of the massive concrete bed and banks by which it is today recognized as the city's river, especially when, often for most of the year, there is little or no water in it. When dry, it resembles a banked speedway; a local legislator once proposed turning it into a bicycle path[33]—and many films have imaginatively done so. In Terminator 2, Arnold Schwarzenegger-as-cyborg drives his motorcycle down it in order to rescue a bicycling boy from a careening diesel truck driven by another cyborg from the future. The film begins with a vision of the nuclear destruction of Los Angeles. The rescue is crucial for the sake of humanity's future, since this boy will grow up to be a kind of savior (this is what cyborgs do: go back to change the view ahead). But it is not that boy's agency here that saves humanity, but the agency of technology, and a nearly unimaginable, highly progressed form of it: we do not see the sequence of events that lead up to this cyborg's invention.

The river-as-freeway for a rescued future is a reversal of the freeway-as-river in Didion's Play It As It Lays, which shows again that what looks like human agency is actually its opposite. Didion writes of Maria Wyeth in the passage excerpted above,

> Once she was on the freeway and had maneuvered her way to a fast lane she turned on the radio at high volume and she drove. She drove the San Diego to the Harbor, the Harbor up to the Hollywood, the Hollywood to the Golden State, the Santa Monica, the Santa Ana, the Pasadena, the Ventura. She drove it as a riverman runs a river, every day more attuned to its currents, its deceptions ... Sometimes the freeway ran out, in a scrap metal yard in San Pedro ... or out somewhere no place at all where the flawless burning concrete just stopped, turned into common road, abandoned construction sheds rusting behind it. When that happened she would keep in careful control, portage skillfully back ... and try to keep her eyes on the mainstream, the great pilings, the Cyclone fencing, the deadly Oleander, the luminous signs, the organism which absorbed all her reflexes, all her attention.[34]

There is much to note here from an environmentalist perspective. The freeways are all place names; they *are* places that substitute for the centered places she escapes from, the unlocatable territory to which she lights out to forget trouble. They are also rivers, anthropomorphized with their "deceptions;" the built environment is metaphorized first as nature, then as human, the agency of which human beings must conform to. But when they occasionally run out we meet a scrap metal yard and abandoned construction sheds—rusting perhaps because of all that river that has run out now that the river's concrete is "burning" (the fire and flood curse etched into LA's apocalyptic imagination). Just as the built freeways are naturalized as rivers that are themselves both personified and named after places, Maria is at first an explorer on her "free way" and yet, by the end of the passage, an entity whose reflexes are entirely absorbed by this man-made "organism" she is in thrall to. What is natural, artificial, and human here, and what has agency? And the one reference to plant or animal life—the oleander—is "deadly." Recall Terminator 2: an entirely artificial man drives on a man-made riverbed to rescue a boy from being killed by another artificial man so that the boy can later rescue humanity from its own nuclear destruction. We can only be in Los Angeles, in a world in which technology takes on the forms of nature and human beings the form of technology.

Maria Wyeth's machine-like subjection to the car, the road, and the traffic currents was perhaps inspired by Christopher Isherwood's 1964 novel A Single Man, which also metaphorizes the freeway as river. Isherwood's environmentalist sense of the interrelations among all existing entities, whether it be nature and the city or the title character George and other human beings, derived from his studies in Vedanta spirituality, which holds that there is only a single reality. George, however, feels cut off from everything and everyone, even his own body. (In freeway terms, this does not make a safe driver: accidents, like traffic jams, reveal the inseparable relations of drivers to their bodies, bodies to their automotive extensions, and all drivers to each other's.)

> As he drives, some kind of auto-hypnosis exerts itself … the reflexes are taking over; the left foot comes down … the eyes, moving unhurriedly from road to mirror, mirror to road, calmly measure the distances … it is a river, sweeping in full flood toward its outlet … more and more [the body] appears to separate itself [from George], to become a separate entity: an impassive, anonymous chauffeur-figure with little will or individuality of its own. George's jaws work, his teeth grind, as he chews and chews the cud of his hate … Rage, resentment, spleen … If we say that he is quite crazy at this particular moment, then so, probably, are at least half a dozen others in these many cars around him, all slowing as the traffic thickens … Is the chauffeur steadily becoming more and more an individual? *Is it getting ready to take over much larger areas of George's life?*[35]
> (emphasis mine)

Loss of agency here produces road rage, as George finds an excuse for "hating three quarters of the population of America." George's state resembles a postmodern syndrome that Celeste Olalquiaga calls in Megalopolis an urban *psychasthenia* (from the Greek for a mental disorder):

> Defined as a disturbance in the relation between self and surrounding territory, psychasthenia is a state in which the space defined by the co-ordinates of the organism's own body is confused with represented space. Incapable of demarcating the limits of its own body, lost in the immense area that circumscribes it, the psychasthenic organism proceeds to abandon its own identity to embrace the space beyond. It does so by camouflaging itself into the milieu. This simulation effects a double usurpation: while the organism successfully reproduces those elements it could not otherwise

apprehend, *in the process it is swallowed up by them, vanishing as a differentiated entity.*[36] (emphasis mine)

In Isherwood's novel, this "organism" is not simply George, who experiences that "unpleasant moment when you drive up the ramp which leads onto the freeway and become what's called 'merging traffic.'"[37] It is also the entire environment in which George circulates: the city itself is imagined as an organism that is not only untamed in the passage below—there is no human agency here—but will become swallowed up by its own reproduction of those elements it blindly usurps. When he first came to California, George had loved the "wildness" of the hills and canyons, Isherwood writes, in a series of descriptions that move from the primitivist to the pastoral and from the progressivist finally to death:

> He felt the thrill of … venturing into the midst of a primitive, alien nature … But this afternoon George can feel nothing of that long-ago excitement and awe; something is wrong from the start. The steep, winding road, which used to seem romantic, is merely awkward now, and dangerous. He keeps meeting other cars on blind corners … The area is getting suburban … he is oppressed by awareness of the city below … it has spawned and spread itself over the entire plain. It has eaten up the wide pastures and ranchlands and the last stretches of orange grove; it has sucked out the surrounding lakes and sapped the forests of the high mountains. Soon it will be drinking converted sea water. And yet it will die … It will die because its taproots have dried up—the brashness and greed which have been its only strength. And the desert, which is the natural condition of this country, will return.[38]

Once acting on nature to create Los Angeles as a suburban paradise for individuals to migrate to, human beings are, in these examples, mere reflexes absorbed into a man-made organism that has usurped nature's place and taken on a life of its own.

Isherwood's narrative takes us back to the future of L. A. as Mike Davis might describe it. But in the booster rendition of the freeway, it is a progressivist site that returns to us the most natural of gifts: as Chapman argued in 1967, "The most important freeway dividend may be life itself," because without them, Los Angeles would be "an impossible place to live."[39] The freeway thus also achieves imaginarily what the pastoral mode had once represented; though unnatural, it reminds drivers of what nature once supplied. The freeway is a site that is both within and without the city, valued for what it is not: those poverty-stricken neighborhoods it protects one from seeing, in which American "mobility" is not achieved by pressing the gas. According to Leo Marx, "the appeal of open spaces, or the natural, has as much to do with what is not there (crowding, poverty, class tensions, militarism, social complexity) as with its actual and potential attributes."[40] This rehearsal of the forms of pastoral desire within the unnatural landscape of the freeway is one of the most remarkable yet overlooked aspects of this site: the machine on the freeway in the garden on the desert revives the drive toward freedom and away from urban tension that the pastoral involved, and it rehearses or recapitulates Los Angeles's booster history, which saw the man-made pastoral triumph over the desert, suburbanites retreat to the pastoral with increased (sub)urbanization, and the increasing mobility of the automobile with the construction of the freeways. The American compulsion to find open spaces is evoked at the beginning of the film L.A. Confidential when a city official uses the rhetoric of Manifest Destiny to dramatize the construction of the last stretch of the Santa Monica freeway to the ocean: this is what Manifest Destiny was driving toward. While the freeway—with its concrete, noise, congestion, and exhaust— may seem the antithesis of the pastoral, it is also its culmination: the overcoming of and escape from the city.

In the "only secular communion Los Angeles has," with its "rapture" and "mystical" state, one that induces "a kind of narcosis,"[41] Los Angelenos experience those very qualities associated with divinity for which, argues Leo Marx, the pastoral served as a repository: "beauty, order, harmony, serenity, transcendence." Just as the movement toward the pastoral was a movement toward freedom, so is entering the freeway in its most commonly romanticized version. But only up to a point, as Marx argues about the pastoral: "If pursued too zealously, this centrifugal motion almost certainly will lead to an encounter with omnipotent natural forces and, ultimately, with death."[42]

The Televised Freeway: In "Hot Pursuit" of Death
Let me begin this section with two thematic citations:

> We call it Hot Pursuit. . . .The highspeed action can be thrilling. But it's fraught with danger—mounting injuries and deaths for officers, suspects, and bystanders ... In L. A., where such pursuits are common, police have pioneered what may be the safest way to chase a fugitive: from the air.
> ("In Hot Pursuit," American Justice [A&E Television Networks, 1996])

> Boy—getting off the freeway makes you realize how important love is.
> ("Cher" in the film Clueless)

They call them the "eyes in the sky," and they have given us a new spectator sport on local Los Angeles television: the freeway chase. Local news (even when unscheduled to be on the air) will "cut to a live chase" and "stay with it" until, as the police call it, the "termination point." "It's like the Wild, Wild West," says one news helicopter pilot. This is the hyperreal freeway—not lived space, not real structure, but a mediated, virtual "high speed" experience whose erotics and narcotic appeal are related to the anticipation of "real" death or injury that won't hurt those of us who are watching, since "our" eyes are in the sky, and not on the road.

The freeway reinforces social divisions not only by making the suburbs accessible from downtown, or in the manner in which automobiles serve as extensions of Angelenos, but also in the manner that television—that other "extension of man" in Marshall McLuhan's phrase—mediates and often narcotically inures them from others' social reality and subjectivity. If the modern crowd produced in the artist a desire, as Baudelaire puts it, to enter into others' personalities, to enjoy "this universal communion" that reveals what "a very small, restricted, feeble thing" love is, compared with the soul "giving itself entire ... to the stranger as he passes," the crowded freeway seems to obliterate the soul-sense.[43]

The freeway-as-narcotic is a dominant motif in the literature of Los Angeles. Its etymological connection to Narcissism is exploited thematically by Thomas Pynchon in his 1965 The Crying of Lot 49 and in his essay "A Journey into the Mind of Watts" a year later. In these works, Pynchon links the freeway to whites' narcissistic numbness to black pain. "While the white culture is concerned with various forms of systematized folly," he writes in his essay on Watts:

> the black culture is stuck pretty much with basic realities like disease, like failure, violence, and death, which the whites have mostly chosen—and can afford—to ignore. The two cultures do not understand each other, though white values are displayed without let-up on black people's TV screens, and though the panoramic sense of black impoverishment is hard to miss from atop the Harbor Freeway, which so many whites must drive at least twice every working day. Somehow it occurs to very few of them to leave at the Imperial Highway exit for a change, go east instead of west only a few blocks, and take a look at Watts ... But Watts is country, which lies, psychologically, uncounted miles further than most whites seem at present willing to travel.[44]

The freeway allows whites to protect themselves from social pain in neighborhoods deemed fit, historically, for the construction of freeways. (The Santa Monica freeway, for example, was built over poor neighborhoods far to the south of Beverly Hills, a fact which now inconveniences that town's residents who need to get downtown.) When Pynchon's Oedipa Maas arrives in the aptly named San Narciso, with its "census tracts, special purpose bond-issue districts, shopping nuclei, all overlaid with access roads to its own freeway," she resolves to pull in at the first motel she sees, stillness and four walls having at some point become preferable to this illusion of speed, freedom, wind in your hair, unreeling landscape—it wasn't. What the road really was, she fancied, was this hypodermic needle, inserted somewhere ahead into the vein of a freeway, a vein nourishing the mainliner L.A., keeping it happy, coherent, protected from pain, or whatever passes, with a city, for pain.[45]

After the 1990's, the televised freeway in L.A.'s imaginary has served a dual role: to protect from pain by eroticizing it and to provoke pain outside its hyperreality. Although I have spent hundreds of hours and thousands of miles driving the freeways in Los Angeles, by far my strongest and only painful memories of the freeway were on and through television: the O. J. Simpson car chase, watched live by a national audience in 1994, and especially the L.A. riots in 1992. In both instances, through its mediation, television intervened in the events, if only in the O. J. chase by drawing thousands of people out of their homes and away from the TV to watch the surreal procession from freeway overpasses, whether to cheer him on or "be there" if he killed himself. In 1992, I spent hours in front of the television from the moment in the afternoon when the not-guilty verdict was announced in the case against the

police officers who beat Rodney King until later that night when I could smell smoke
coming through my windows. But the turning point in that televisual experience
came when it was clear that "the eyes in the sky" were no longer looking. The news
helicopters reported the "breaking story" that the police had left the scene at what
turned out to be the "flashpoint" of the riots, the intersection of Florence and
Normandie. It was left to news helicopters to chart the steady progression of
violence, as reporters, watching in the studios, called out (in racialized identification
with the victim) for "someone" to do something about the "animals" brutalizing
Reginald Denny. All of these events, of course, came about because the violence in
the videotape that was replayed on television—against Rodney King—not only
appeared bodily and unjust, and something more real than a "live pursuit", but had a
physical impact on others both before and after the verdict, when the city erupted in
violent rage. Whites across the country were familiarized with what was too familiar
to many minorities. George Holladay's videotape of what happened to Rodney King
off the freeway escaped simulated reality and intervened in social reality, in large
part because the jury members (in the prosecution of the police offers who beat
King) were trained to see it as a series of freeze-frames by the defense. In her
performance piece <u>Twilight: Los Angeles, 1992</u>, Anna Deavere Smith records
Reginald Denny's memories before he was brutalized in a racialized chain reaction.
When he got off the Harbor Freeway on his daily delivery route, Denny, who
admitted that he had not been keeping up on what was going on in California,
surveyed the scene near the flashpoint of the riots and said to Smith: "It was just like
a scene out of a movie—total confusion and chaos. I was in awe."[46] From mediated
to immediate experience, Denny fell brutally into the history of a city that was
swallowing him up.

What Pynchon and many black leaders had warned in 1966 after the Watts riots
came true: because they would be forgotten and the pain of the urban poor forgotten,
or simply remembered as a scene from a movie, the riots would erupt again. After
1992, many have forgotten already, many have not, but the televised freeway, like
the riots themselves, does not make discriminations regarding drivers' subjectivities.
That is perhaps the most curious aspect of the "hot pursuit": drivers being chased
have become the cars that extend them at high speed; their subjectivity, their
memories of the police, are left to the spectator to surmise. Police motives toward the
driver, on the other hand, are understood only by means of the initial fact of evasion:
"There is a general feeling among cops that a person who runs must be hiding
something," the video "Hot Pursuit" claims. And so, when a woman who is an Indian
national was straddling two lanes on Vine in Hollywood and she fled the cops who
tried to pull her over, a long-winding pursuit was underway. As the once live,
televised footage replays, the narrator provides an imaginary history:

> Soon she takes the entrance ramp to the 405, one of L. A.'s busiest
> freeways. This chase was just eight months after the L. A. riots, an outburst
> sparked by another LAPD hot pursuit, the chase and subsequent beating of
> drunk driver Rodney King. The police officers in the King beating would
> later be accused of succumbing to a common pitfall of hot pursuits—

letting adrenaline built up in the chase get the best of them in the capture. [This woman] would later say that one of the reasons she fled was that she feared she would be beaten, like Rodney King.

Just one of the pitfalls of being a Third World woman in Los Angeles: one is not made allowances for the adrenaline built up over history. "Hot Pursuit" leaves us with the cryptic information that as she left her vehicle, "she oddly said 'Vote for Ross Perot'" and was eventually ordered to serve time in a mental facility—but was quickly released and is quite normal, according to her lawyer. The eyes in the sky have it: the woman on the ground has no voice or reason.

Like the freeway experience, the televised freeway offers a communal experience, but one that divides people; it reveals and hides both historical causality and human pain. It is at once deeply personal and terrifying to some and entertaining in its hyperreality to others. One of its curiosities, in the context of the O. J. chase and the L.A. riots, is the possibility that some of these pursuits are themselves "actually" hyperreal: copies without an original. It is precisely in their disembodied, dehistoricized gaze that these numerous chases-from-the-air on TV take on an impersonal life of their own, reproducing themselves as lived experience that has been mediated through the eyes in the sky.

Such a disembodied gaze is the subject of the only book cover among books on Los Angeles (that I am aware of), which represents the freeway from the driver's seat. James Doolin's 1986 painting Highway Patrol (figure 5) presents the freeway from the driver's seat of a patrol car driving in the fast lane: but no one, it seems, is at the wheel—unless the viewer is. Positioned as the subjective gaze in a disembodied space, the viewer is made to seem an extension of a vehicle that has a mind and will of its own—and even its own eyes, by virtue of the two illuminated circles on the control panel. Headlights in the rear view mirrors resemble eyes and stand in for drivers in other cars. On the passenger side stands a rifle: though it is preoccupied with sight and lines of sight, there is no one looking and no one to look at in the image. And there is no stable horizon line in this image of a downward-left curving interchange overpass that is about to pass under an upward-left climbing interchange overpass (there are at least three other divergent angles). The image is threatening precisely because it visualizes a city without subjectivity or situatedness: we lose our bearings in this bodiless view from a highway patrol car.

The televised police chase is only one of the latest of freeway phenomena that challenge us to rethink how we transport ourselves generally into others' subjectivities—and into history—within urban and post-urban environments of the real, the imagined, and the hyperreal. In a very real sense, there is no social space without that transportation. Yet whenever lived social space is mediated for us, whether by maps or movies, we are necessarily made blind to what Benjamin's angel of history (itself a figure of mediation) sees. A goal of this paper has been to understand how such mediations work, how they both enable and limit our vision, in the hope that there are yet richer routes ahead to being in Los Angeles.

James Doolin, <u>Twilight</u> (1999). Courtesy of the Koplin Gallery.

Rand dust jacket (1967). Courtesy of Oxford Univ. Press.

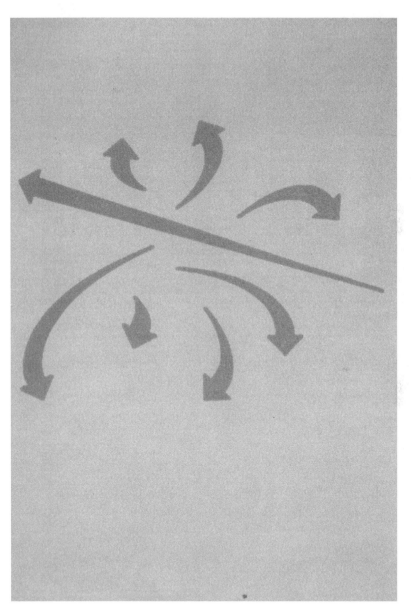

Rand cover board. Courtesy of Oxford Univ. Press (1967).

Keil book cover. Courtesy of Roger Keil (1998).

James Doolin, "Highway Patrol," (1986). Courtesy of the Koplin Gallery.

NOTES

[1] "Miles": International Times, 14 March 1969. Qtd. in Banham below, 17.

[2] Grahame Clarke, "The Great Wrong Place?: L. A. as Urban Milieu," in Clarke, ed., The American City (London, 1988): 142. Qtd. in Mike Davis, City of Quartz (London: Verso, 1990): 83.

[3] Reyner Banham, Los Angeles: The Architecture of Four Ecologies (Middlesex: Penguin Books, 1971): 219.

[4] John L. Chapman, Incredible Los Angeles (New York: Harper & Row, 1967): 82.

[5] Martin Wachs, "The Evolution of Transportation Policy in Los Angeles" in Allen J. Scott and Edward W. Soja, eds., The City: Los Angeles and Urban Theory at the End of the Twentieth Century (Berkeley: University of California Press, 1996): 106. Wachs' article is a more comprehensive historical analysis of transportation in Los Angeles than Banham's study (below). See also: Martin Wachs, "Autos, Transit and the Sprawl of Los Angeles," Journal of the American Planning Association 50, no. 3(1984): 297-310; Wachs and Crawford, eds., The Car and the City: The Automobile, the Built Environment, and Daily Life (Ann Arbor: University of Michigan Press, 1992).

[6] Norman M. Klein, The History of Forgetting: Los Angeles and the Erasure of Memory (London: Verso, 1997). See his appendix, "Where is Forgetting Located?": 301-317. Among the first to be forgotten, of course, are the thousands of people who lost their homes during the construction of the freeways. 15,000 people alone lost their homes for the construction of the Santa Monica freeway. It is said that one apartment owner was "bumped" three times as the route threaded its way through western L.A. See Chapman, 82. Oral histories of these losses are hard to come by.

[7] Leonard Pitt and Dale Pitt, Los Angeles A to Z: An Encyclopedia of the City and County (Berkeley: University of California Press, 1997): 157-161. This appears to be the encyclopedia's longest entry.

[8] Banham, 213, 214.

[9] Scott and Soja, The City, 106.

[10] Roger Keil, Los Angeles: Globalization, Urbanization, and Social Struggles (Chichester, U.K.: John Wiley & Sons, 1998): xv.

[11] Edward Soja, Postmodern Geographies (New York: Verson, 1989): 243-244. See also Fredric Jameson, "Postmodernism, or, The Cultural Logic Late Capitalism." New Left Review 146:53-92.

[12] See Jean Baudrillard, America (London: Verso, 1988).

[13] Joan Didion, After Henry (New York: Simon & Schuster, 1992: 110-111.

[14] Didion, After Henry, p. 110.

[15] Chapman, 87.

[16] Christopher Isherwood, A Single Man (New York: Farrar, Straus, & Giroux, 1964): 36, 40.

[17] J. Nicholas Entrikin, The Betweenness of Place: Towards a Modern Geography (Baltimore: The Johns Hopkins University Press, 1991): 43.

[18] The cover of Mike Davis's Ecology of Fear: Los Angeles and the Imagination of Disaster (New York: Henry Holt, 1998) does, however, present a singular (graphically designed) image of the freeway. Yet, curiously, in neither this book nor his City of Quartz does Davis discuss the freeway system or freeway culture at any length.

[19] Walter Benjamin, Illuminations: Essays and Reflections, trans. Harry Zohn and ed. Hannah Arendt (New York: Schocken Books, 1969): 257-258.

[20] Shotgun Freeway: Drives thru Lost L. A.. A documentary film by Morgan Neville and Harry Pallenberg, 1995.

[21] Banham, 75.

[22] Keil, 60.

[23] Banham, 77-78.

[24] Martin Wachs calls the corporate conspiracy theory a gross oversimplification of the causes of the railway's demise. Citing statistics and newspaper accounts, Wachs argues persuasively that long before these companies intervened by acquiring stock in the street railways and converting trolley cars into buses, the street railways were losing the competition with the automobile. See Scott and Soja, The City, 112-115.

[25] Los Angeles A to Z, 374.

[26] Frederick Jackson Turner, "The Significance of the Frontier in American History," in The Frontier in American History (Tucson: University of Arizona Press, 1986): 12.

[27] Carey McWilliams, Southern California: An Island on the Land (Layton, UT:

Gibbs Smith, 1973; orig. pub. 1946): 15.

[28] Leo Marx, "Open Spaces, City Places, and Contrasting Versions of the American Myth," in Judy Nolte Temple, Open Spaces, City Places: Contemporary Writers on the Changing Southwest (Tucson: University of Arizona Press, 1994): 34-36. This section derives its title from Marx's influential study The Machine in the Garden: Technology and the Pastoral Idea in America (New York: Oxford University Press, 1964).

[29] Mary Austin, Stories from the Country of Lost Borders. Ed. Marjorie Pryse (New Brunswick: Rutgers University Press, 1987): 180.

[30] Joan Didion, Slouching Towards Bethlehem (New York: Farrar, Straus, & Giroux, 1995; orig. pub. 1968): 159.

[31] Raymond Chandler, Trouble Is My Business (New York: Vintage, 1992; orig. pub. 1939): 162.

[32] Slouching Towards Bethlehem, 217.

[33] Al Martinez, City of Angles: A Drive-by Portrait of Los Angeles (New York: St. Martin's Press, 1996): 98.

[34] Joan Didion, Play It As It Lays (New York: Farrar, Straus, & Giroux, 1970): 15-17.

[35] Christopher Isherwood, A Single Man (New York: Farrar, Straus, & Giroux, 1964): 40.

[36] Celeste Olalquiaga, Megalopolis: Contemporary Cultural Sensibilities (Minneapolis: University of Minnesota Press, 1992): 1-2. Qtd. in Edward Soja, Thirdspace: Journeys to Los Angeles and Other Real-and-Imagined Places (Oxford: Blackwell, 1996): 198. Soja points out that the term *psychasthenia* originates with Roger Caillois, a figure in the dissident surrealist movement that influenced the spatial thinking of Walter Benjamin and Henri Lefebrve. (Sofa, 198n.)

[37] Isherwood, 34.

[38] Isherwood, 111.

[39] Chapman, 83.

[40] Open Spaces, City Places, 34.

[41] Joan Didion, The White Album (New York: Farrar, Straus, Giroux, 1979): 83.

[42] Open Spaces, City Places, 35.

[43] Charles Baudelaire, Paris Spleen. Trans. Louise Varčse. (New York: New Directions, 1970; orig. pub. 1869): 20

[44] Thomas Pynchon, "A Journey Into the Mind of Watts," in Dennis Hale and Jonathan Eisen, eds., The California Dream (New York: MacMillan, 1968): 252-253. The essay was originally published in The New York Times Magazine, June 12, 1966.

[45] Thomas Pynchon, The Crying of Lot 49 (New York: Harper & Row, 1986; orig. pub. 1965): 24, 26.

[46] Anna Deavere Smith, Twilight: Los Angeles, 1992 (New York: Doubleday, 1994): 103.

WORKS CITED

Austin, Mary. <u>Stories from the Country of Lost Borders</u>. Ed. Marjorie Pryse. New
    Brunswick: Rutgers University Press, 1987.

Baudelaire, Charles. <u>Paris Spleen</u>. Trans. Louise Varèse. New York: New
    Directions, 1970.

Baudrillard, Jean. <u>America</u>. London: Verso, 1988.

Banham, Reyner. <u>Los Angeles: The Architecture of Four Ecologies</u>. Middlesex:
    Penguin Books, 1971.

Benjamin, Walter. <u>Illuminations: Essays and Reflections</u>. Trans. Harry Zohn and ed.
    Hannah Arendt. New York: Schocken Books, 1969.

Chandler, Raymond. <u>Trouble Is My Business</u>. New York: Vintage, 1992.

Chapman, John L. <u>Incredible Los Angeles</u>. New York: Harper & Row, 1967.

Clarke, Grahame. <u>The American City</u>. London: Verso, 1988.

Davis, Mike. <u>City of Quartz</u>. London: Verso, 1990.

---. <u>Ecology of Fear: Los Angeles and the Imagination of Disaster</u>. New York:
    Henry Holt, 1998.

Didion, Joan. <u>After Henry</u>. New York: Simon & Schuster, 1992.

---. <u>Play It As It Lays</u>. New York: Farrar, Straus, & Giroux, 1970.

---. <u>Slouching Towards Bethlehem</u>. New York: Farrar, Straus, & Giroux, 1995.

---. <u>The White Album</u>. New York: Farrar, Straus, Giroux, 1979.

Entrikin, J. Nicholas. <u>The Betweenness of Place: Towards a Modern Geography</u>.
    Baltimore: The Johns Hopkins University Press, 1991.

Isherwood, Christopher. <u>A Single Man</u>. New York: Farrar, Straus, & Giroux, 1964.

Keil, Roger. <u>Los Angeles: Globalization, Urbanization, and Social Struggles</u>.
    Chichester, U.K.: John Wiley & Sons, 1998.

Klein, Norman M. <u>The History of Forgetting: Los Angeles and the Erasure of
    Memory</u>. London: Verso, 1997.

Martinez, Al. City of Angles: A Drive-by Portrait of Los Angeles. New York: St. Martin's Press, 1996.

Marx, Leo. Open Spaces, City Places: Contemporary Writers on the Changing Southwest. Ed. Judy Nolte Temple. Tucson: University of Arizona Press, 1994.

McWilliams, Carey. Southern California: An Island on the Land. Layton, Utah: Gibbs Smith, 1973.

Olalquiaga, Celeste. Megalopolis: Contemporary Cultural Sensibilities. Minneapolis: University of Minnesota Press, 1992.

Pitt, Leonard and Dale. Los Angeles A to Z: An Encyclopedia of the City and County. Berkeley: University of California Press, 1997.

Pynchon, Thomas. The Crying of Lot 49. New York: Harper & Row, 1986.

---. The California Dream. Eds. Dennis Hale and Jonathan Eisen. New York: MacMillan, 1968.

Shotgun Freeway: Drives thru Lost L. A.. Dirs. Morgan Neville and Harry Pallenberg. King Pictures, 1995.

Smith, Anna Deveare. Twilight: Los Angeles, 1992. New York: Doubleday, 1994.

Soja, Edward. Thirdspace: Journeys to Los Angeles and Other Real-and-Imagined Places. Oxford: Blackwell, 1996.

Turner, Frederick Jackson. The Frontier in American History. Tucson: University of Arizona Press, 1986.

Wachs, Martin. The City: Los Angeles and Urban Theory at the End of the Twentieth Century. Eds. Allen J. Scott and Edward W. Soja. Berkeley: University of California Press, 1996.

Los Angeles, Epicenter of the Cinematic Spectacle

Susanne Rieser
University of Vienna

"Everyone gets really excited . . . about lava engulfing LA," said Mick Jackson, director of Volcano. "It's really about the chaos of Los Angeles. We have earthquakes and mudslides and fires . . . . It's the great thing about [Volcano]—you can never exaggerate too much about Los Angeles. You should have seen us on our location scouts, 30 of us tumbling out of a huge van, with a cell phone glued to our ear." Jackson takes out a note pad and scribbles down a reminder, "A new image for the movie," he says brightly. "Molten lava oozing over a cell phone."
                                                   Patrick Goldstein

Los Angeles, a global center for the media industries, is the default location of most US film and TV-productions. As such, it remains almost invisible. However, when films explicitly address the city, they tend to present it as an ever more spectacular post-Blade Runner environment. It is films like Terminator II: Judgment Day, Escape from L.A., The Crow, Volcano, Independence Day, or Strange Days, which epitomize Los Angeles' nightmarish self-representation at the turn of the millennium.

Los Angeles is also the home of scores of highly spirited independent film and video communities who produce alternative cityscapes. Yet the L.A. indies— recently spotlighted in the April 2000 issue of the film and video monthly The Independent ("Greetings from Los Angeles")—hardly make it outside the local art crowd. It is "mainstream films from Chinatown to L.A. Confidential which represent the key field of inquiry for analyzing how film works to construct the popular [mythology] of Los Angeles," as even Karen Voss in her wonderful analysis "Screening the Other Los Angeles" asserts (157).

Mainstream film teams are hyperactive, as the above quoted interview with Mick Jackson, director of Volcano, suggests. Yet while their sheer activity is somehow comprehensible—we are in Los Angeles, after all—it is puzzling to watch their zealousness in creating a dark and dangerous Lokalkolorit that wildly differs from what the average on-site tourist experiences: Enchanted by sunshine and palm trees, s/he will probably browse around designer outlets and fancy art galleries, have dinner in one of the stylish restaurant, visit any of the glitterati dance clubs and recuperate under the palm trees on one of the beautiful beaches the next day. And while Hollywood bombshells movie audiences around the globe with an ever more violent and apocalyptic screen self, the same visitor, when going to the movies in the evening, may indeed wonder: "But, are we in the same city of Los Angeles, after all?"

In <u>Ecology of Fear: Los Angeles and the Imagination of Disaster</u>, Mike Davis adds a further twist to this already schizoid experience:

> No other city seems to excite such dark rapture. . . . Indeed, as one goes back further in the history of the urban disaster genre, the ghost of the romantic Sublime—beauty in the arms of terror—reappears. The destruction of London—the metropolis once most persecuted in fiction between 1885 and 1940—was imagined as a horrifying spectacle, equivalent to the death of Western civilization itself. The obliteration of Los Angeles, by contrast, is often depicted as . . . a victory for civilization. (277)

This apocalyptic mannerism is very much in sync with action cinema. Action films routinely present carnage and obliteration as a component of their spectacular visual style, and they usually do so to thrill and titillate rather than to shock the audience. In the face of social and cultural crises, action films are a most successful genre in that they seem to offer conventional solutions to otherwise insurmountable problems.

In the following pages I will seek to explore Los Angeles' self-portrait as a cinematic disasterville as well as to contextualize the apocalyptic imagery within the metropolis' geographical and social particularities. Prefatory outlines will comprise theories on action film and a reflection on the affinity of violence, spectacle, and amnesia. The central focus of the essay is on the city's topography and on Hollywood's translation of natural and social traumas into cinematic dramas. These natural and social traumas, ranging from earthquakes and wildfires to poor neigh-borhoods and Hispanic immigration, generate the very explosive apocalyptic city-scape and its seemingly insurmountable problems that action films are designed to resolve.

Spectacular Action Cinema

Action film is top ranking in the multimillion-dollar business of the entertainment industries. It gained this champion position in the 1980s and has further consolidated it throughout the 1990s. Outsized fees, outrageous budgets and profits, together with star merchandizing, hi-tech special-effect industries, and multimedia by-markets continue to break new records. Transnational distribution systems provide almost global box-office presence. Action films—especially the Pacific-Rim productions of Hollywood and Hong Kong—have become an apotheosis of a postfordist popular culture.

Action film, says Larry Gross, is "food for the eyes." Although it does come in many different wrappings, its modes of operation are invariably tantamount to a breath-taking and ear-splitting filmic roller coaster. An adrenaline rush of action that Roland Barthes once called a sumptuous "festival of affects." Chases and crashes, wall to wall-violence, spectacular bodies and hi-tech weaponry are further enhanced by being displayed against the bleak background of urban warscapes and dystopian wastelands. The hyperkinetic and supersonic discourse nosedives the audience into roaring masses of icy water or glowing lava, into flaring flames, gruesome abysses or just into the very "line of fire." Fatal tornados, ferocious beasts, murderous aliens, and lethal meteor showers are further bits of the Hollywood semantics signifying the violent, mostly ultraviolent, break-in of the forces of the "wild" into civilization.

Action film is the contemporary form of a cinema of sensationality and speed. And the more futuristic it behaves, the more it revokes its own origins. "Whether or not it is true," Richard Dyer once commented on Speed, "that the first audiences ducked down in terror at Lumiere's Train Arriving At a Station, is irrelevant—the idea that they did has often seemed to be emblematic of what film is about." Action film has indeed become synonymous with an ever more extravagant engineering of sensations—its formula being the reduction, if not elimination, of complex political and psychological situations and their transformation into the simple moment of extreme physical danger. And it is precisely this narrative austerity as a central stylistic device of the "Big Loud Action Movies" (Gross) which in turn fully releases their true power—the power of suspense surplus, the power of the spectacular excess, and finally, the audio-visual overkill.

Its *leitmotif*—"damn the logic, full speed ahead"—is also how action film reacts to analytical attempts—with "armed response"—forcing what Kathleen Murphy calls a "bloody confetti screenstorm deconstructing image/content into techno-nihilism, a welcome-to-the year-2000 random scatter of pixels" onto aficionados and academic critics alike (51). Action film is highly successful in luring the audience not into identification or intellectual negotiation, but into immersion and affective-somatic response. I will nonetheless attempt to zoom into the politics of the spectacle, because, as their prime position in the entertainment industries suggests, action films are certainly more than "big toys for big boys."

Since only the big-budget blockbusters can generate real grosses at the box-office, films for the global market have to rely on spectacle and gloss and must be appealing in action to sell themselves to the consumer, Wheeler Winston Dixon has pointed out in "Disaster and Memory:" While dialogue-driven films can often translate poorly in overseas markets, "the common language of spectacle, violence, and destruction cuts across all territorial and linguistic boundaries, surviving even the exigencies of dubbing and/or subtitling to reach the widest possible audience base" (92). In this sort of economic environment, the film itself becomes "answerable to a plethora of bankers, investment syndicates, focus groups, audience-testing session" and "looses the opportunity to be responsible for itself" (94). Even more, I want to suggest that it is action films' lavish budgets for the monumental sets and their equally luxurious annihilation alone that display affirmative system value: The super-expensive triumph over the apocalyptic forces of disaster, so popular in Hollywood products from Volcano to Independence Day, itself affirms the survival capacities of the very system that brings forth these action films. The sheer excessiveness of the visual plethora glorifying the apocalyptic scenarios suggest that is almost impossible, at least while in the movie theater itself, to discern the various agendas that are eclipsed within the powerful imagery of the spectacular overdose.

The imagery is so powerful, because action films at heart do not feature crises, but always catastrophes. In her article "Information, Crisis, Catastrophe" Mary Ann Doane distinguishes crises and catastrophes along their temporal dimension: the crisis then is a process, the catastrophe is the most critical moment of a crisis—without duration that is, where everything happens at once (223). Catastrophic time stands still. If progress, as Doane suggests, is the "utopian element" in technological development, then the catastrophe is the dystopia, the always unwelcome interruption of this forward movement. Catastrophe thus signals the failure of an ever-escalating technological desire to conquer nature. However, I will later argue that catastrophes or other disasters are—at least in the action cinema—not always that unwelcome.

Whereas in storytelling meaning has time to linger, to be subject to unraveling, the imagery of the catastrophe is, to borrow another term from Doane, "shot through with explanation" (227). And it is these catastrophic moments in action films, only seconds or split-seconds in duration, where the films unfold their true visual splendor—scenes that I term absolut action (Rieser): when the conventional imagery turns into an iconographic anarchy of explosions and implosions, of violent impacts and the ensuing nihilist images. In the moments of frenzy and ejection, rapture and redemption, where hi-speed editing changes into slo mo, noise into silence, representation into abstraction. Absolut action is the diamond lane on the autobahn of action film. Absolut action relates to action film as does the kiss to romance: brevissimo, but a meaning grenade nonetheless, which structures the entire film—both in a retrospective and (by way of genre-experience) also in a prospective manner. It is this spectacular overdose, which overhauls meaning and leaves us dazed and confused. In fact, there seems to be a powerful alliance between spectacle and amnesia.

Total Recall? Spectacle and Amnesia

The spectacular overdose can be analyzed within a variety of very different theoretical references, the more prominent of which are concepts of surplus, of jouissance, and—with reference to the "explosion of Otherness"—Bakhtin's conception of the carnivalesque. The most sweeping theorization of the spectacle, however, has been supplied by Guy Debord in his landmark book Society of the Spectacle. Debord, the revolutionary member of the Situationist International, who died in 1994 after shooting himself in the heart, claimed that the spectacle is a grandiose maneuver of distraction and deception, which overpowers every other appearance in order to seize the "monopoly of appearance." The role of the spectacle, as he puts it, is to be louder, more powerful and more violent than any other voice. Through the spectacle, Debord concludes, hegemony discourses upon itself in an "endless monologue of self-appraisal." The spectacle, in all its appearances from the court of Versailles to the Apollo landing and the Gulf War, is nothing less than a "self-portrait of power." (13-24)

In other media and cultural studies theories the spectacle is variously conceptualized as a "symptom," as a manifestation of the information overload, as an allegory (in the tradition of Benjamin), or as an entrance valve for differences (as in Bhabhas' notion of postcolonial temporality). For the purpose of this article I would like to mention in particular the postmodern notion of image dominating narrative, as theorized by Josh Cohen in Spectacular Allegories. This postmodern image, which not only overpower the narrative but is also characterized by discontinuity and disruption (in difference to the earlier comparably compact imagery of the Fordist area), reminds Cohen of the Baroque allegory. A new, postmodern multiperspectivity has transformed images into fragments (such as in absolut action)—which are supposedly open to infinite meanings. In the allegorical imagery then the "masculine" vision—masculine in the sense of viewing or subject position—and its attempt to control and dominate the "feminine" sphere of images—as object position—is challenged and deeply frustrated when object-worlds begin to dynamize and to live a life of their own. This dynamization is exactly what viewers experience when confronted with the disaster scenarios of films like Backdraft, Twister, Volcano and action films' general imagery: A reversing process which potentially opens up new grounds for visual agency and an eventual re-distribution in the symbolic relation between the visual subject- and object-positions. This is also what Lyotard refers to with his concept of the figurative, which inter-rupts the system of knowledge by transgressing perspectivical representation. But as long as we just end up with a "neoliberal pluralism of indeterminacy" (Benhabib), the progressive potential of the allegory/figurality remains inactivated.

This is why I want to contextualize the spectacle within hegemonic discourse, in particular within official memory. Because the spectacle—the violent rupture of the audio-visual sequitur—is, I presume, often designed as a consciously arranged fissure in the official memory.

In his article "'Make My Day!' Spectacle as Amnesia in Imperial Politics" Michael Rogin analyzes the spectacle as the in/visible link between contemporary political practices and their historical roots. By referring to the works of Richard Slotkin and others, he traces the spectacular US foreign policy back to the large-scale violence that has always been part of American history, ever since the first European settlers began to wrest land away from natives and through the times of Manifest Destiny which by now might as well be called "ethnic cleansing".

"Go ahead, make my day!" President Reagan warned the Congress, threatening to veto a petition on tax-increase. Reagan was quoting Clint "Dirty Harry" Eastwood who speaks that line in Sudden Impact (1983) to an African American hoodlum pressing his gun on a female hostage's head. Eastwood provokes the murder of the hostage, in order to kill the hoodlum. The lives that Eastwood puts at risk are black and female, not his own. The president as well had made women and people of color his targets, notably through the tax cuts that were meant to axe parts of their social security benefits. According to a survey done by Rogin, almost everyone was familiar with the "Go ahead! ..."-expression, but hardly anybody could recall the context in which it had been said. Amnesia, he concludes, makes it possible to remember the white hero—and simultaneously forget the context which produced him: "In the American myth we remember, white men alone risk their lives in equal combat. In the one we forget, white men show how tough they are by resubordinating and sacrificing their race and gender others" (505).

The notion of "white heroes above suspicion," reminds me of the film The Big Hit. The Big Hit is an LA-based action movie featuring a hyperkinetic imagery and some of the most dazzling visuals when Mark Wahlberg throws a bomb somewhere in the thirtieth floor of an L.A. high-rise and bungee-jumps out off the window. After cutting the rope he splashes deep down into a conveniently located swimming pool, the quite blue water of which is forcefully torn to drops by Wahlberg's massive impact and turns, only split-seconds later, into a blazing inferno caused by the powerful detonation of the bomb.

It is hard not to like the hero and sympathize with him, for he is a sensitive, cute and shy guy—who "unfortunately" has to make his living as a killer on demand, because of his two gorgeous but equally greedy girl-friends—one of them African American, the other a "Jewish princess." While about half of the action is in fact caused by his frantic attempts to hide this double life (as he doesn't want to "hurt either's feelings"), the other half of the action is caused by his Hispanic side-kick, who tries to set him up. The nauseating representation of Wahlberg's "race and gender others" however gets lost in the course of a spectacle which fuses one image into another with blinding speed and razor-sharp cutting: a spectacle so overwhelming that the viewer can do little but submit to the film's seamless mesh of violent chases and grandiose killings. Mark Wahlberg is essentially the sexy brother of Forrest Gump, on whom Jane Caputi remarks that he, an emblem of American innocence, never actively hurts anyone. Yet, significantly, "most of those around him serve him in some way or another and then drop dead. Forrest Gump is a smiley face stamped on the violence and injustice in American history" (157).

Amnesia in this sense is a cultural strategy of selective repression. Rogin: "Since amnesia means motivated forgetting, it implies a cultural impulse both to have the experience and not to retain it in memory. It signifies not simply memory loss but a dissociation between sensation and ego that operates to preserve both." Amnesia supports guilt-free pleasures: The spectacle allows the sensual (re-)enactment of repressed (usually violent) events. Rogin's observation, that "amnesia disconnects from their objects and cuts off from memory those intensified, detailed shots of destruction, wholesaled on populations and retailed on body parts" (507)—can be validated in action movies from Rocky to Saving Private Ryan.

Amnesia serves as a filter for the "return of the repressed," which in the wrappings of surface entertainment—films, TV-series, talk shows—permits the scopophilic indulgence into the "illegitimate" original scenario, in that "it lets the spectacular imagery alone rise to the more memorable symbolic order" (507). The spectacular slaughtering and dismemberment in action films is reflected by the formal dis-memberment (the absolut action-sequences) and is thus (to speak with Irigaray) in total opposition to a political claim for re-membering. The spectacular imagery of action film—in its superficiality, sensationality, ephemerality and reproducibility—is a perfect arena for the manipulation of amnesic desires.

Disasterville

Los Angeles, the self-proclaimed capital of catastrophes, is the natural habitat of disaster imagery. And the discourse on the topography of the city is one of the central issues determining the imagery of Hollywood action cinema.

Mike Davis has argued that the clustering of natural disasters in the L.A. region has generated a discourse within which the former "Land of Sunshine" is reinventing itself as an "Apocalypse Theme Park". Paranoia about nature—about earthquakes, droughts, floods, and hurricanes—helps to conceal the "social construction of natural disaster" and deflects attention away from the fact that L.A. has deliberately put itself in harm's way. Actually, the majority of natural disasters, says geographer Kenneth Hewitt, "are characteristic rather than accidental features of the places and societies where they occur."

The works of Norman Klein and Mike Davis present excellent accounts of how urbanization in L.A. has been violating environmental common sense for generations. Historic wildfire corridors have been turned into suburbs, wetland zones into marinas, and floodplains into industrial districts. An estimated amount of three billion tons of concrete—or 250 tons per inhabitant—have been poured over prime land. Moreover, the dilemma with extreme events—such as quakes, droughts, floods—is that they tend to organize themselves in causal chains. Droughts, for example, favor wildfires, which, in turn, remove ground cover and make soils impermeable to rain. This in turn increases the risk of flooding. Sheet flooding and landslides, then, result in dramatic erosion. Davis: "The Southern California land-scape epitomizes the principle of nonlinearity where small changes in driving vari-ables or inputs—magnified by feedback—can produce disproportionate, or even discontinuous, outcomes" (19).

Yet when Davis claims that Southern California has experienced natural disasters that were "as unnatural as the beating of Rodney King and the ensuing riots," one is left to wonder about the curious "Biblical Disaster?"-table he has put together in Ecology of Fears (see fig. 1). Although rightfully acclaimed as a highly original and meticulous critic of the disaster discourse in Los Angeles, the renowned sociologist certainly joins in the very discourse he is critical of. Ironically or not, the table suggests that it seems almost impossible, even for the most conscientious scholars, to escape the apocalyptic rhetoric of the city.

BIBLICAL DISASTERS?

Date	Disaster	Dead	Damage (millions)
1992 February	Storm/flood	8	$ 150
1992 April	Riot	54	$ 1,000
1992 June	Earthquake	1	$ 50
1993 January	Storm/flood	9	$ 150
1993 October	Firestorm	3	$ 1,000
1994 January	Earthquake	72	$42,000
1995 January	Storm/flood	4	$ 200

Source: Figures from the Los Angeles Times.

Fig. 1. Biblical Disasters?
(Davis 8).

Fear of depth and of aridity

LA is built on top of sand-filled ancient ocean basins full of hollow spaces, which enhances the vulnerability of the city's exposure to earthquakes in terms of depth stability. The region had been mostly a desert until, long before the construction of the aqueduct, subterranean water basins were discovered. The subsequent cultivation of thousands of orange, lemon and avocado groves turned Southern California into a new "Garden of Eden." Local promoters in the 20s and 30s accordingly classified the L.A. region as "Our Mediterranean! Our Italy!" (Davis 12). The Mediterranean metaphor, well known from the TV-series Falcon Crest, which features an old-established Italian American wine-growing dynasty, has successfully superinstalled a fictional European history over the original Native-American and Mexican cultures. Similarly, Chinatown, the film portraying the social dimensions and private disasters connected to the planning of a huge dam, is both the "ur-text for L.A. political history" (Klein 247), and an "indictment of the city's refusal to accept L.A.'s real identity as a *desert*" (Voss 176).

Not surprisingly, two cardinal fears of the L.A. region are fear of depth and fear of aridity. The paranoia about earthquakes certainly has a realistic context—with seismologists warning that the recent quakes have been too infrequent to relieve the accumulated strain of the Pacific Rim, so that apprehension about The Big One is only reasonable. But the paranoia may also reflect a kind of sub-surface/subconscious guilt over the reckless conquest of the Native American/Mexican soil, which might at any moment—and here goes the projection—go on a vendetta-trip, wiping out the falsifiers of history in a big seismic blow-out.

Also the fear of aridity, or (to put it the other way round)—the desire for humidity—has a metaphorical quality to it. Humidity, as the billion dollar cosmetic industry with its obsessive "moisture, moisture, moisture"—fetishism suggests, certainly not only refers to skin moisture, but to the horrifying idea of losing out on capital features of the bodily fluids of sexuality: humidity/fluidity/fertility. Just as the fear of depth in Southern California may be linked to an (admittedly very funky) obsession with surfaces and superficiality, so may the fear of aridity be associated to one of the world's largest sex industries in L.A.

I however want to insist that the earthquake paranoia is the really obscene of the two: Although devastation is a realistic threat to Southern California, the hitherto death toll is infinitely small when compared to other earthquakes in the rest of the world (such as in Armenia, Japan, Turkey, or China). The same is true for floods, droughts or volcanoes, which are devastating—in Mozambique, Ethiopia and Indonesia.

Fire Alarm

Other popular fears, such as fear of fire, are more explicitly connected to human agents. Fires in Los Angeles have a unique discursive quality, with the fires of the Watts Rebellion, the fires of the 1992 riot and the frequent natural chaparral fires being melted into one single phenomenon. And while the human responsibility for tenement fire, affecting mostly poor immigrants in run-down and overcrowded buildings, is persistently "naturalized," wildfire—a natural cyclical phenomenon of the desert flora—is, in a reverse logic, suspected to be manmade (Davis). Hysteria about wildfire in Malibu has led to open speculations that black gangs were "burning rich white neighborhoods"—some even hinting at a possible "Muslim connection" to New York's World Trade Center bombing. T. C. Boyle's Tortilla Curtain gives a fascinating account of how paranoia turns the protagonist of the novel from liberal into an almost fascist citizen in a gated Anglo community situated in one of the fire-prone valleys. In the early 1990s, the Los Angeles Times summarized the fear: "Fire prevention and crime prevention in California are becoming one and the same. . . . Californians need to stop viewing brush fires solely as acts of God and start thinking of them as sometimes acts of criminal—even pathological—man. . . . We are no longer fighting 'it;' we are fighting 'them'" (5 November, 1993).

Davis presents a fascinating social history of the "arsenic Other": While the arsonist was formerly suspected to be an Indian, a tramp, a Wobbly, or (in the 1950s) a sexual pervert who "sets fire at night in order to see women run out of their homes in a state of undress," the contemporary arsonists are believed to be either inner-city black gangs or homeless people dwelling in illegal encampments in the L.A. hinterland (133).

Outlawing the Wildlife

The Los Angeles Times regularly features news items of wild animals intruding into the urban region—live snakes washed upon beaches, mountain lions in backyards, coyotes somewhere down the streets in the suburbs. The many in-accessible canyons around the metropolis sustain a large wildlife population, which more and more frequently seems to take pleasure in visiting also inner city parks and hills.

Mountain lion hysterias and similar panics about black bears in hot tubs, plague-carrying squirrels or killer bees are symptomatic of a precarious relationship between the metropolis and its environment. While humans' urban pathologies—such as trash-dumping or paramilitary training—are intruding ever deeper into wildlife's habitat, the wild is adapting to what Davis calls the "pet-and-garbage ecology of the suburbs" (246).

Predators in the city are a hallmark of a new and unwanted intimacy of humans and wildlife. And while the urban poor and non-white populace is put into the same category with beasts, the startled predators on their search for food are criminalized as trespassers. Predators, as also the film Predator II depicts them, are signifiers of a return of the repressed.

In psychoanalysis, repression is the alternative to integration. And the refusal to integrate in fact results in playing the dualistic drama—the showdown between human and nature. Stacy Alaimo argues that it is paradoxically the very establishment of "nature" or of "the wild" as fixed outside human space that renders it most securely bound within human discourse. One needs only to remember, Alaimo elucidates, that the star of Free Willy was "none other than a very captive whale"—to realize that human fantasies of animal freedom mark rather than disrupt the captivity of nonhuman nature (238). Quoting Baudrillard, who claims that in a universe of increasing speech "the fact that animals do not speak—weighs more and more heavily on our organization of meaning" (238), Alaimo introduces new perspectives on the dinosaur films (a sub-genre of action film). The destabilization of the discursive fixity of wilderness, she says, is enhanced by invoking predators not only as monsters and spectacles, but also as media-stars and pajama patterns which by and through representation "speak for and within the discourses of the human" (238). When nature and culture are conceptualized as opposing rather than interfacing processes, predatory monsters—in their various guises as dinosaurs, carnosaurs, giant ants or godzillas—may emanate from this strained dualism.

Lost Angeles

Aside from earthquakes, fires, and the rampant fauna, it is also certain segments of the human society who are imagined as threatening Los Angeles' "old"—established identity.

Barrios and hoods, home to large segments of the Hispanic and African American Angelites, are discursively associated to warscapes by urban apocalypse movies. Post-apocalyptic L.A. as popularized by movies such as Blade Runner or Escape from L.A. is a city occupied by assassinators, terminators, mutants, and gangs. These scenarios constitute postmodern versions of film noir: endless nights and endless (presumably acid) rains signify urban wastelands and a climate gone industrially mad (Klein).

Since the 1980s there has been a dramatic trend toward the merging of all L.A. fiction with the disaster or survivalist narrative. With the decay of L.A.'s Anglo identity, notes Davis, race hysterias have shifted from images of invading hordes of aliens to images of "the city as the Alien itself," the destruction of which affords an illicit pleasure not always visible in previous annihilations. Territorial anxieties and the instability of the white hegemony, however, lead to bizarre overreaction and mystification not only in action cinema, but also in family entertainment.

In his book Cinematic Political Thought: Narrating Race, Nation and Gender Michael J. Shapiro spotlights white Angeleno anxiety as a core element in the film Father of the Bride II. Los Angelites are certainly less old-established and more mobile than many other populations. Nonetheless, they are, just like all other non-nomadic people, territorially organized. And because "territorially organized people understand themselves on the basis of autonomy they ascribe to their spatio-temporal limits and constraints," Shapiro maintains, "alterations of boundaries or new cross-boundary transactions can threaten to attenuate collective identity" (82).

Although FOB II is not an action film, it is a useful example of how territorial anxieties and threatened Anglo identities are not an exclusive domain of the action cinema, but diffuse also into standard family entertainment: FOB II could be described as a sugar-coated paraphrase of Predator II, an exceptionally savage action film that will be highlighted later in this essay. When L.A. resident George Banks, the father of the bride, learns he is to become a grandfather, he experiences an identity crisis and decides to make a bold move and sell the house that has been the family home for 18 years. The buyer, Mr Habib, is a predatory Arab businessman who comes across as the bogey of culture clashes straight out of a Samuel-Huntington chamber of horror. Shapiro: "[The Arab] is symptomatic of a more general con-temporary anxiety, the construction of the Cultural Other as a threat to the domestic space of the nation as a whole" (83). When Bank finally understands that for Habib the house is simply an inconvenience on a "valuable piece of land" he screams: "This is not a piece of land, this is my home! Don't bulldoze my memories," he pleads. Habib relents but charges him much more than he had paid for the house the previous day. While Habib is thus represented as an economic predator, the wealthy lifestyle of the Banks family remains undiscussed. "Habib is more than an item of script modernization," says Shapiro, "he is a threat to the territorial/cultural space of a nation:" He is the "dangerous cultural Other," who operates with a different commitment "with respect to what is exchangeable versus singular or non-exchangeable because of its special cultural and emotional significance" (84). Habib is, as I would like to emphasize, essentially an Angeleno in that he represents the dark, avaricious side of the legendary L.A. boosterism. Habib is nothing but the alter ego of George Banks, a potential protagonist out of Norman Klein's The History of Forgetting: Los Angeles and the Erasure of Memory, which provides not only first-class research data but also striking insights into the long-standing L.A. practice of "bulldozing memory."

The Cartography of HelL.A.

While Father of the Bride II only "plays" with territorial anxieties, disaster fiction and film have begun to openly exploit Anglo anxiety. The discourse of multi-culturalism in LA, writes Lisa Lowe, "constructs the white citizen against the back-ground of a multicultural dystopia" (85).

Falling Down (Joel Schumacher, 1992), the shooting of which ironically had to be interrupted during the L.A. up-rising, became "the first film remapping L.A. according to the new Los Angeles myth—the city as Hispanic hell" (Klein). The route that D-FENS takes constitutes a fantasy of the "the browning," "thirdworlding" or "Latinization" of Los Angles. D-FENS' epic journey across the city manipulated into El Lay reminds Elana Zilberg of psychotic disturbances associated with the contemporary recomposition of "space-time-being" in Los Angeles at the turn of the millennium: "Film director Schumacher employs an array of filmic devices to produce an awesome schizophrenic accumulation of energy in his protagonist, and indeed, in his audience—the sort of madness born of late capitalism's excess depicted in Deleuze and Guattari's 'Schizo Out for a Stroll' in Capitalism and Schizophrenia" (185).

The film presents the barrio infinitely larger than it really is—a neo-noir strategy "which makes for better suspense thrillers, is better for dirty kills," comments Klein on the portrait of L.A. "falling down from an Anglo point of view."

As much as I love noir, and find it exotically compelling, it is nevertheless often utterly false in its visions of the poor, of the non-white in particular. It is essentially a mythos about white male panic—the white knight in a cesspool of urban decay.... The booster myths (sunshine, climate, Protestant Eden) generate an emptiness that leads to violence and despair, in the form of urban fables. The crime on dark streets stands in for the fears about foreigners, jobs, speculations, and cheap hype. It pits the white, usually Protestant, shamus against a world that is utterly transient, as if no poor communities exist except as a hangout for crooks and addicts. What results is a posse really; it distracts memory away from community life as it existed inside the city. (79-80)

Yet while the poverty of hoods and barrios once guaranteed them the pole position for locating crime dramas, a new competitor has evolved: public space itself. Crime dramas, especially those on TV, have indeed been undergoing substantial changes. Elayne Rapping in "Alien, Nomads, Mad Dogs and Road Warriors" analyzes the most recent transformations both of the figure of the delinquent and of the areas of delinquency.

In media representations, delinquents once tended to be big criminals (drug lords, child murderers, or ruthless gang members) who, according to Rapping, are increasingly being replaced by small trespassers such as petit thieves, prostitutes, sexual deviants, or drug users. People, who are harming themselves rather than others—essentially the ethnic poor and the "white trash" in the streets. While criminals were formerly presented essentially as people "just like us," pathological but still subjects who could be analyzed and were suitable to correctional treatment, the criminals in new TV-tabloids such as COPS are presented as not only irredeemable but also as increasingly "other" and "alien" (256). Ideas of reform, correction, or cure seem wildly anachronistic for these inhuman freaks:

> Crime itself . . . is radically reconstructed. No more do criminals plot and scheme towards nefarious goals; act out of jealous rage, greed, or anger; hide out and attempt to cover their tracks as in traditional narratives. Now we have a new set of characters, apparently driven not by reasonable, if reprehensible, desires and goals, but by brute instinct or chemical derangement; these criminals lurk, wander, and simply break down a spiritual and physical wasteland somewhere outside society's orderly borders. . . . In place of the orderly plot structure of conflict, crises, and resolution, we now have a series of endless irrational disruption. (259)

The presentation of these new crime characters as inscrutable, irresponsible, uncontrollable, and random, is utterly dehumanizing and barbarizing. When questioned by police officers, their stories appear either incoherent or meaningless— due to lack of English, to mental illness or their being under the influence of alcohol or drugs. Their crime essentially is "not being capable of comprehending the rules by which we live" (267). They are not so much deviant from normal behavior as simply "aliens hovering at our borders," held back only by surveillance systems and the ever-present police forces (266). COPS is not a grand narrative of spectacular crimes, but a series of and about little dispersed spectacles. COPS essentially tells people to feel safe only in gated communities and—in the case of LA—in the secured shopping districts of Santa Monica's Third Street Promenade and Universal's City Walk or the shopping malls of Westwood, Century City or Beverly Hills.

White supremacism

In the dystopian city genre, an increasing number of writers experiment with genocides. The new survivalism of the dystopian city genre is one that Davis terms "gourmet survivalism" (318), with reproduction organized on strict eugenic principles in order to provide "executive-quality genes" (323). And although there are certainly progressive post-apocalyptic scenarios, re-fashioning L.A. with alternative genders, ethnicities and topographies, many disaster films feature elements of white supremacism. Davis warns that ethnic cleansing programs as laid out in the infamous Turner Diaries (written by the American Nazi Andrew MacDonald in 1978), have become to be understood as an instruction manual for neonazis of how to stage a Holocaust in Los Angeles:

> Concentrating on the city's vulnerable infrastructure, they cripple LAX, blow up freeway overpasses, set the harbor ablaze, and cut the aqueduct. White liberals are shot on the spot. . . . The first act of the new regime is the brutal expulsion of seven million blacks and Latinos from the Los Angeles area. . . . Meanwhile, hundreds of thousands of Jews and people of mixed ethnicity are marched into the mountains north of Los Angeles, where they are slaughtered with machine guns and hand grenades. Finally . . . the organization turns to white race traitors. Sixty thousand are hung from tens of thousands of lampposts, power poles, and trees. After the purification of Southern California, the Organization nukes the "contaminated" cities of Miami, Toronto, and New York, killing at least 60 million people. (333-35)

It is in fact hardly possible to enjoy survivalist narratives after learning about the Turner Diaries. The same holds true also for imaginations of an environmental collapse as "nature's final solution" to "overpopulation" and "race decay" as jointly invoked by the New Right and Christian ministers, who call for a divine genocide against a Sodom and Gomorra-Los Angeles.

Aliens sell

Threats to territories and identities are further developed in the alien invasion genre, where immigration and invasion are presented as exchangeable terms. The belief that "aliens are already among us," as portrayed in the film Tujunga Canyon Contacts, has produced dozens of support groups for self-proclaimed victims of alien sexual predation (Davis 341): Sexual hysteria about alien impregnation in the "Alien-versus-Aryan story"—essentially infused with fear about miscegenation—is also provided by the underlying equation between alien invaders and illegal immigrants in films like Alien/Nation (1988). Lianne McLarty is rightfully disturbed by the fact that Alien/Nation puts marginalized racial and sexual identities into positions of superhuman power and simultaneously poses dominant power as a form of powerlessness, thus reversing the relations of power between victim and prosecutor. The film, more radically even than the above-mentioned film The Big Hit, constructs hegemonic segments as "not only disempowered but also violently victimized precisely because of the (monstrous) identities of Others" (356). The alien thus both ignites and justifies the violence enacted upon it: "Recent alien invasion films construct identity as a matter of biological essentialism, promoting a kind of purity which depends not only on a violent defense of boundaries, but on the obliteration of differences altogether" (356).

Fig. 2. LAX – Los Angeles International Airport Theme Building: The aliens have already landed.
Source: The Postcard Factory, Canada.

Predator II

Predator II (not to be confused with Predator, starring Arnold Schwarzenegger) opens with an all black screen and a distant soundtrack of African drum music and animal sounds. Ululation intensifies as the camera rapidly moves in an aerial shot over jungle woods until it hits the high-rises of downtown L.A. emerging suddenly out of the wildwood. Except for the yellowish gray smog layers, the image with the locating text "Los Angeles 1997" bears resemblance to common postcard views of the downtown area (fig. 3). A sudden cut then offers us a curious red and blue thermal vision of downtown L.A. Only later on will we learn that this is the point-of-view of a mysterious and monstrous Predator, who has a heat-sensitive vision. The next cut throws us right into the middle of a firepowered street warfare between Jamaican and Colombian drug syndicates, destitute police officers and hysterical news reporters, while the animal noises slowly transform into the noises of the city wilderness—shootings, sirens, cars, screams. The Predator, all the while watching from above, is both a high-tech and ultraprimitive creature, endowed with super-human power, dreadlocks and vagina dentata facial features. In this film, Yvonne Tasker points out, L.A. is nothing but "an urban jungle . . . the hunting ground for the Predator on his safari" (50). The Colombians are presented as gunslingers and the fantasized voodoo barbarity of the Jamaicans is exotic and shocking—but still surpassed by the atrocious bestiality of the Predator himself, who usually doesn't leave a party without skinning his victims from head to toe and hanging them upside down.

Fig. 3. Downtown Los Angeles.
Source: California Scene Postcard.

In "Angels Dinosaurs Aliens" Tomas DiPiero and Rajani Sudan suggest that the real trauma with monsters, aliens—or predators, for that matter—is that something about them remains un-incorporated into subjectivity (6). Traditional trauma theories which believe in overcoming traumatic (repressed or otherwise unconscious) experiences by integrating them, are thus considered inadequate by DiPiero and Sudan: because the alien monsters are precisely constructed as non-assimilable entities, as beings from another order of signification, as "standing at meaning's limits." Aliens are in fact rarely imagined as joining in with those whom they visit, but rather as forcing a new way of being onto the people. They are "radically, absolutely other"—as is the case in Men In Black, which suggests that weirdos such as Dennis Rodman, Elvis Presley or Newt Gingrich are in fact aliens—even if they look like humans. Since absolute alterity is however unthinkable, we have to invent discourses that articulate alien morphology. Aliens, who regularly enter in moments of logical or political crises (in action cinema that is in the moments of the rupture of the audio-visual sequitur, where absolut action unfolds its splendor) are, according to DiPiero and Sudan "invented to suture the gaps created by their own logic" (10). Aliens, monsters and predators are, to put it with Zizek, symptomatic. Because the symptom, although it can be interpreted as a knot of significations (significations being subject to symbolic interpretation)—is always more than that. There is a remainder, an excess not reducible to the symbolic network. It is this remainder, this residue, which the alien encounter is meant to exploit. The fascination of the catastrophe rests on the desire to confront the remainder—or to be confronted with that which is the excess of signification.

The Riot as Symptom

Alienization is a popular and powerful strategy to naturalize social disaster. The 1992 riot, inaccurately and insufficiently attributed to outrage over LAPD brutality after the Rodney King beating and to anti-Koreanism, was in fact driven primarily by the "empty bellies and broken dreams" of the victims of the early 1990s' recession. Irrespective of vast evidence (cf. Davis, Klein) verifying that the riot was a "class issue," media's obsession with Hispanic and especially with Black violence has persistently represented the uprising as a "race issue."

It was an almost unrealistic moment when I caught sight of a certain illustration in Davis' Ecology of Fear (fig. 4): the reproduction of an image from a satellite operated by the National Atmospheric Association from April 30th, 1992 which shows a large thermal anomaly spreading over Los Angeles, extending over almost 90 square kilometers—with the hottest spots in Downtown and some smaller anomalies in the north and south.

The riot, although "composed of tens of thousands of individual acts of anger and desperation, was perceived from the orbit as a unitary geophysical phenomenon" (Davis 422).

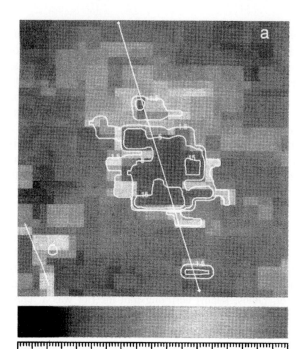

The L.A. riot from
space

Fig. 4
Source: Davis (421).

The satellite images thus amounts to a spectacular overdose—a symptom, if you want, from the heat-sensitive point-of-view of the Predator in the film Predator II. By fusing the many individual acts of outbursts into one grand phantasm, the image— once as a meaning-loaded opening sequence to a Hollywood action film (1990) and once as a dispassionate high-tech recording from a satellite (1992)—is a most perfect example of a postmodern image "dominating the narrative" (Cohen): An allegory, which lives a life of its own, and which exemplifies the fusion of social trauma and cinematic drama—in Los Angeles, epicenter of the spectacle.

WORKS CITED

Alaimo, Stacy. "Endangered Humans? Wired Bodies and Human Wilds in Carnosaur, Carnosaur 2, and 12 Monkeys." Camera Obscura 40/41 (May 1997): 227-44.

Caputi, Jane. "Small Ceremonies: Ritual in Forrest Gump, Natural Born Killers, Seven and Follow Me Home." Sharrett 147-74.

Cohen, Josh. Spectacular Allegories: Postmodern American Writing and the Politics of Seeing. London: Pluto Press, 1998.

Davis, Mike. Ecology of Fear: Los Angeles and the Imagination of Disaster. New York: Vintage Books, 1998.

Debord, Guy. The Society of the Spectacle. New York: Zone Books, 1994.

DiPiero, Tomas and Rajani Sudan. "Angles Dinosaurs Aliens." Camera Obscura 40/41 (May 1997): 5-15.

Dixon, Wheeler Winston. Disaster and Memory: Celebrity Culture and the Crisis of Hollywood Cinema. New York: Columbia UP, 1999.

Doane, Mary Anne. "Information, Crisis, Catastrophe." Logics of Television: Essays in Cultural Criticism. Ed. Patricia Mellencamp. Bloomington: Indiana UP, 1990: 222-39.

Goldstein, Patrick. "Volcanic Convergences." Los Angeles Times, 19 August 1996, F7.

Klein, Norman M. The History of Forgetting: Los Angeles and the Erasure of Memory. London and New York: Verso, 1997.

Lowe, Lisa. "Imagining Los Angeles in the Production of Multiculturalism." Immigrant Acts: On Asian American Cultural Politics. Ed. Lisa Lowe. Durham: Duke UP, 1996.

McLarty, Lianne. "Alien/Nation: Invasions, Abductions, and the Politics of Identity." Sharrett 345-60.

Murphy, Kathleen. "Black Arts." Film Comment 31.5 (September/October 1995): 51-53.

Rapping, Elayne. "Aliens, Nomads, Mad Dogs and Road Warriors: Tabloid TV and the New Face of Criminal Violence." Sharrett 249-74.

Rieser, Susanne. Action Film: The Politics of the Spectacle. Work in progress.

Rogin, Michael P. "'Make My Day!' Spectacle as Amnesia in Imperial Politics." Cultures of United States Imperialism. Ed. Amy Kaplan and Donald Pease. Durham: Duke Up, 1993: 499-534.

Shapiro, Michael J. Cinematic Political Thought: Narrating Race, Nation and Gender. New York: New York UP, 1999.

Sharrett, Christopher, ed. Mythologies of Violence in Postmodern Media. Detroit: Wayne State UP, 1999.

Tasker, Yvonne. Spectacular Bodies: Gender Genre and the Action Cinema. London: Routledge, 1993.

Voss, Karen. "Replacing L.A.: Mi Familia, Devil In a Blue Dress, and Screening the Other Los Angeles." Wide Angle 20.3 (July 1998): 157-81.

Zilberg, Eleana. "Falling Down in El Norte: A Cultural Politics and Spatial Poetics of the ReLatinization of Los Angeles." Wide Angle 20.3 (July 1998): 182-209.

Filmography

Backdraft (Ron Howard, USA 1991)
Blade Runner (Ridley Scott, USA 1982)
Chinatown (Roman Polanski, USA 1974)
Falling Down (Joel Schumacher, USA 1992)
Father of the Bride II (Charles Shyer, USA 1995)
Free Willy (Simon Wincer, USA 1993)
Escape from L.A (John Carpenter, USA 1996)
Independence Day (Roland Emmerich, USA 1996)
Men In Black (Barry Sonnenfeld, USA 1997)
Predator II (Steven Hopkins, USA 1990)
Rocky (Robert Chartoff, Irwin Winkler, Sylvester Stallone, USA 1976-1985)
Saving Private Ryan (Steven Spielberg, USA 1998)
Speed (Jan De Bont, USA 1994)
Strange Days (Kathryn Bigelow, USA 1995)
Sudden Impact (Clint Eastwood, USA 1983)
Terminator II: Judgment Day (James Cameron, USA 1991)
The Big Hit (Che-Kirk Wong, USA 1998)
The Crow (Alex Proyas, USA 1993)
Twister (Jan De Bont, USA 1996)
Volcano (Mick Jackson, 1997)
Waterworld (Kevin Reynold, USA 1995)

ABSTRACTS
Working Sites: Texts, Territories, and Cultural Capital in American Cultures

Robert Lawson-Peebles, "Foucault's Mirror, the Amazon Basin, and the Topography of Virginity"
The starting point for this essay is Foucault's lecture "Of Other Spaces." Foucault discusses the mirror as an object, which exists in one space while reflecting another. It is both a utopia, its silvered surface containing "no real place" (Gr. Eutopos) and also a heterotopia (it occupies a unique space that is "absolutely real"). Foucault's mirror can be adapted to represent a dynamic between the utopian (using the term in its more modern sense) and the heterotopian in the first European accounts of the Amazon River. The utopian elements (sometimes inverted into the dystopian) consist of transported Eastern imagery drawn from a wide range of precedent texts including The Alexander Romance, Polo's Travels, and Mandeville. Heterotopian elements are represented by an awareness that Brazil's features are *sui generis,* beyond the image-bank of the precedent texts. The first writers of the Amazon, e.g. Friar Gaspar de Carvajal, therefore adapt some simple heuristic structures, including the Roman Catholic calendar and the genre of Epic, to convey the shock of the new. As the written accounts multiply and are spread and translated throughout Europe, their utopian elements become disputed. Amazons and Anthropophagi are pushed to the boundaries of the Amazon. Foucault's mirror becomes multifaceted, revealing a debate between competitor nations as well as the dynamic between old and new. Spanish accounts of the Amazon had commented on the nudity and sexuality of the natives. Raleigh's The Discoveries of Guiana, in contrast, adapts an allegory of chivalry to attack tales of Spanish atrocities, and to propose an ideology of virginity in the service of Elizabeth I. The essay concludes with Raleigh reasserting the utopian imagery in his The History of the World, which examines a number of classical sources to "prove" the existence of Amazons in Guiana.

Mario Klarer, "Sealing Anuses and Devouring Men: Utopia, Gender and Incorporation in the Early Image of America"
A significant number of early modern narratives of discovery and travel about America comment on and contrast the utopian, idyllic or paradisiacal landscape with the utter cruelty and depravity of its indigenous inhabitants, notably their cannibalistic practices. This apparently paradoxical coexistence of a topic found, for example, in the travelogues of Columbus and Vespucci, in various 16th century ewewitness accounts, as well as in 18th and 19th century novels. Working "America" as the ideal site for representations of cannibalism, this essay will show how notions of the physical body—in this case the mutilated and incorporated body—constitute an integral part of the early pre-national image of what was to become the United

States. The ritually incorporated body is stylized as a realistic manifestation of utopian thought in religion and myth as it is projected onto the New World.

John R. Leo, "Land of Consuming Passion: Thomas Moran's 'Mountain of the Holy Cross' and the Signifying of Perspectives"

Thomas Moran's and W.H. Jackson's visual collaborations in the 1870s depicting Yellowstone and the Rockies (painting, photography, engraving) did immense cultural and ideological work. Their work helped establish Yellowstone as a national park and to instrumentalize popular icons and populist fantasies as nation-making visual media (cf. Benedict Anderson). This paper looks closely at late 19th-century American cultural production as a postcolonial adventure and takes as a case study Moran's engraving of the "Mountain of the Holy Cross," published in the series Picturesque America (1874 and after, edited by William Cullen Bryant). My focus is on how Moran deployed perspectival apparatuses to create both the *similitude* of cultural and geographical unity—America as the "one land" of Manifest Destiny produced by popular reproduction of visual topi—and the *simulacrum* of "being there" by the effective power of art discourse ("realism") and popular reproductions. Several arguments impinge and depart. The first deals with how an "original" work becomes a circulated "copy" in another medium, e.g. Moran traced Jackson's photograph of the Holy Cross Mountain in order to produce his own elaborated engraving, a move resembling the displaced tracings of biblical narratives onto the American landscape, and one reflecting the mass media dispersion of any message's source, dispersion, and consumption. The second main argument extends and deconstructs the very basis for Manifest Destiny, mainly by confronting the contradictions between a biblical "textualizing" of landscape and of lived experience, of fantasies of divine "presence" against the physical realities of a shrinking wilderness: a "shrinking divinity," or perhaps a futuristic "divinized boosterism." The third main argument itself displaces the biblical narrative investing the land with national/cultural capital onto perspectival schemes built into art discourse and illusion (e.g. three-point perspective and the illusion of distance, which are the basis for "realistic" landscape art). The *figural* perspectivism of landscape writers and travelogues is briefly noted by comparison.

Anthony Marasco, "Nature in Ruin: The Rephotographic Survey Project as a View of History and a Study of a Site"

Between 1977 and 1979, the Rephotographic Survey Project repeated 122 photographs made during the great geological surveys of the American West of the 1870s. As presented in the Project's published report, I believe the Project to be a missed opportunity pointing to an opening. It is a missed opportunity because what was initiated as a study of survey photography evolved into a complex ritual of participation with nature whose jeremiads finally are not of any heuristic use. It points to an opening because if approached with an awareness of the techniques, aesthetics (including critiques of representations), and ideological interrogations occasioned by much contemporary rephotography, the sites occupied by (past, present) survey photographers become available to historical analysis and reveal the intricacies of their tense and contradictory natures.

William Boelhower, "The Spirit of Chicago: Abundance and Sacrifice in Nature's Metropolis"

By the beginning of the 20th-century, Chicago had become the nation's second metropolis in size and importance. In a single generation it grew from a nondescript town on the south shore of Lake Michigan to a city with global pretensions. Accounts of what it was like to enter Chicago for the first time are as fascinating as they are abundant. Frank Lloyd Wright, Theodore Dreiser, Sherwood Anderson, Hamlin Garland, Ben Hecht, and many others recounted their sense of wonder and amazement as they approached the great city and then sought to live and work in it. All of them were ultimately possessed by the spirit of Chicago and got caught up in its whirlwind of business and wild amusements.

In his study of Chicago, William Cronon examines the process by which first nature (the raw products of the land) was converted into second nature (meat products, standard cuts of lumber, steel). In effect, he describes what can be called a semiotics of grain when he explains how this raw material passed from being handled in bags owned by individual farmers to a fixed number of grades stored in grain elevators. And in the process the flow of grain up the Chicago River was converted into the speculative flow of the Board of Exchange. Using the metaphor of flow as a master-word for embracing any number of conversion processes, this paper builds on Cronon's insights by enlarging his description of first and second nature to embrace a broader understanding of the definition of economy. For what was happening in post-fire Chicago from the 1870s to the early decades of the 20th-century goes well beyond the confines of the restricted economy (the money economy) to embrace all cultural practices, what George Bataille called the general economy.

It is, therefore, the dialectic between these two economies—monitored by the metaphor of flowing—that allows us to glimpse the workings of Chicago's spirit of place. This spirit, Marcel Mauss would call it an atmosphere, can be traced not only in the collective life of the city but also in the individual activities of its inhabitants. Focusing on the narrative moment of the entrance topos in several autobiographies by Chicago authors, this paper provides a phenomenological and genealogical description of urban "self/sites" and then proceeds to study the process by which they become artistic capital. The work and writings of Louis Sullivan provide us with an exemplary case of the symbolic conversion to which the metaphor of flowing alludes.

Martha Banta, "Buckongahelastown, Munseytown, Middletown"

Robert and Helen Lynd's <u>Middletown</u> (1929) and <u>Middletown in Transition</u> (1935), classics in the field of social anthropology, are considered "pioneering" studies of "a typical American town." Continued attempts to pry meaning from a site selected for its averageness have turned Muncie, Indiana, into a site for ongoing academic enterprises. The tap by Muncie's cultural capitalists into late 20th-century forms of cash-flow was as important to the scholar-entrepreneur, as was the flow of natural gas in the 1880s that lured industries from the East to this small Delaware

County site in east-central Indiana. Current Middletown projects continue to focus on the town's demographic significance as the statistical "mean" by which cultural analysts hope to gauge what "Americaness" is. To take this approach, however, drops one into Muncie *medias res,* while largely ignoring the earlier stratifications that provide the literal groundwork of its engrossing narratives.

"The Three Muncies" corrects this oversight. It goes back to origins; to narratives exposed by geology and archaeology; to prehistory as well as to later historical accounts. The discoveries are surprising as one traces the connections among Buckongahelastown (established by a chief of the Delawares, a tribe cast out by the Iroquois from its original homeland in the East); "Munseytown" (set up as a trading post in 1827); "Muncie" (the official name since 1845, but replaced in popular terms by "Middletown" once the Lynds arrived with the intention to annotate what was "typical" and "average"). That the Lynds got a number of things wrong is only part of the saga of how a town becomes famous for being ordinary. Muncie could not count on Hoosier authors such as Theodore Dreiser, Kurt Vonnegut, or A.B. Guthrie to tell its story. This task was handed over to outsiders (sociologists, photographers, television dramatists, journalists), yet most have left unresolved the questions that could better be put to the site by practitioners of sociological archaeology, geology, and cultural and literary history. "The Three Muncies" raises these questions and brings answers to each of the singular narratives it offers.

Tadeusz Sławek, "'Mathematics of Creation': Lane, Olson, and the Problem of Loss"

Using Merleau-Ponty's terminology, this essay claims that the movement of vision takes place in the field of polarities between the frontal view (in the everyday) and in-depth perception (in poetry or painting): "There is that which reaches the eye head on, the frontal properties of the visible; but there is also that which reaches it from below—the profound postural latency whereby the body raises itself to see— and that which reaches vision from above like the phenomena of flight, of swimming, of movement, where it participates no longer in the heaviness of origins but in free accomplishments." One can see the idea of *placing* inherent in GRAMMOgraphy inserts an invisible ("postural latency") into the structure of the visible, a figure that punctures the present with the absent. Furthermore, this "postural latency" allows for a placing and thickening of the sign that, on the one hand, takes into account all dimensions and directions ("frontal," "below," "above"), but on the other hand does not lock up *place* in the irreversibility of one specific place or site, of one topos. Rather the sign's work liberates the working site both from a strict unidirectionality of reasoning (which always wants to get back to a clearly determined "origin") and from the permanence of one location in which the accepted (conventional) meaning seals off the sign (Ponty's Nietzschean critique of "heaviness"). Grammography discovers the importance of place in the placelessness of the everyday (Olson: "a place as a term in the order of creation…is worth more than a metropolis").

This essay argues then that description is inevitably perforated by sub-scription. To see a painting, or to read a poetic image, is to simultaneously describe its contents, retell what is there, and to deal with what has not been done by the image-maker. Sub-scription refers to the power of small (shall we say, "invisible?") print which, by providing the represented object with further perspectives and wildly distant points of view, relates it not only to the immediate scene of event (a port of Gloucester, for instance, depicted either at the time of Lane or Olson) but to the invisible scene of non-event (what Olson called "the mathematic of Creation"), from which the represented objects have emerged. In Olson's analyses of Lane's work, or in his own formings and referencings to the rock formations upon which Gloucester was built, or in his archaeological references to Dogtown (a part of Gloucester famous as the "only ruined town of America"), Olson "transfers" or rather places Gloucester in/to the ancient Middle East, more particularly Phoenicia (Olson: "Lane's eye-view of Gloucester/Phoenician eye-view"). In sub-scription perception does not erase memory but is strengthened by its hidden operations.

William R. Handley, "Freeways in the City of Angels"

This paper examines the Los Angeles freeway as a specific yet amorphous site that both erases historical memory and produces a wide range of literary and visual representations. It explores this site with regard to its function as totalizing form for the city; as a palimpsestic text-territory that yet elides a history of land speculation; as the intersection between LA's natural and built environments (when one considers its metaphorization as river and the L.A. river's rematerialization as roadway); and finally with regard to the more recent spectator sport of the high speed police chase and to how the "eyes in the sky" mediate Los Angeles's racial and class tensions and transmediate them into hyperreality.

Associated with its freeways more than any city in the world, Los Angeles developed according to powerful capitalist interests that favored suburban development dependent on private automotive transportation. All of these influences worked to the disadvantage of an inner city that never integrated according to traditional industrial patterns. As a result, the freeway both maps and often stands in for Los Angeles's postmodern geography, one without center, beginning, or end. The freeway's indeterminacy and resistance to mapping (if one considers the drivers it is meant to serve) is a major reason for its many contradictory meanings and representations in culture. Among these, the freeway experience is seen as one of mobility and stasis, mystical revelation and unconscious aggression, isolation and communion, salvation and narcotic numbness, as this demonstrates in the writing of Joan Didion, Christopher Isherwood, and Thomas Pynchon and films such as Terminator 2, among other sources.

These states of being can in part be understood with regard to the racial divisions in Los Angeles, given that the freeway seems to bring people together (as in Frederick Jackson Turner's sense of the egalitarian effects of the "frontier") and keeps them above the ethnic and poor neighborhoods through which powerful interests chose to build it. The contradictory states of mind on the freeway in LA's literature and film derive not simply from the freedom and risks of the road or the artificial communion on a freeway that divides neighborhoods, classes and races. They also derive from the convoluted history of LA's relation to the natural and the man-made. Such prevalent confusions of the natural and the built in Los Angeles history and culture invert three dominant American myths, as described by Leo

Marx: pastoralism, primitivism, and progressivism. These inversions produce in literature and film a reversal of conventional lines of causality and influence among human beings, nature, and technology. The freeway stands for the "real" Los Angeles because, despite its metaphorical name, it "really" and metaphorically transports meaning between Los Angeles's contradictions.

Susanne Rieser, "Los Angeles, Epicenter in the Cinematic Spectacle"

Los Angeles, a global center for the media industries, is probably the world's biggest producer of sight and sound archives. Hollywood, and the action film industry in particular, reproduce Los Angeles' ever more spectacular, apocalyptic and nightmarish self-representation at the turn of the millennium. This essay seeks to explore the city's self-portrait as a cinematic disasterville as well as to contextualize the apocalyptic imagery with the metropolis' social and geographical particularities. Prefatory outlines will comprise theories on action film and a reflection on the affinity of violence, spectacle, and amnesia. The central focus of the essay is on the city's topography and on Hollywood's translation of natural and social traumas into cinematic dramas. These natural and social traumas, ranging from earthquakes and wildfires to issues of class and ethnicity, generate the very explosive cinematic cityscape and its seemingly insurmountable problems that action films are designed to resolve.